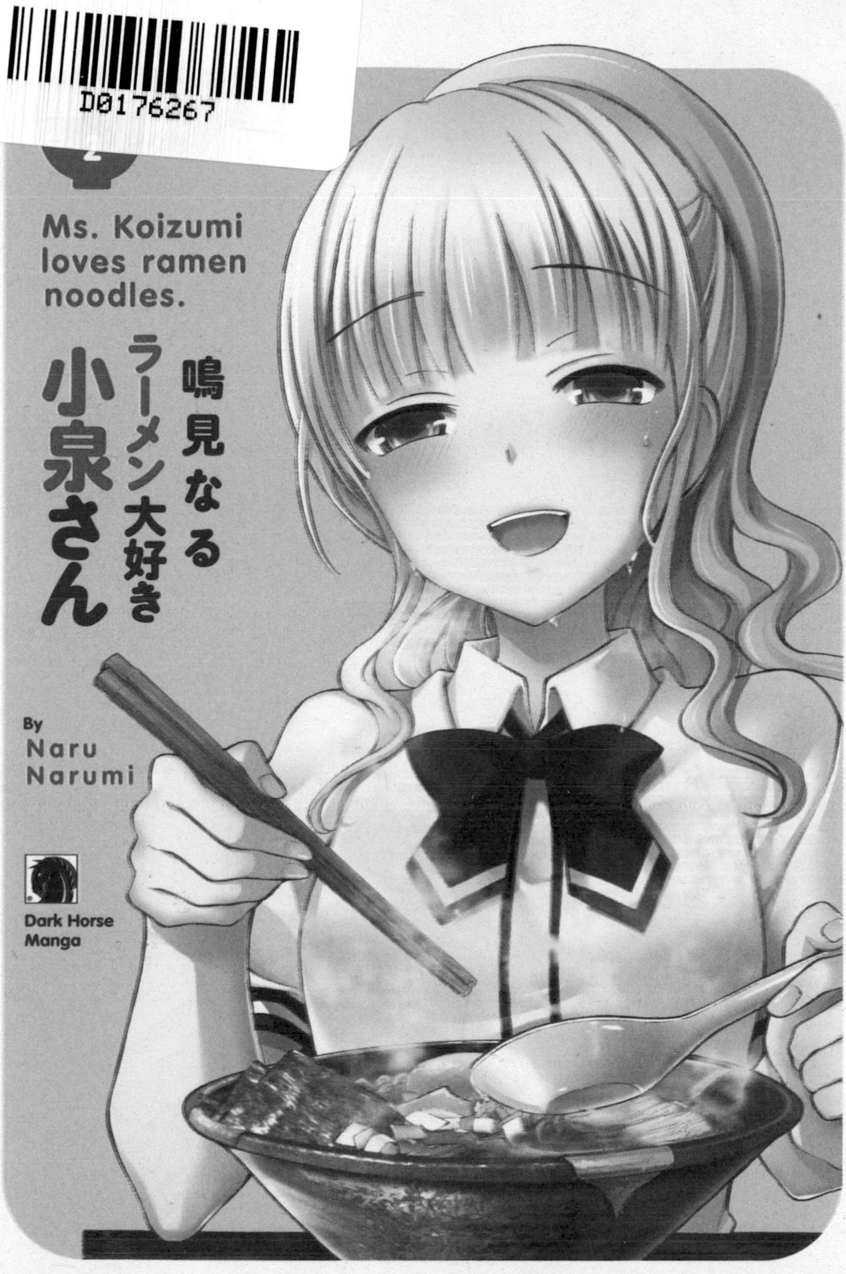

2

Ms. Koizumi loves ramen noodles.

鳴見なる

ラーメン大好き小泉さん

By
Naru Narumi

Dark Horse Manga

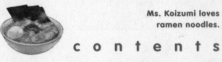

Ms. Koizumi loves
ramen noodles.

contents

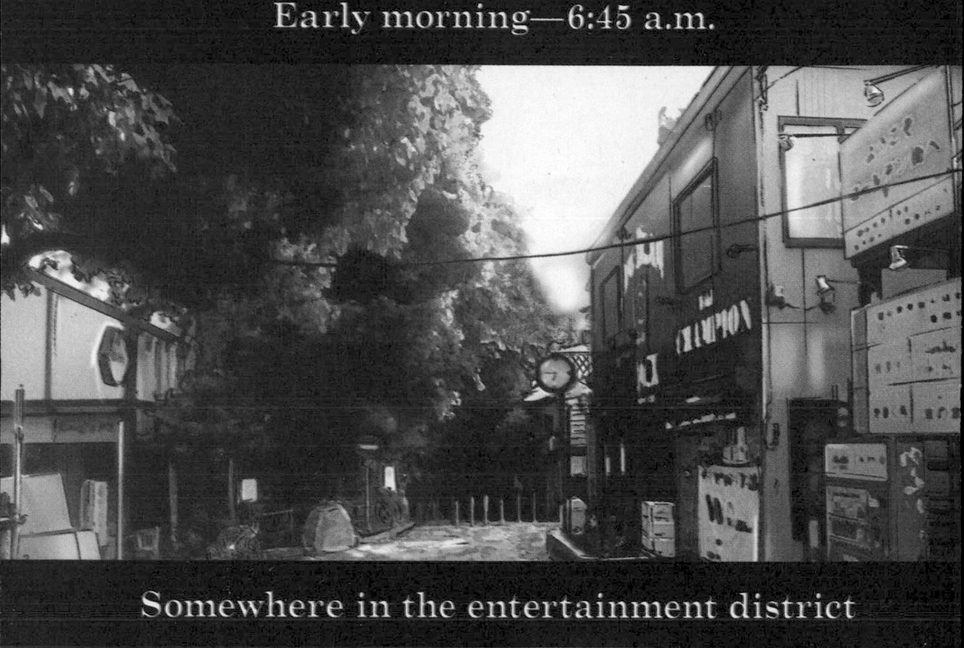
Early morning—6:45 a.m.
CHAMPION
Somewhere in the entertainment district
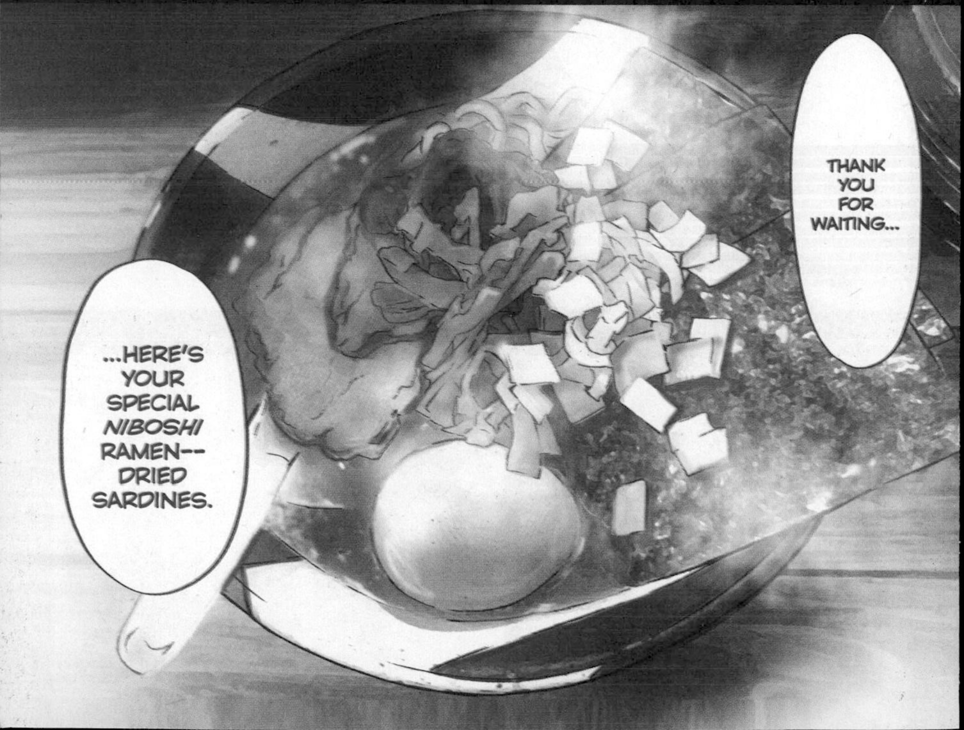
THANK YOU FOR WAITING...
...HERE'S YOUR SPECIAL *NIBOSHI* RAMEN-- DRIED SARDINES.

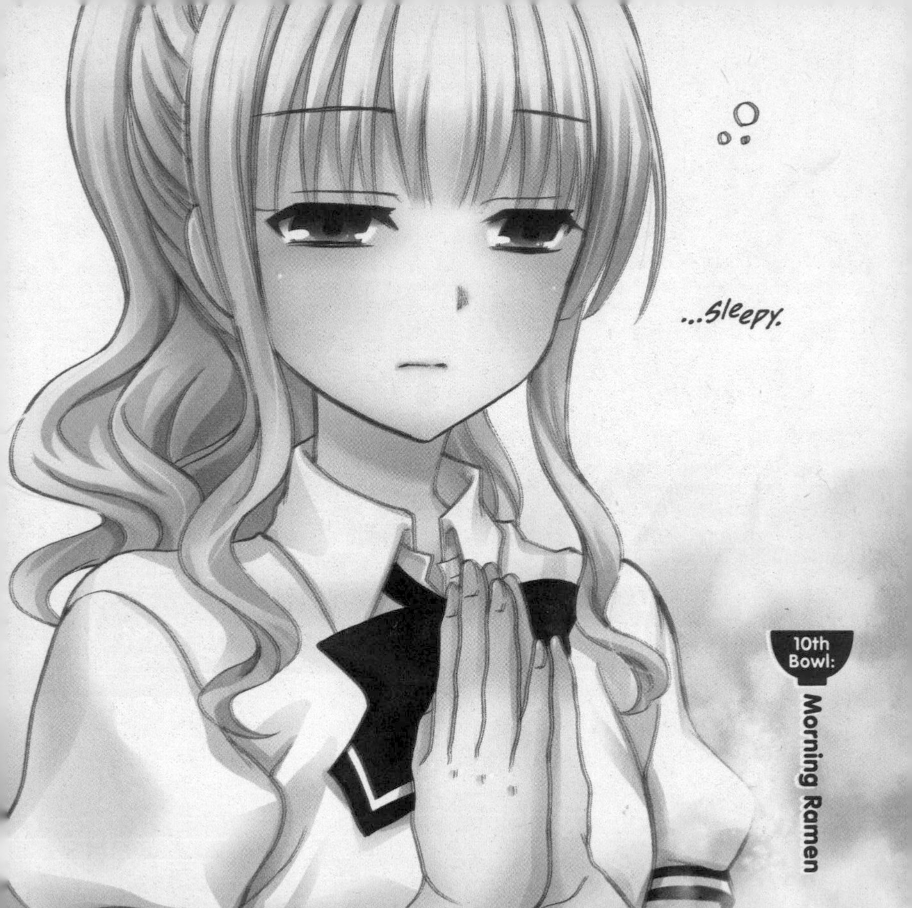
...Sleepy.
10th Bowl:
Morning Ramen

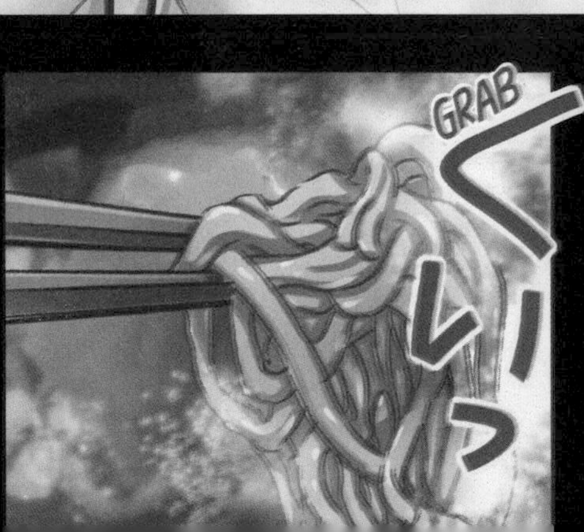
GRAB

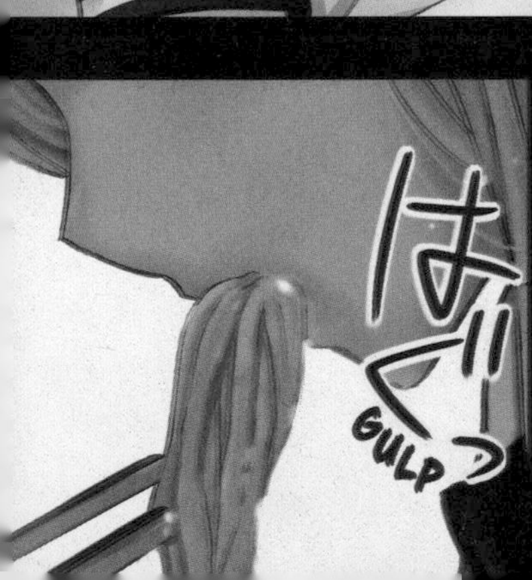
GULP

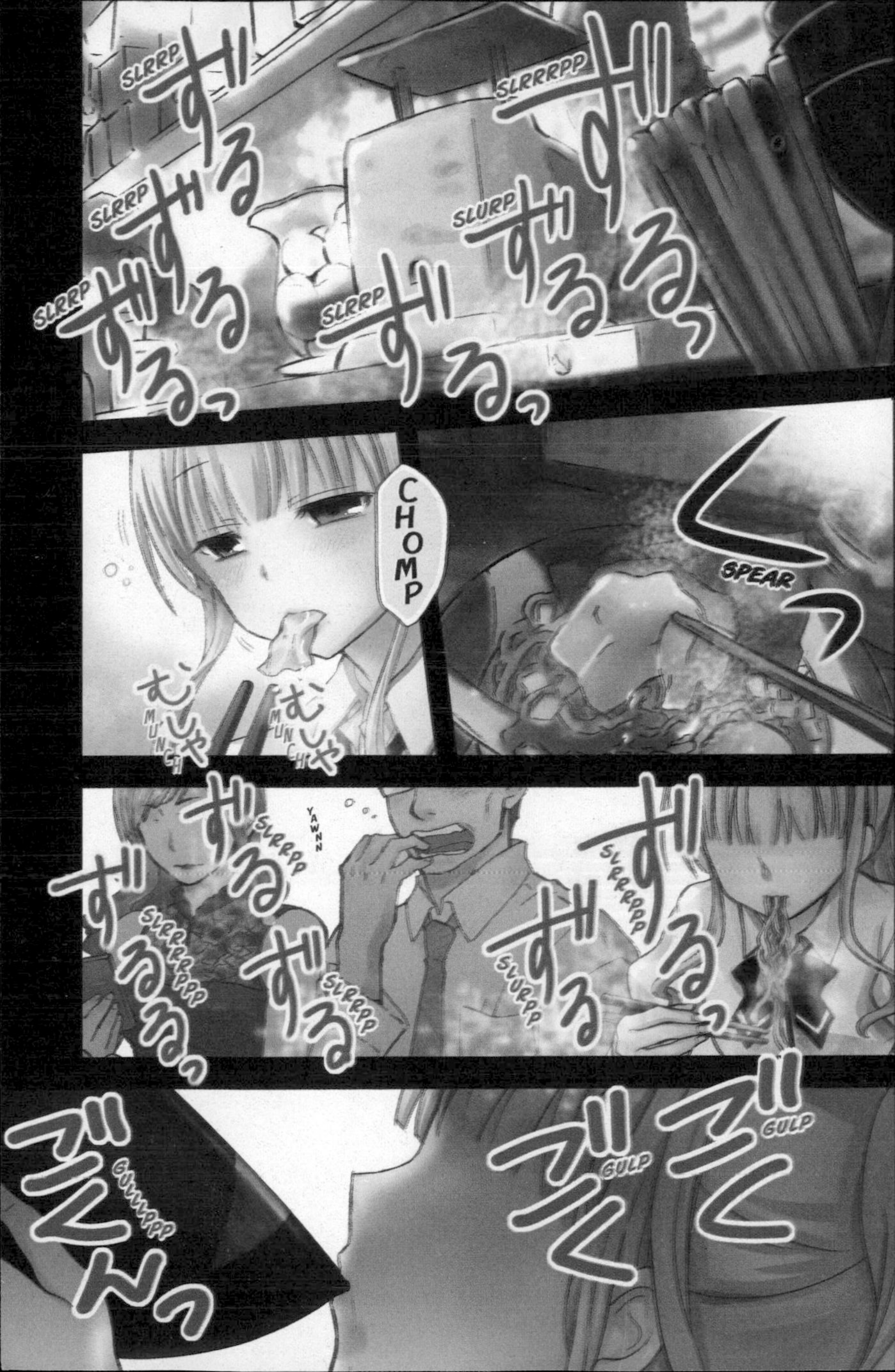

ず SLRRRPP
ずるっ SLURP
ずるっ SLRRP
ずる SLRRP
ずる SLRRP
ずるっ SLRRP
くっ SPEAR
CHOMP
むしゃ MUNCH
むしゃ MUNCH
ずるっ SLRRRPPP
ずる SLURPP
YAWNN
ずる SLRRPP
ずる SLRRPP
ずるるっ SLRRRRPPP
ごく GULP
ごく GULP
ごくんっ GULLLPPP

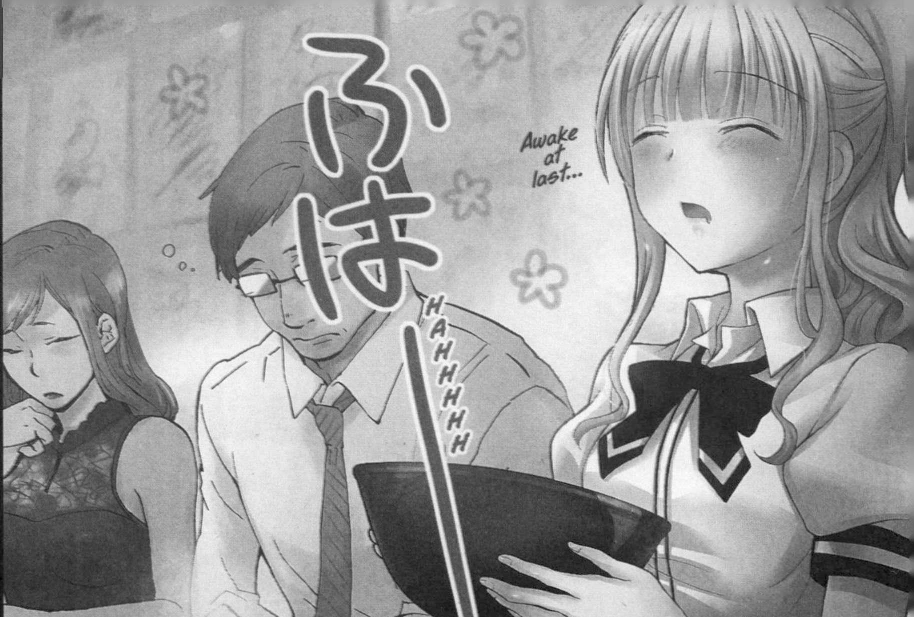
Awake at last...
ふは
HAHHHHHH

6:57 A.M.

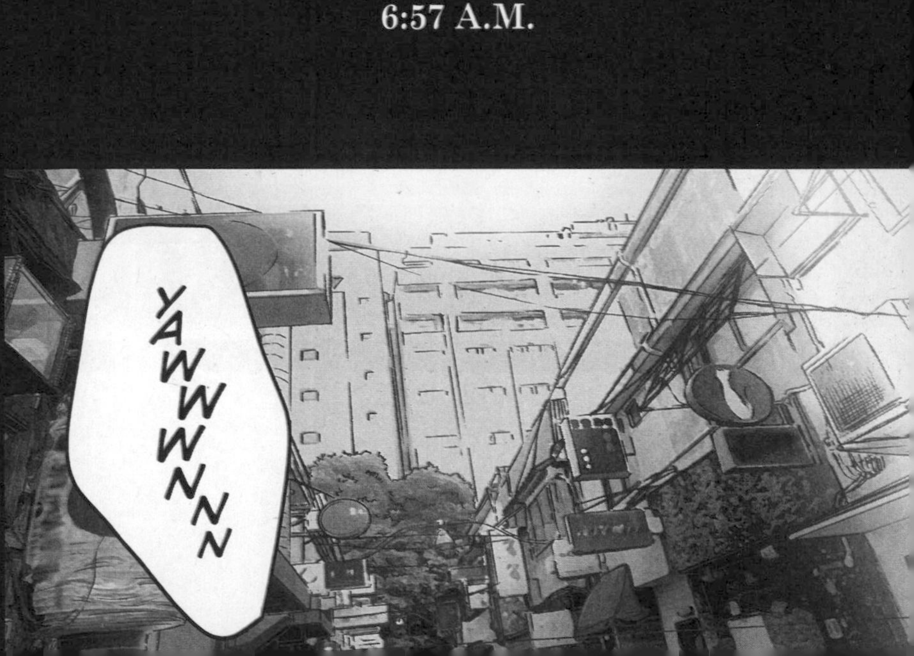
YAWWWNNN

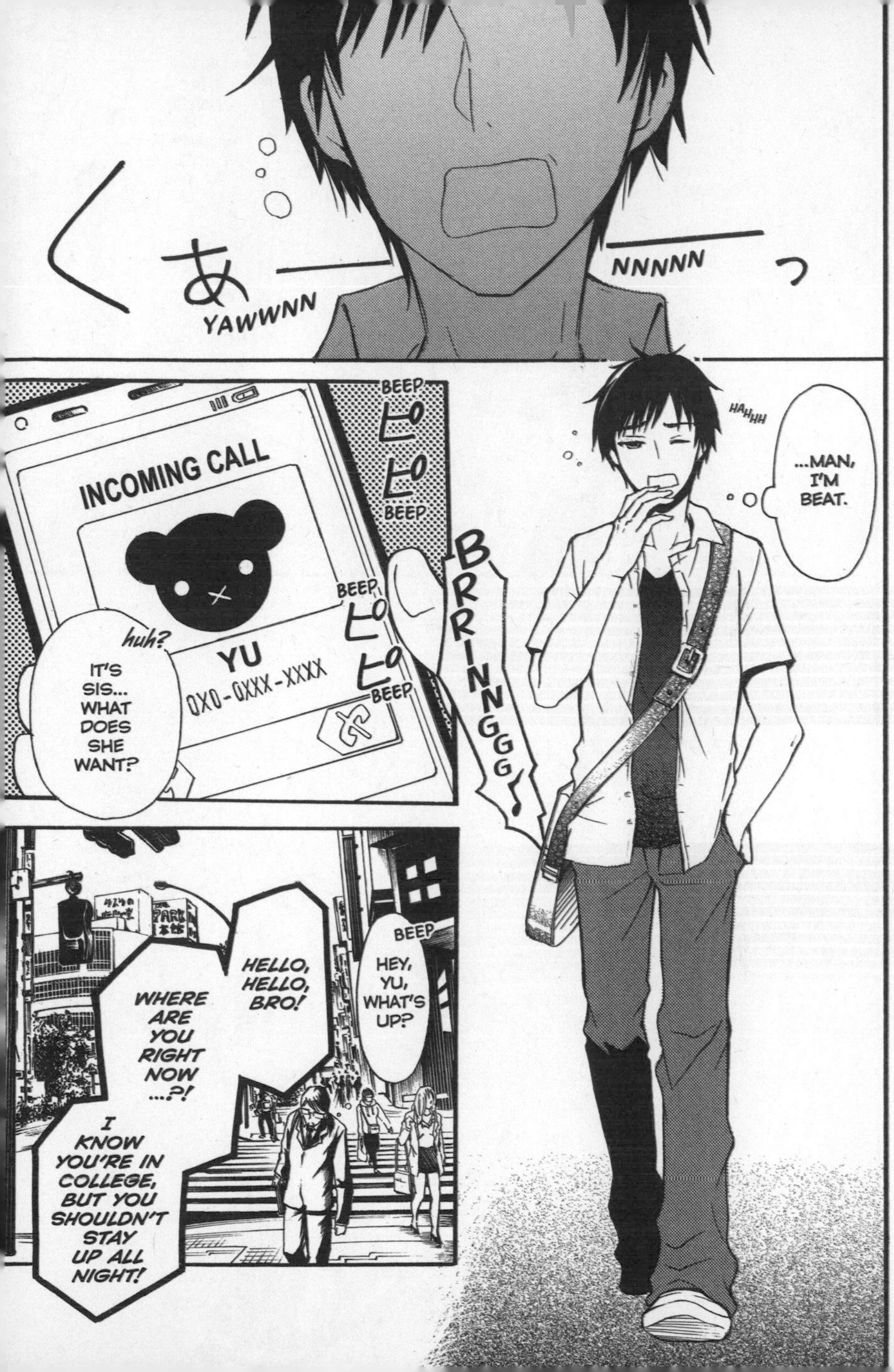
くあーーっ
YAWWNN
NNNNN
HAHHH
...MAN, I'M BEAT.
BEEP ピロピロ BEEP
BRRINNGGG
INCOMING CALL
YU
0X0-0XXX-XXXX
BEEP ピロピロ BEEP
huh?
IT'S SIS... WHAT DOES SHE WANT?
BEEP
HEY, YU, WHAT'S UP?
HELLO, HELLO, BRO!
WHERE ARE YOU RIGHT NOW ...?!
I KNOW YOU'RE IN COLLEGE, BUT YOU SHOULDN'T STAY UP ALL NIGHT!

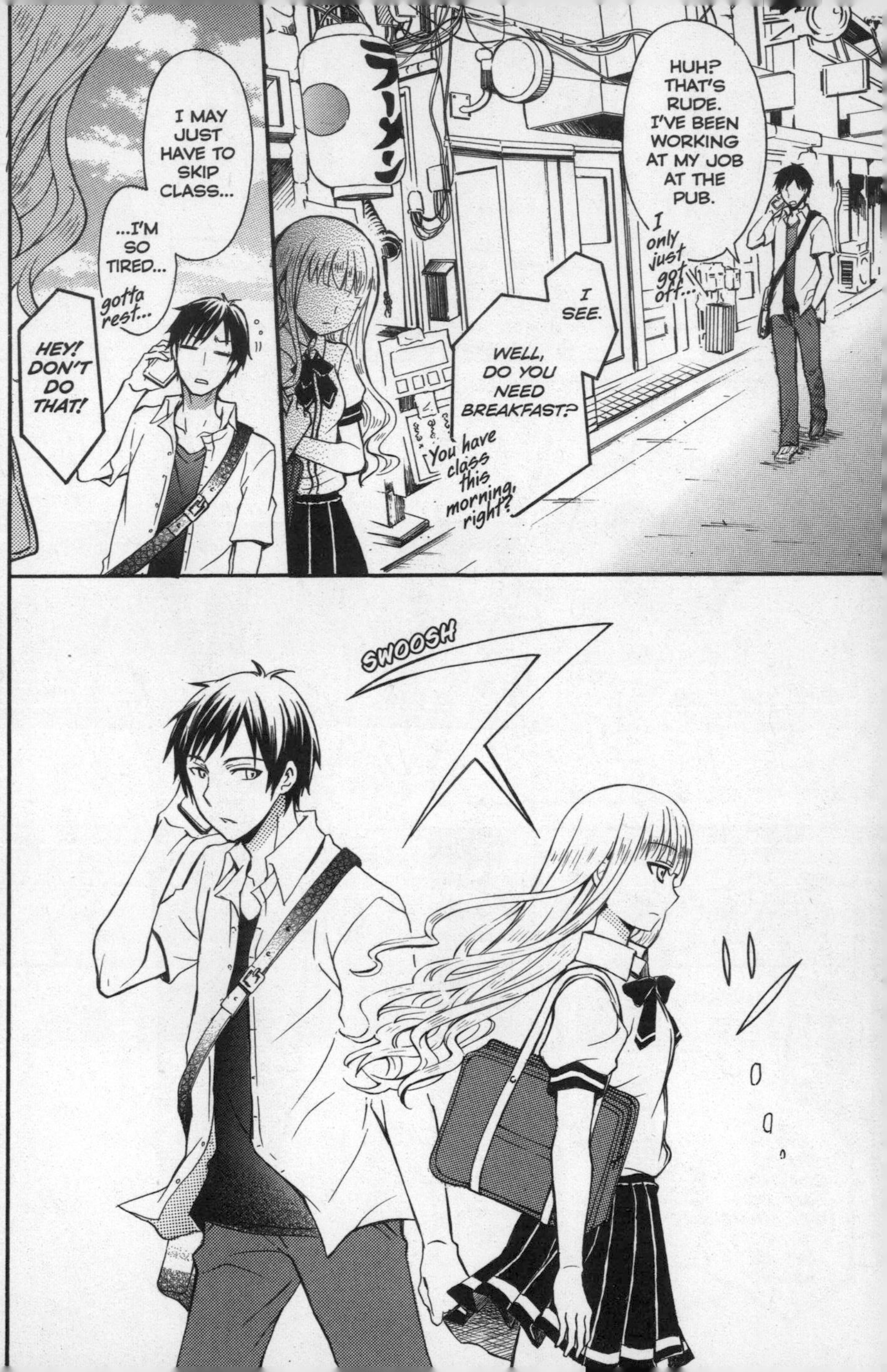
HUH? THAT'S RUDE. I'VE BEEN WORKING AT MY JOB AT THE PUB.
I only just got off...
I SEE.
WELL, DO YOU NEED BREAKFAST?
You have class this morning, right?
I MAY JUST HAVE TO SKIP CLASS...
...I'M SO TIRED...
gotta rest...
HEY! DON'T DO THAT!
SWOOSH

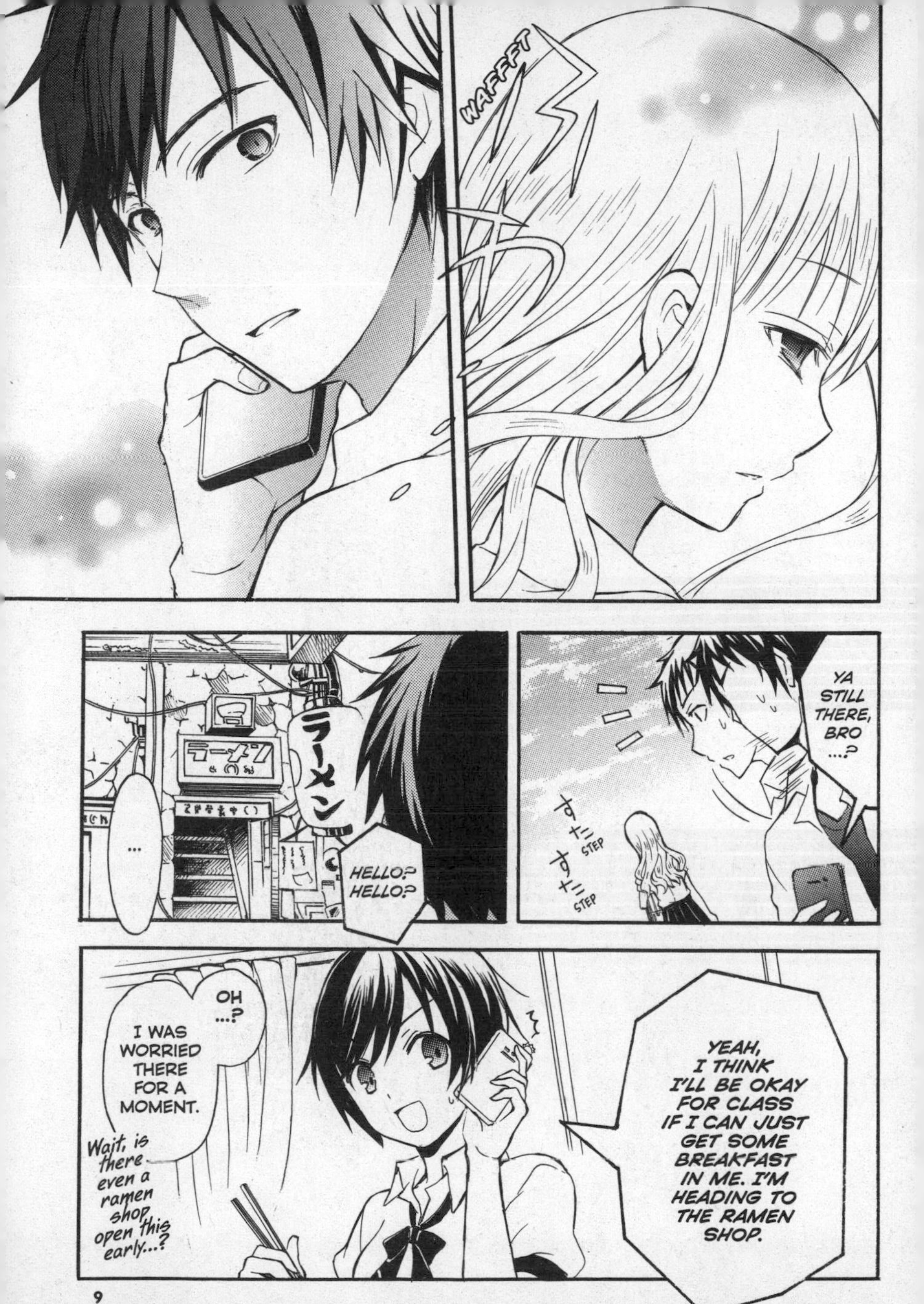
WAFFFT
YA STILL THERE, BRO ...?
すたすた STEP
すたすた STEP
ラーメン
ラーメン
...
HELLO? HELLO?
YEAH, I THINK I'LL BE OKAY FOR CLASS IF I CAN JUST GET SOME BREAKFAST IN ME. I'M HEADING TO THE RAMEN SHOP.
OH ...?
I WAS WORRIED THERE FOR A MOMENT.
Wait, is there even a ramen shop open this early...?

7:00 A.M.

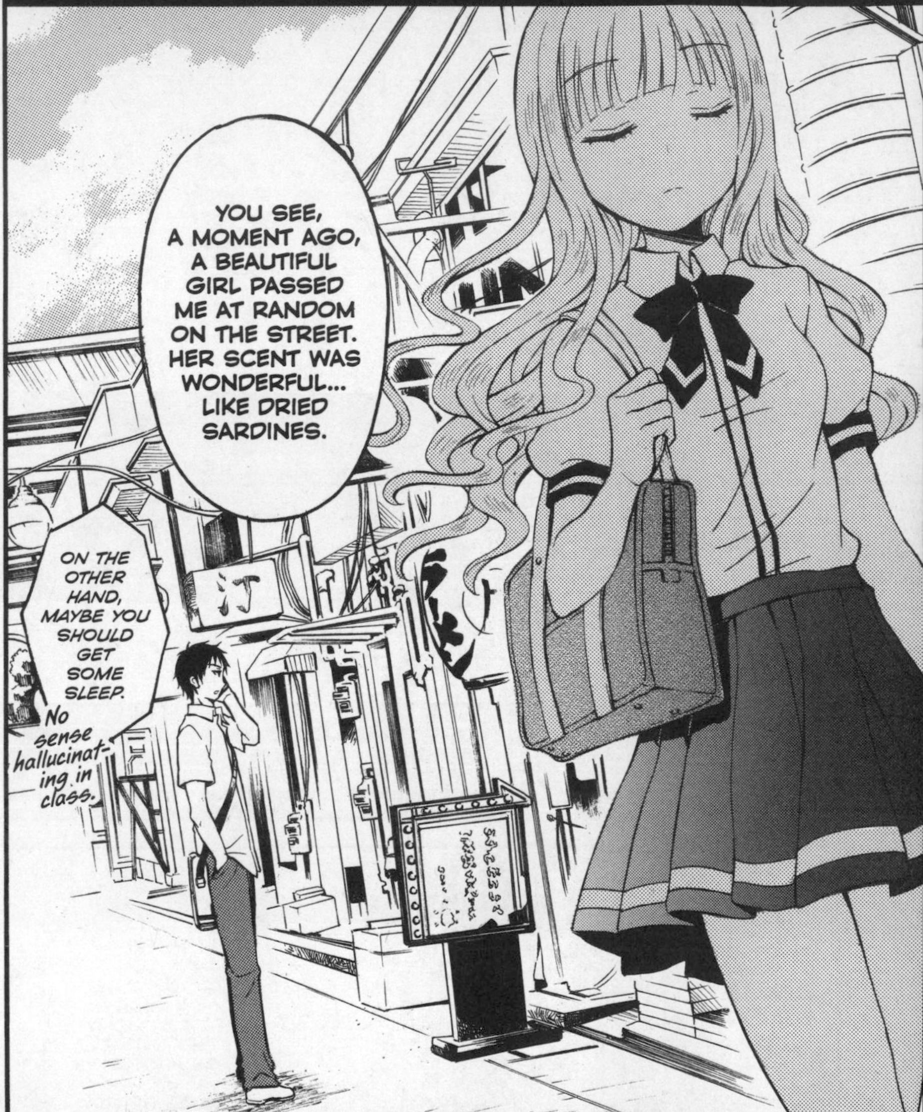
YOU SEE, A MOMENT AGO, A BEAUTIFUL GIRL PASSED ME AT RANDOM ON THE STREET. HER SCENT WAS WONDERFUL... LIKE DRIED SARDINES.
ON THE OTHER HAND, MAYBE YOU SHOULD GET SOME SLEEP.
No sense hallucinating in class.

It's not actually typical in Japan to eat ramen for breakfast. However, in the Shizuoka and Fukushima areas, it's become quite popular—so much so that people there talk about having their bowl of asa ra (asa = morning, ra = ramen)!!

munch
munch
THIS SHOULD WAKE YOU UP

Recently there have even been sweets showing up claiming that Morning Ramen flavor...

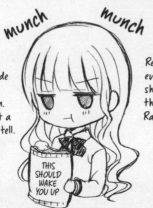

Like in the bag here...mochi made to taste like Kitakata ramen. Maybe it's just a fad? Time will tell.

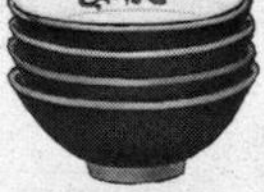

Ms. Koizumi loves
ramen noodles

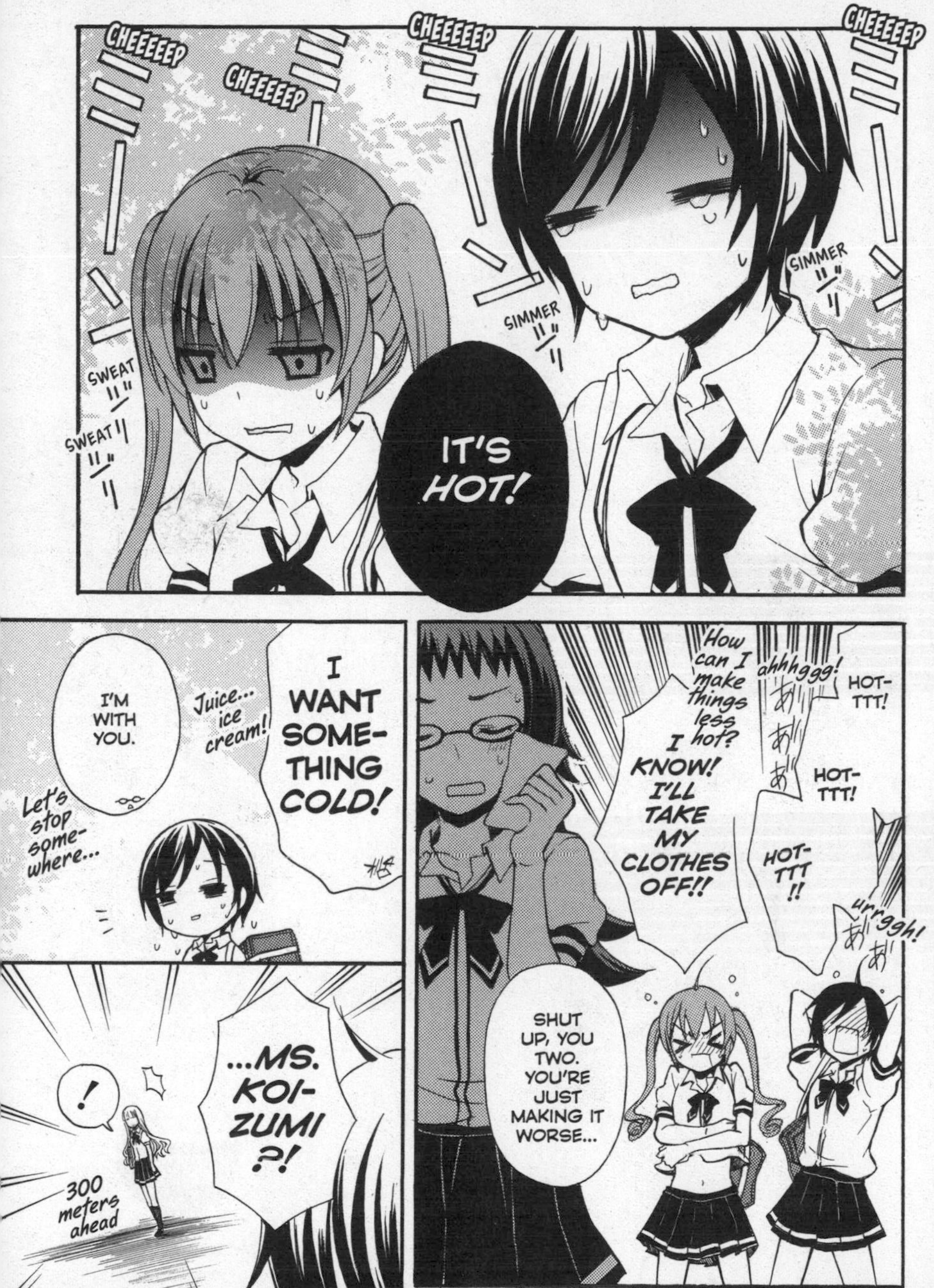
CHEEEEEP
SIMMER
SIMMER
IT'S HOT!
CHEEEEEP
CHEEEEEP
CHEEEEEP
SWEAT
SWEAT
HOT-TTT!
ahhhggg!
How can I make things less hot?
I KNOW! I'LL TAKE MY CLOTHES OFF!!
HOT-TTT!
HOT-TTT!!
urrgggh!
SHUT UP, YOU TWO. YOU'RE JUST MAKING IT WORSE...
I WANT SOME-THING COLD!
Juice... ice cream!
I'M WITH YOU.
Let's stop some-where...
...MS. KOI-ZUMI?!
!
300 meters ahead

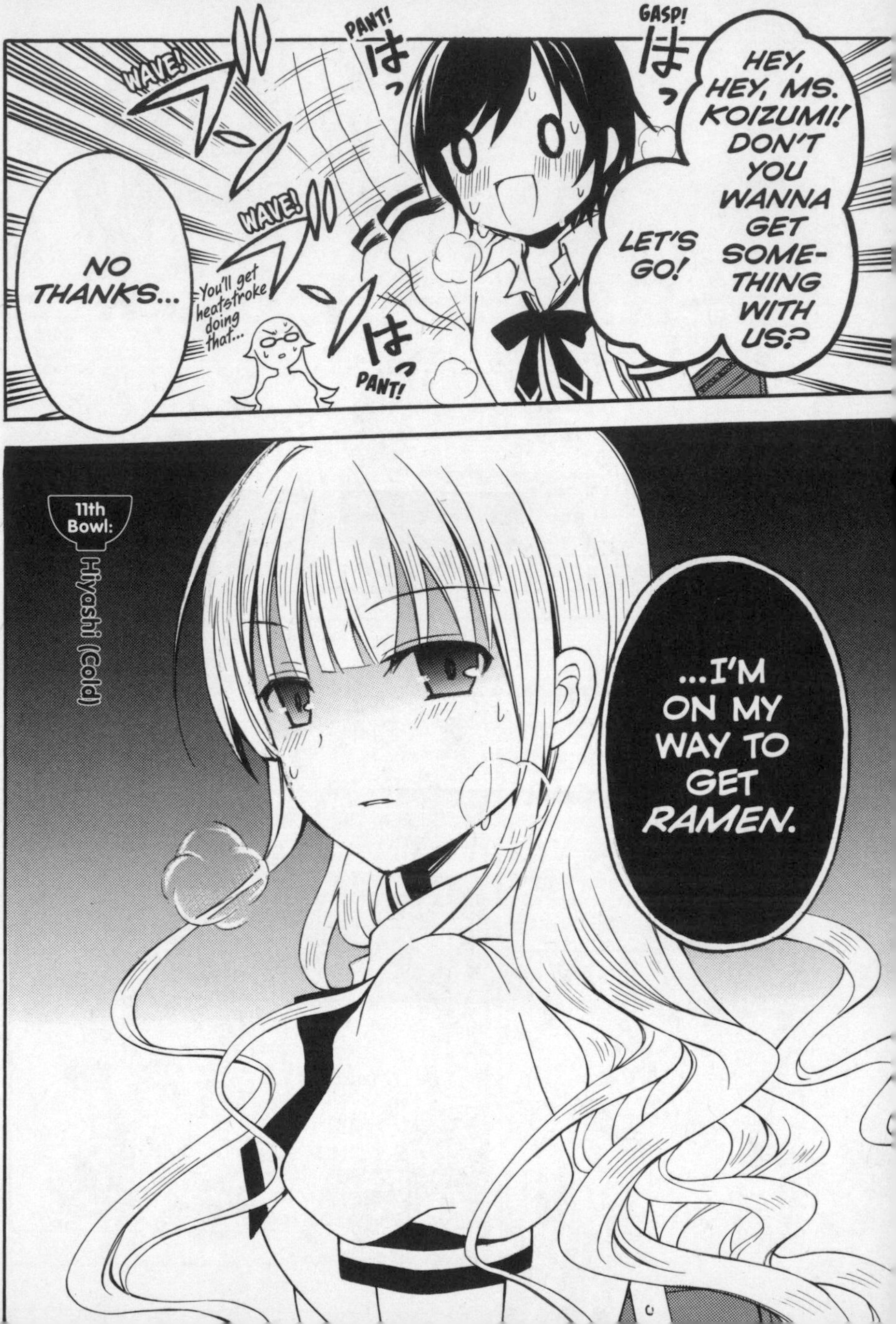
GASP!
はっ
HEY, HEY, MS. KOIZUMI! DON'T YOU WANNA GET SOME-THING WITH US?
LET'S GO!
PANT!
はっ
WAVE!
WAVE!
はっ
PANT!
You'll get heatstroke doing that...
NO THANKS...
...I'M ON MY WAY TO GET RAMEN.
11th Bowl:
Hiyashi (Cold)

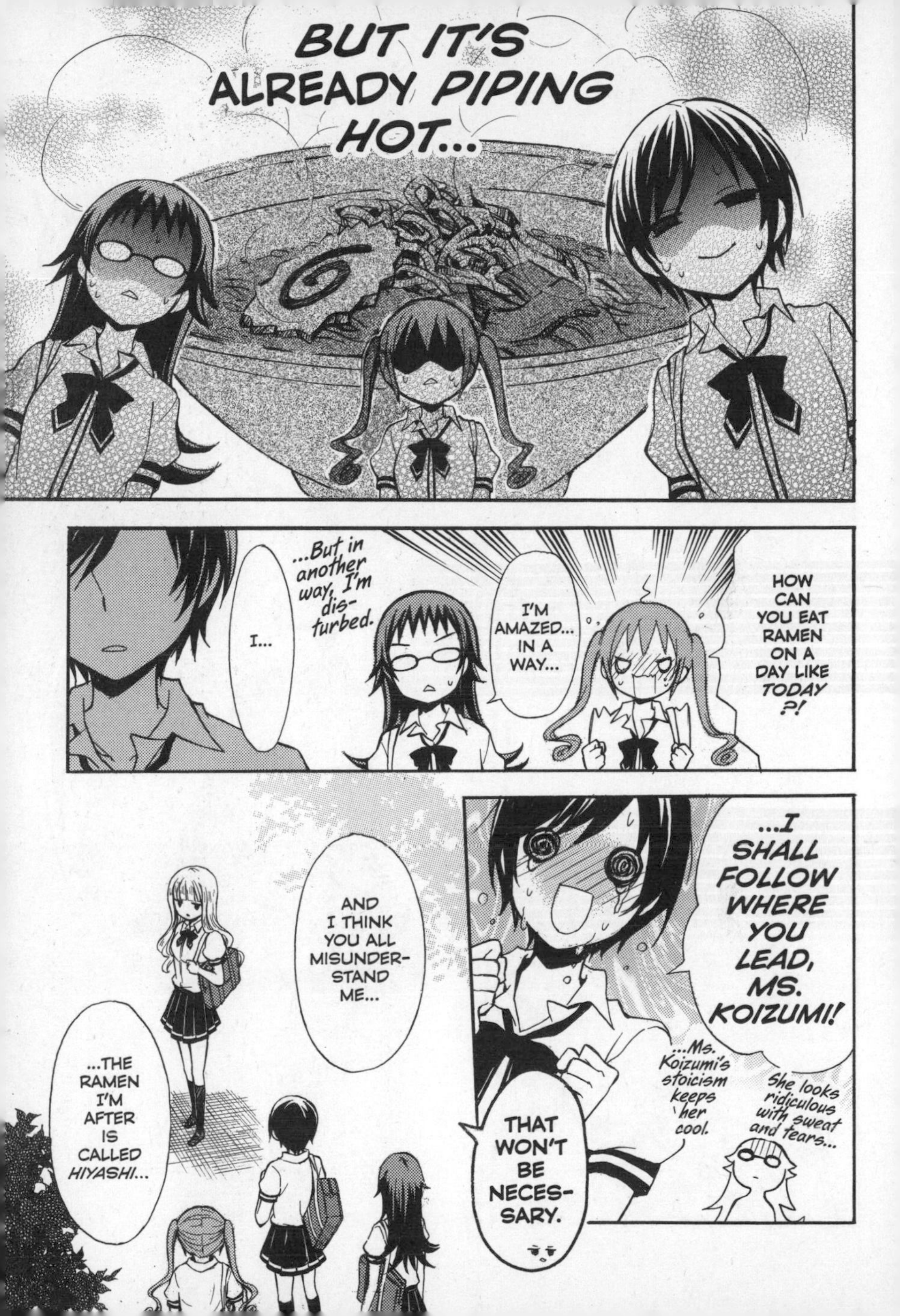
BUT IT'S ALREADY PIPING HOT...
HOW CAN YOU EAT RAMEN ON A DAY LIKE TODAY?!
I'M AMAZED... IN A WAY...
...But in another way, I'm dis-turbed.
I...
...I SHALL FOLLOW WHERE YOU LEAD, MS. KOIZUMI!
She looks ridiculous with sweat and tears...
...Ms. Koizumi's stoicism keeps her cool.
THAT WON'T BE NECES-SARY.
AND I THINK YOU ALL MISUNDER-STAND ME...
...THE RAMEN I'M AFTER IS CALLED HIYASHI...

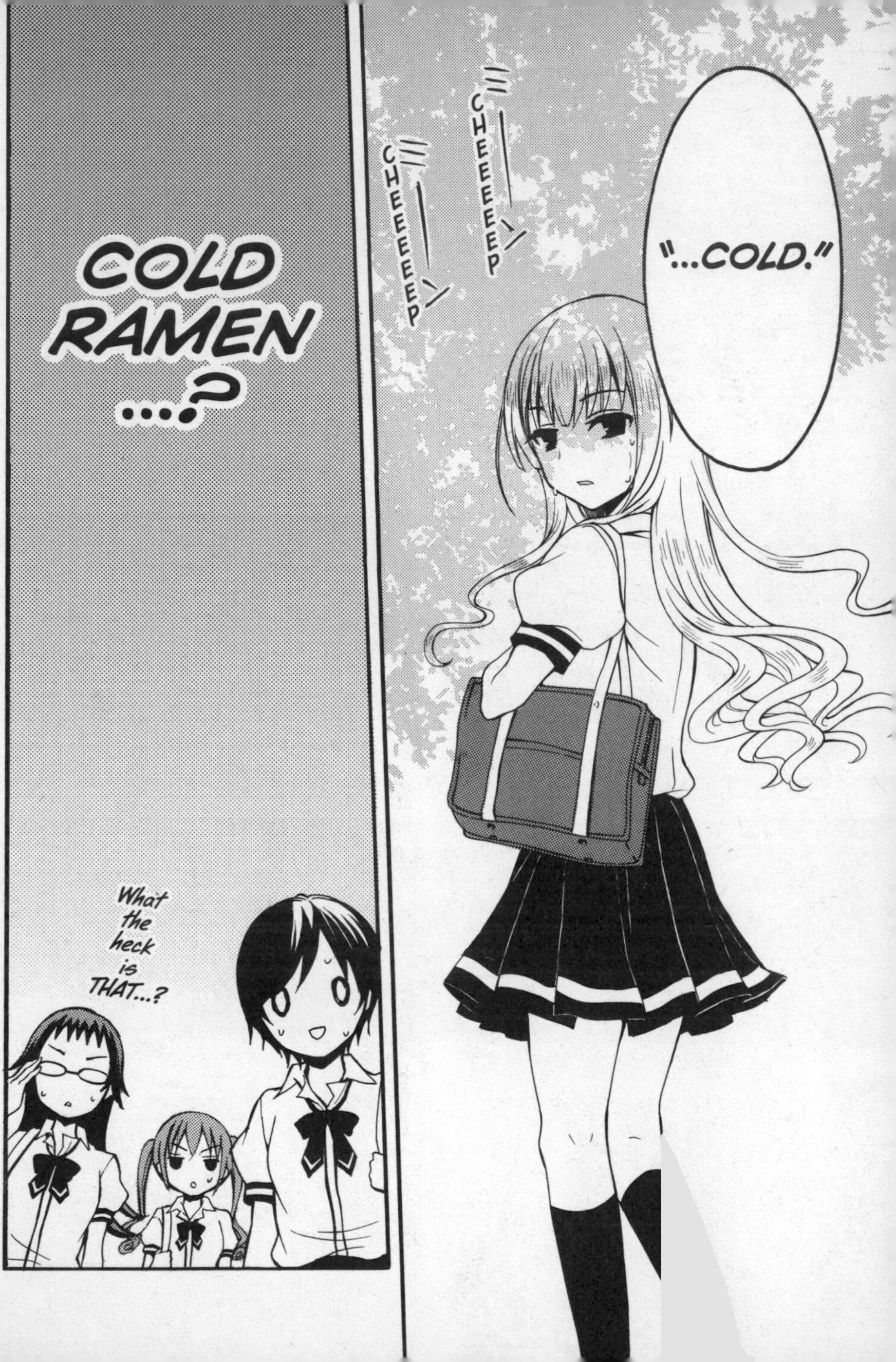
"...COLD."
CHEEEEEP
CHEEEEEP
COLD RAMEN ...?
What the heck is THAT...?

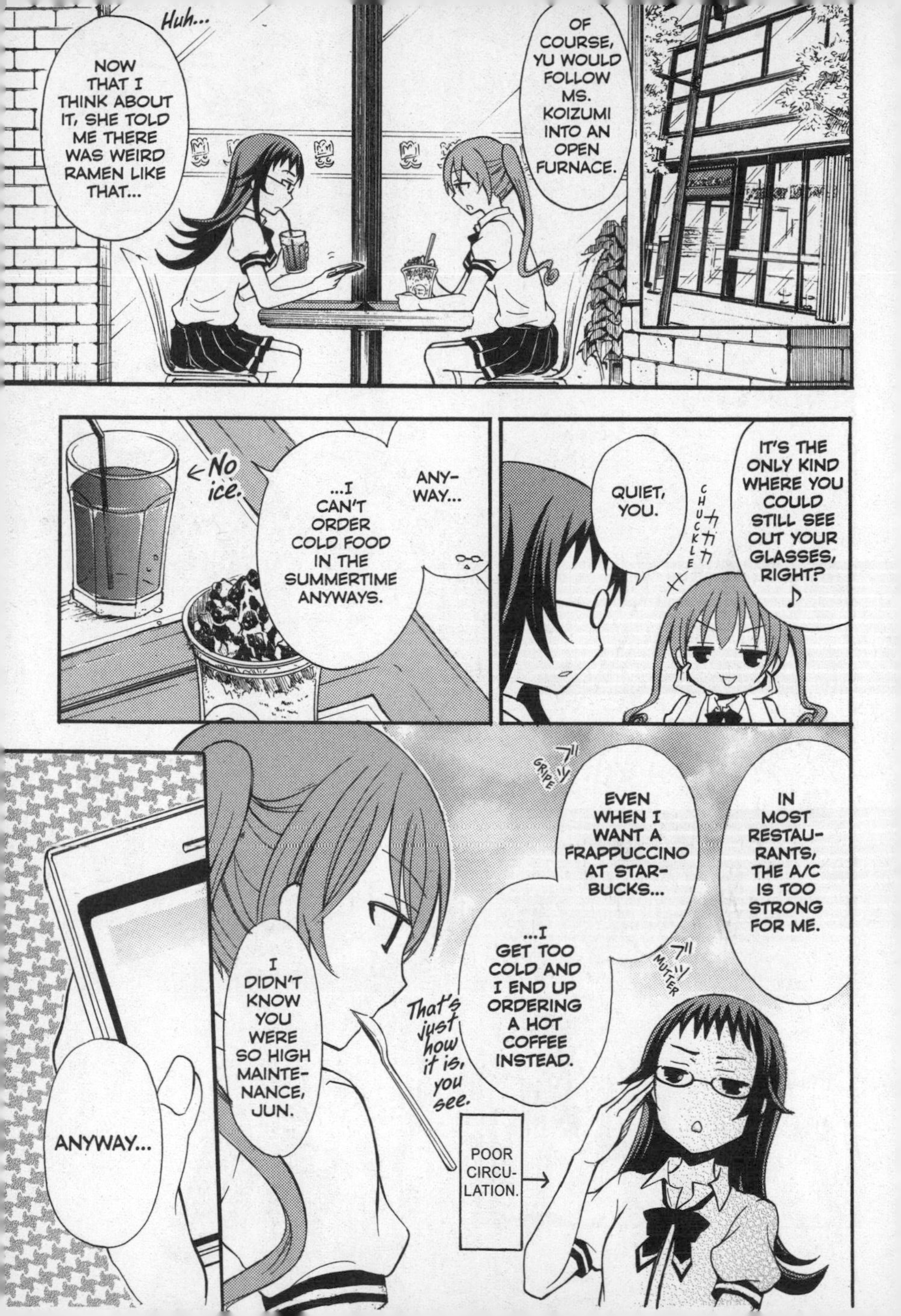
OF COURSE, YU WOULD FOLLOW MS. KOIZUMI INTO AN OPEN FURNACE.
Huh...
NOW THAT I THINK ABOUT IT, SHE TOLD ME THERE WAS WEIRD RAMEN LIKE THAT...
IT'S THE ONLY KIND WHERE YOU COULD STILL SEE OUT YOUR GLASSES, RIGHT? ♪
CHUCKLE
QUIET, YOU.
ANYWAY...
...I CAN'T ORDER COLD FOOD IN THE SUMMERTIME ANYWAYS.
← No ice.
IN MOST RESTAURANTS, THE A/C IS TOO STRONG FOR ME.
GRIPE
EVEN WHEN I WANT A FRAPPUCCINO AT STARBUCKS...
MUTTER
...I GET TOO COLD AND I END UP ORDERING A HOT COFFEE INSTEAD.
That's just how it is, you see.
POOR CIRCULATION. →
I DIDN'T KNOW YOU WERE SO HIGH MAINTENANCE, JUN.
ANYWAY...

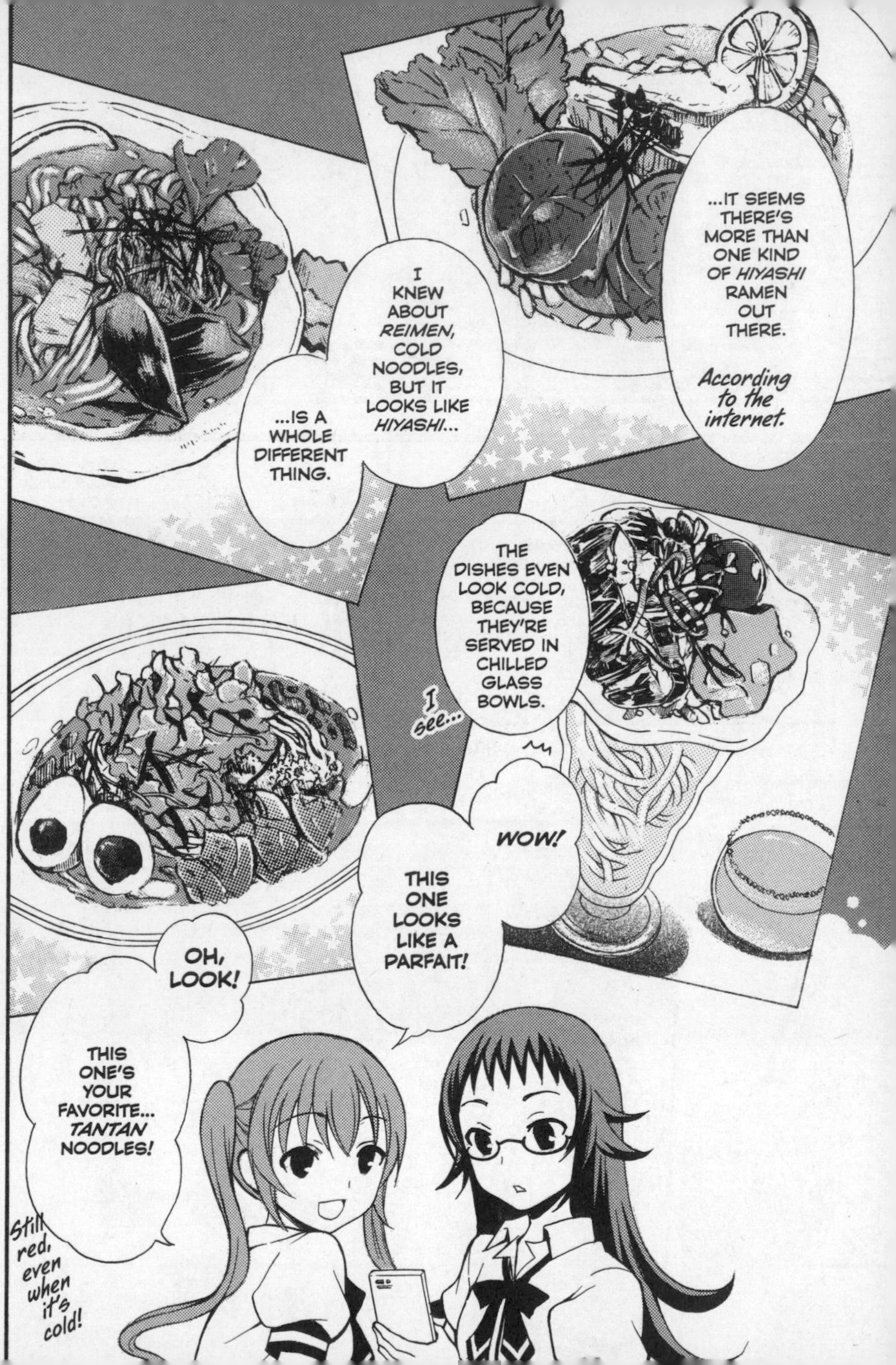
...IT SEEMS THERE'S MORE THAN ONE KIND OF *HIYASHI* RAMEN OUT THERE.
According to the internet.
I KNEW ABOUT *REIMEN*, COLD NOODLES, BUT IT LOOKS LIKE *HIYASHI*...
...IS A WHOLE DIFFERENT THING.
THE DISHES EVEN LOOK COLD, BECAUSE THEY'RE SERVED IN CHILLED GLASS BOWLS.
I see...
WOW!
THIS ONE LOOKS LIKE A PARFAIT!
OH, LOOK!
THIS ONE'S YOUR FAVORITE... *TANTAN* NOODLES!
Still red, even when it's cold!

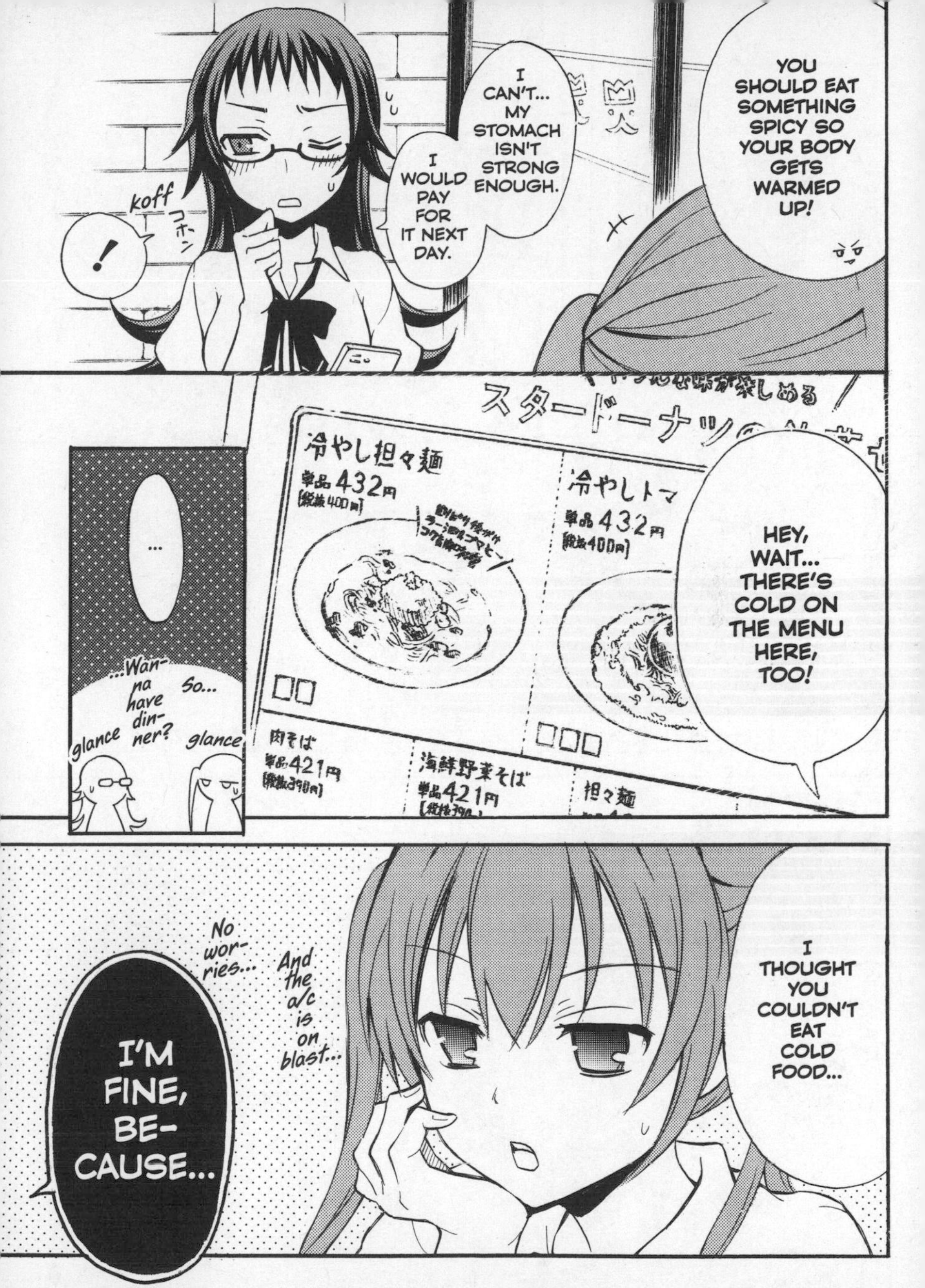
YOU SHOULD EAT SOMETHING SPICY SO YOUR BODY GETS WARMED UP!
I CAN'T... MY STOMACH ISN'T STRONG ENOUGH.
I WOULD PAY FOR IT NEXT DAY.
koff
コホン
!
スタードーナツの
冷やし担々麺
単品432円
[税抜400円]
冷やしトマ
単品432円
[税抜400円]
肉そば
単品421円
[税抜390円]
海鮮野菜そば
単品421円
担々麺
HEY, WAIT... THERE'S COLD ON THE MENU HERE, TOO!
...
So...
...Wanna have dinner?
glance
glance
I THOUGHT YOU COULDN'T EAT COLD FOOD...
And the a/c is on blast...
No worries...
I'M FINE, BECAUSE...

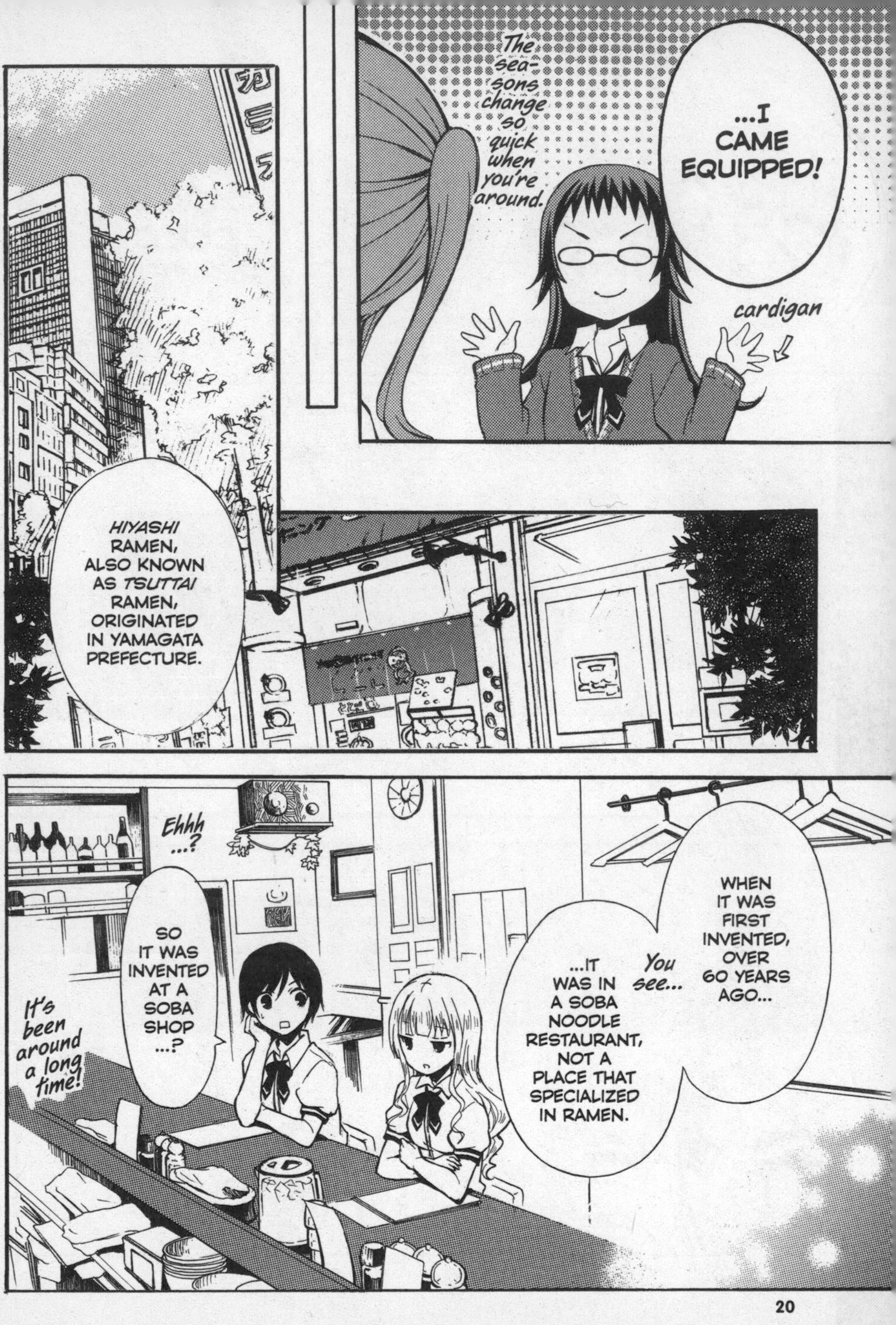
...I CAME EQUIPPED!
The seasons change so quick when you're around.
cardigan
HIYASHI RAMEN, ALSO KNOWN AS TSUTTAI RAMEN, ORIGINATED IN YAMAGATA PREFECTURE.
WHEN IT WAS FIRST INVENTED, OVER 60 YEARS AGO...
You see...
...IT WAS IN A SOBA NOODLE RESTAURANT, NOT A PLACE THAT SPECIALIZED IN RAMEN.
SO IT WAS INVENTED AT A SOBA SHOP ...?
Ehhh ...?
It's been around a long time!

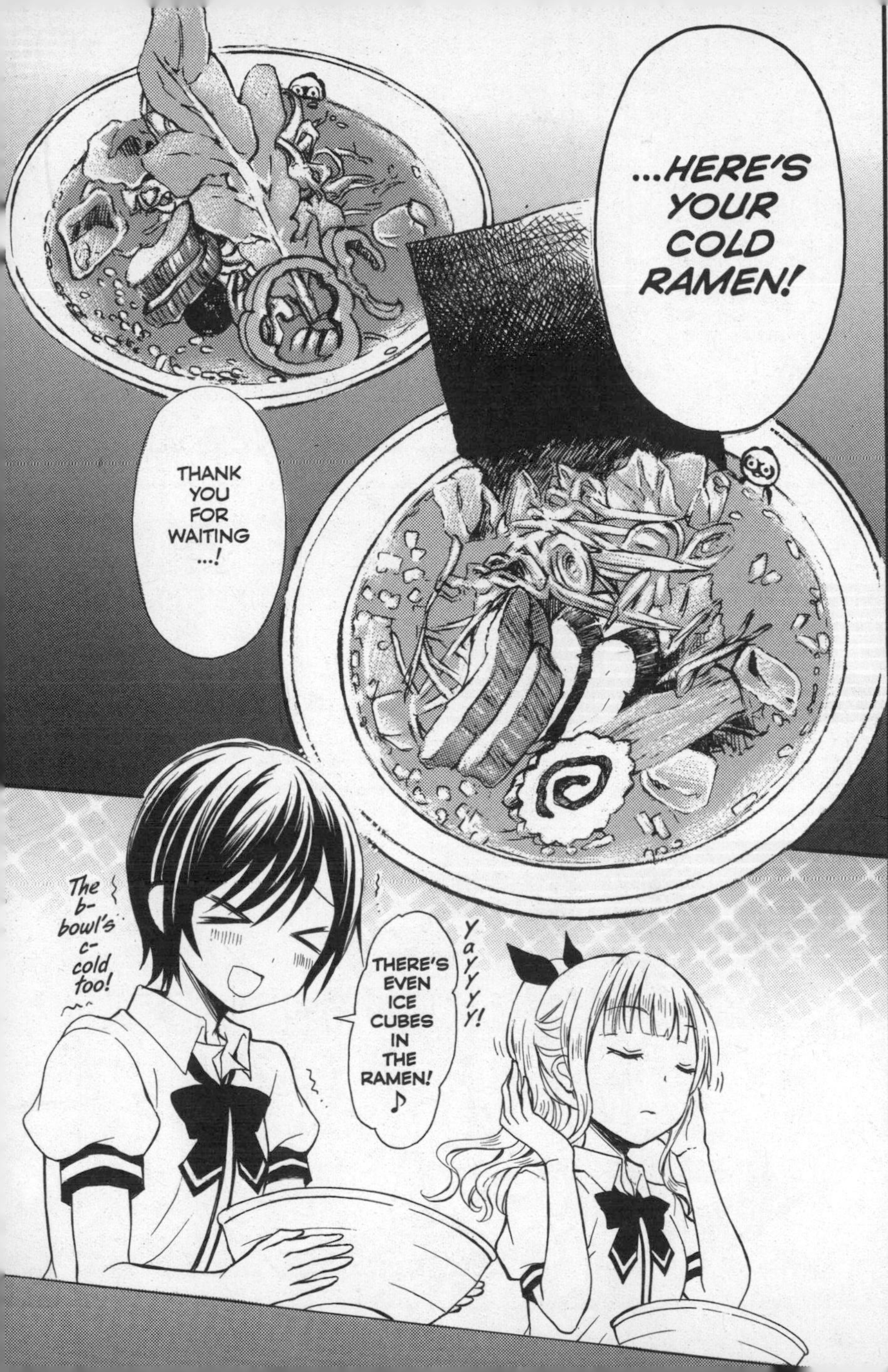
...HERE'S YOUR COLD RAMEN!
THANK YOU FOR WAITING ...!
YaYYYYY!
THERE'S EVEN ICE CUBES IN THE RAMEN! ♪
The b-bowl's c-cold too!

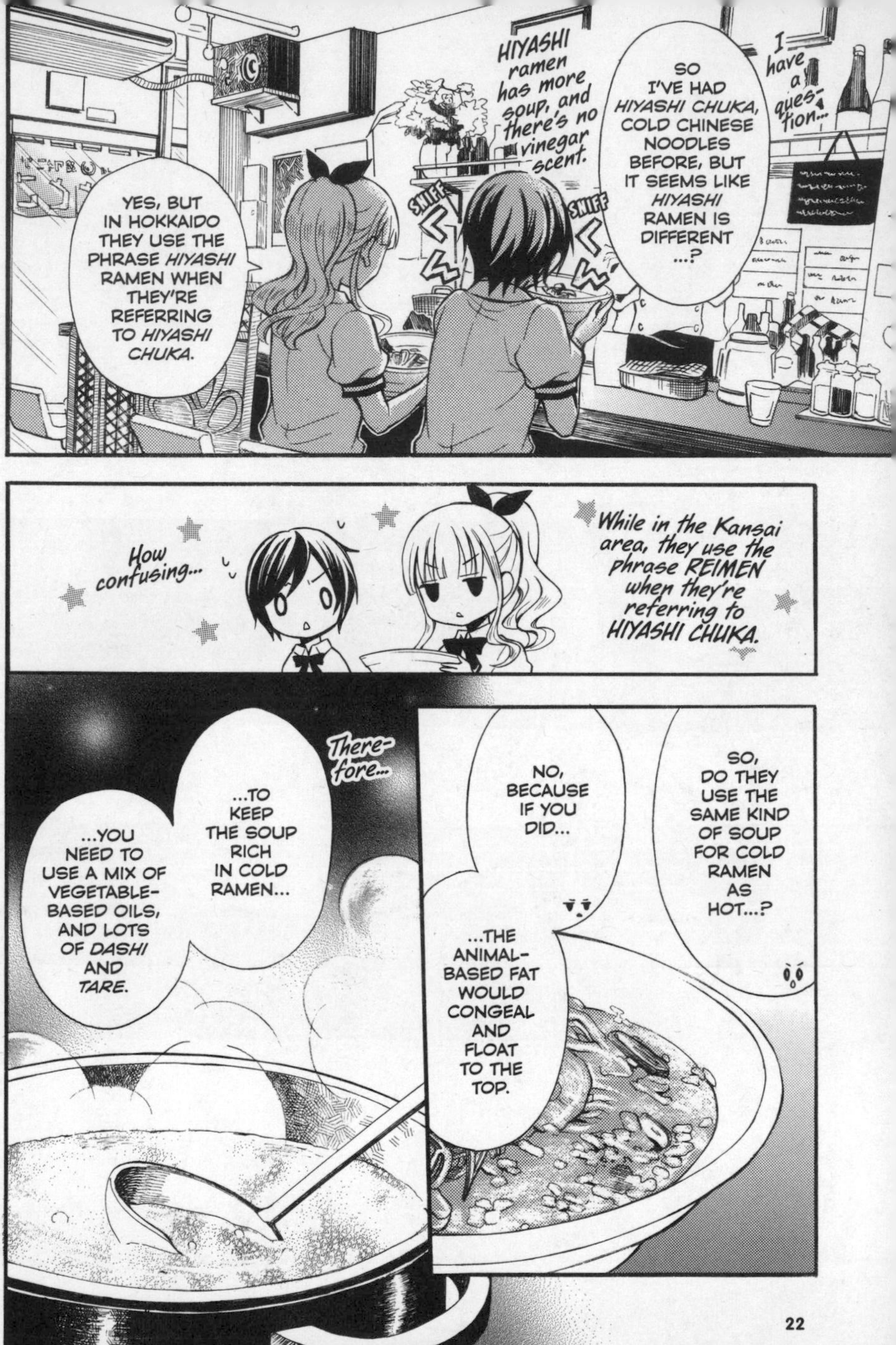
I have a ques-tion...
SO I'VE HAD HIYASHI CHUKA, COLD CHINESE NOODLES BEFORE, BUT IT SEEMS LIKE HIYASHI RAMEN IS DIFFERENT ...?
SNIFF
HIYASHI ramen has more soup, and there's no vinegar scent.
SNIFF
YES, BUT IN HOKKAIDO THEY USE THE PHRASE HIYASHI RAMEN WHEN THEY'RE REFERRING TO HIYASHI CHUKA.
While in the Kansai area, they use the phrase REIMEN when they're referring to HIYASHI CHUKA.
How confusing...
SO, DO THEY USE THE SAME KIND OF SOUP FOR COLD RAMEN AS HOT...?
NO, BECAUSE IF YOU DID...
...THE ANIMAL-BASED FAT WOULD CONGEAL AND FLOAT TO THE TOP.
There-fore...
...TO KEEP THE SOUP RICH IN COLD RAMEN...
...YOU NEED TO USE A MIX OF VEGETABLE-BASED OILS, AND LOTS OF DASHI AND TARE.

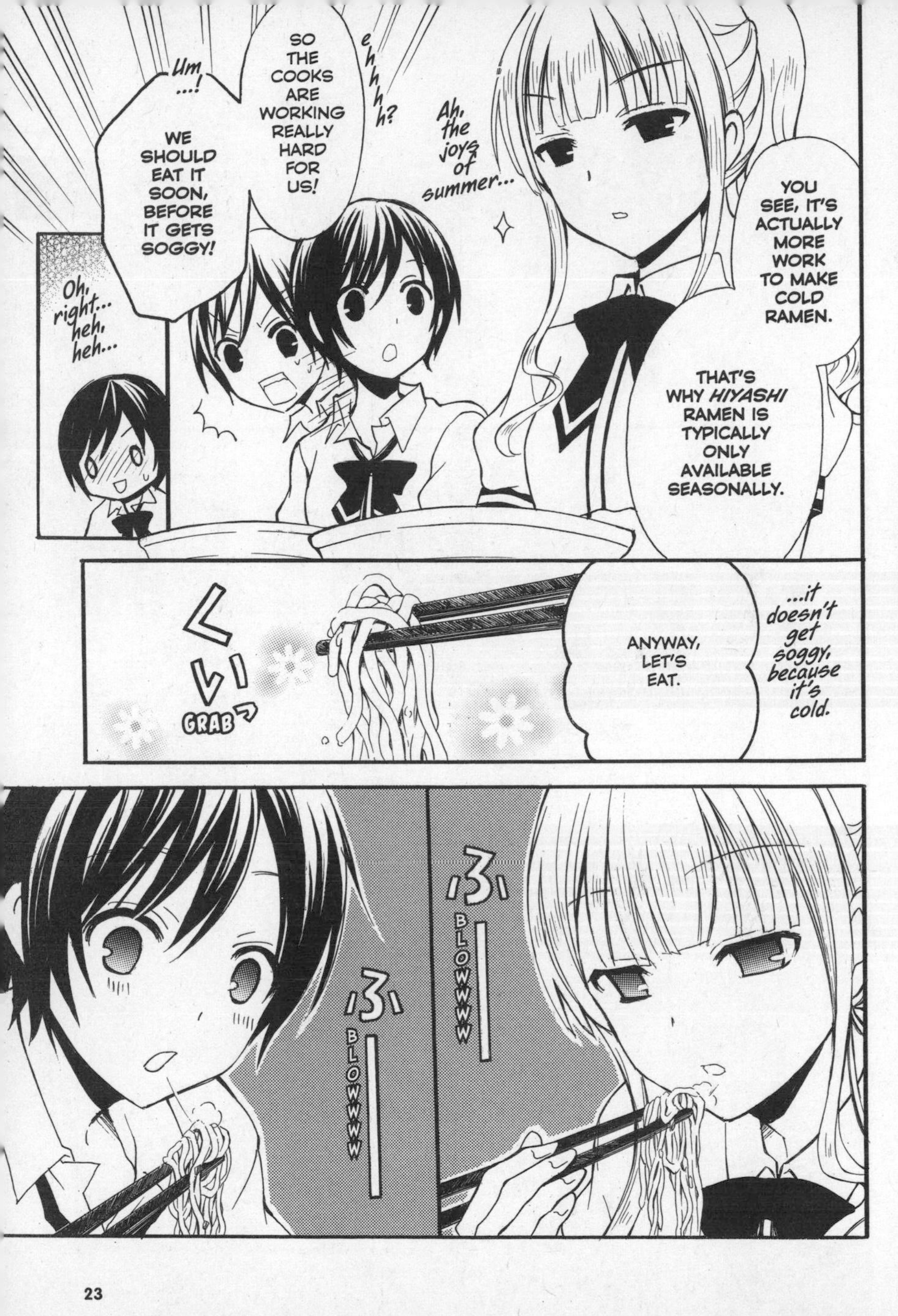
YOU SEE, IT'S ACTUALLY MORE WORK TO MAKE COLD RAMEN.
THAT'S WHY *HIYASHI* RAMEN IS TYPICALLY ONLY AVAILABLE SEASONALLY.
Ah, the joys of summer...
ehhhhh?
SO THE COOKS ARE WORKING REALLY HARD FOR US!
Um ...!
WE SHOULD EAT IT SOON, BEFORE IT GETS SOGGY!
Oh, right... heh, heh...
...it doesn't get soggy, because it's cold.
ANYWAY, LET'S EAT.
GRAB
BLOWWWW
BLOWWWW

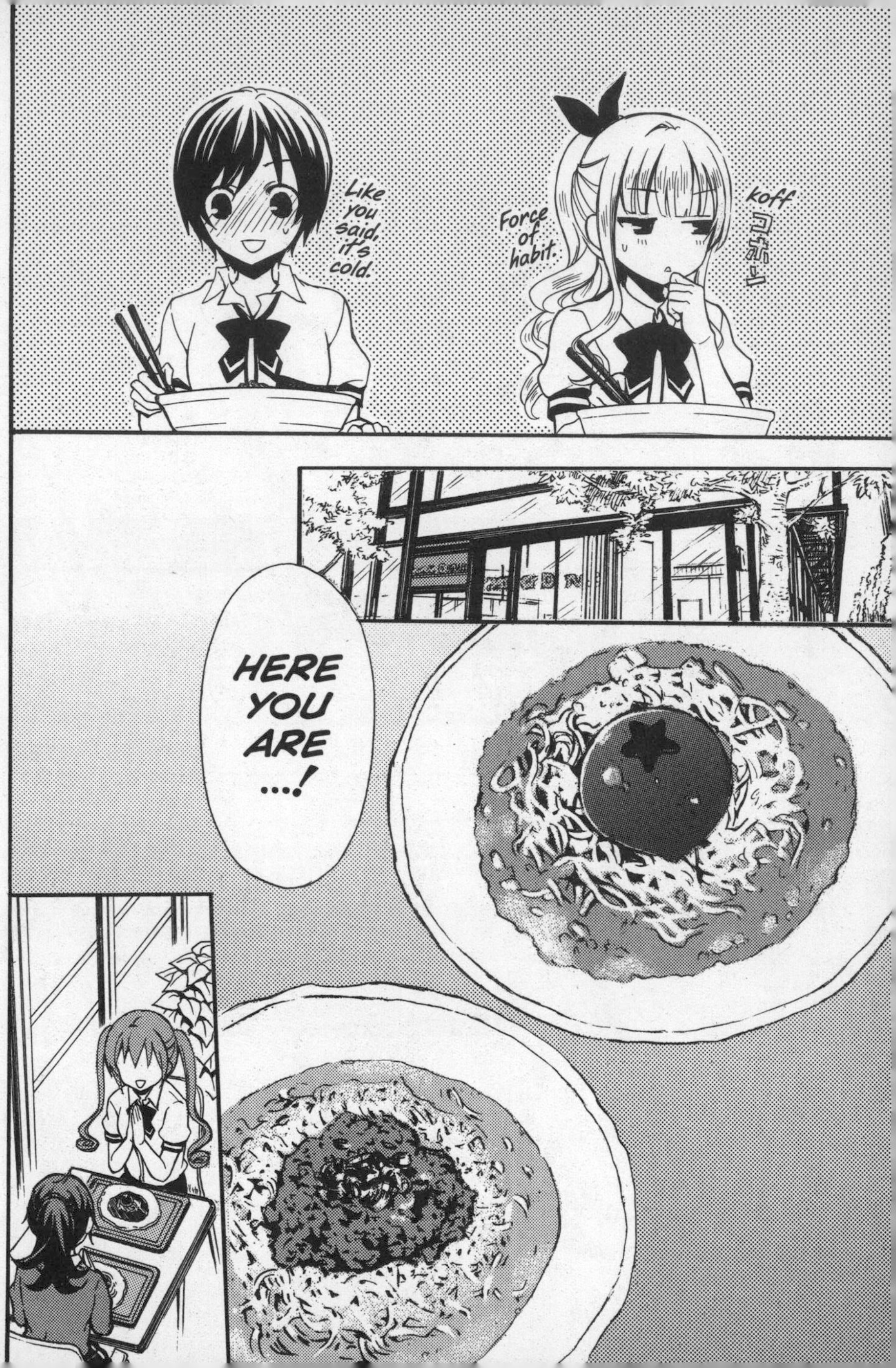

koff
コホッ
Force of habit.
Like you said, it's cold.
HERE YOU ARE ...!

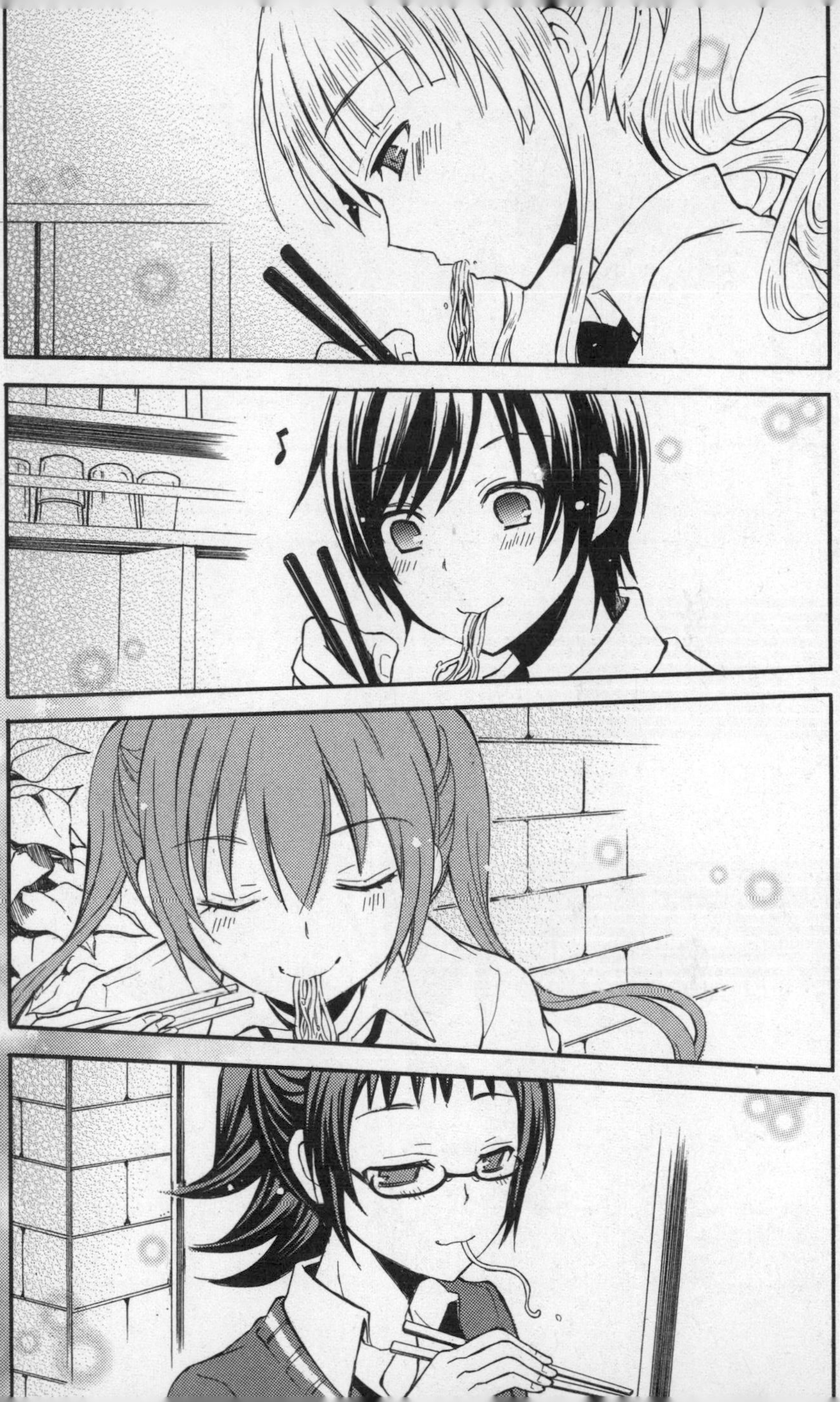

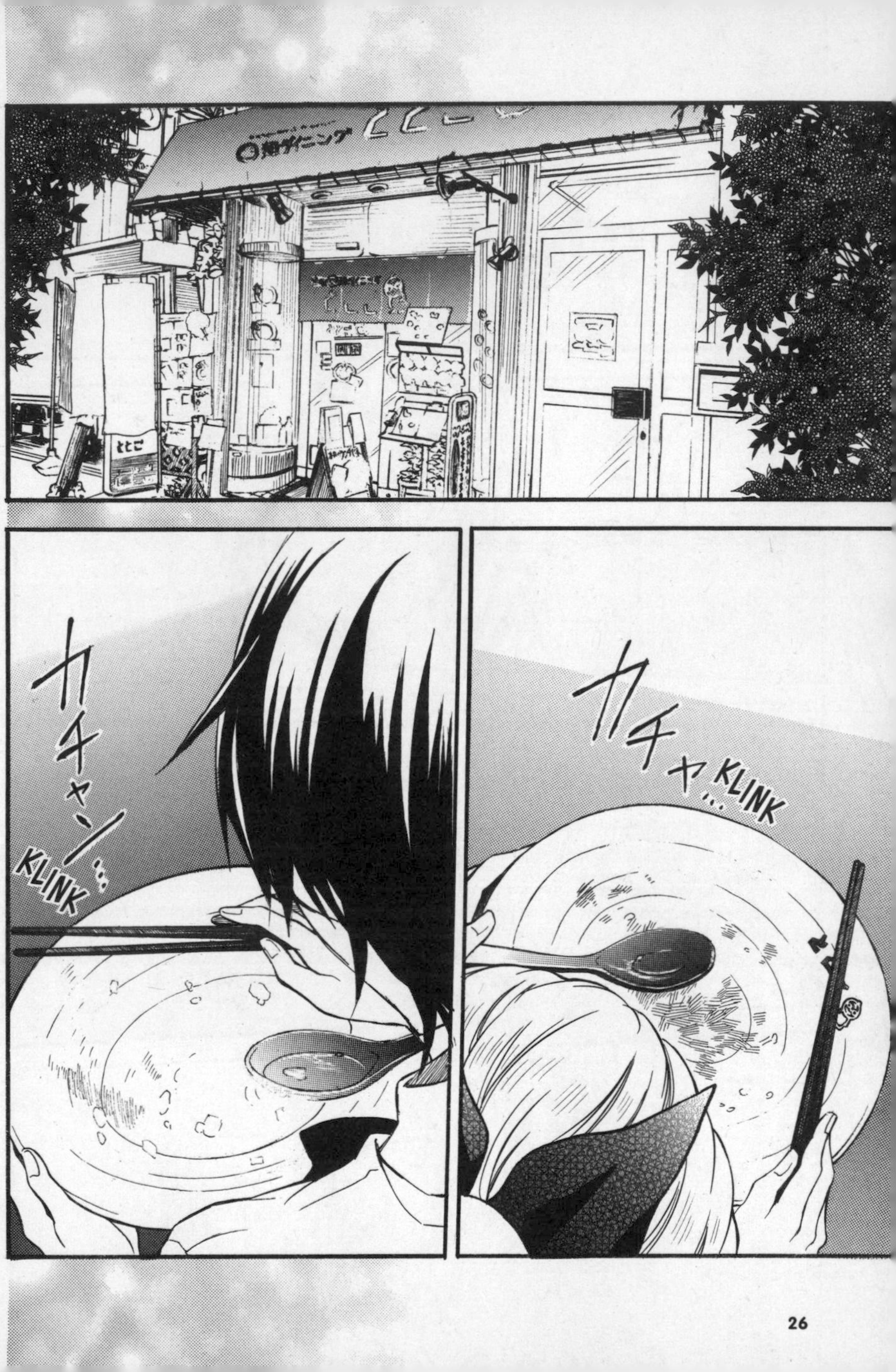
カチャ…
KLINK
カチャン…
KLINK

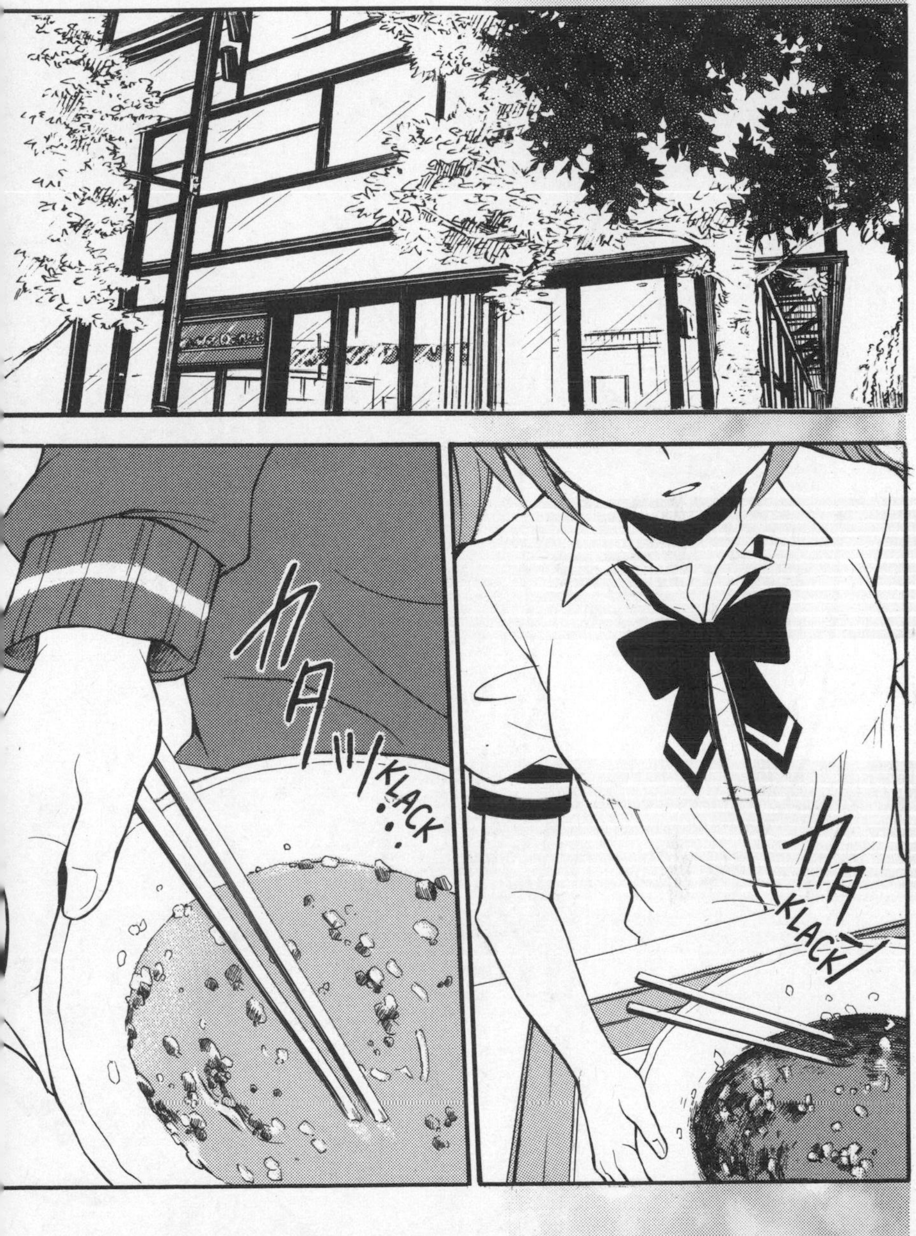
カタ
KLACK
カタッ
KLACK

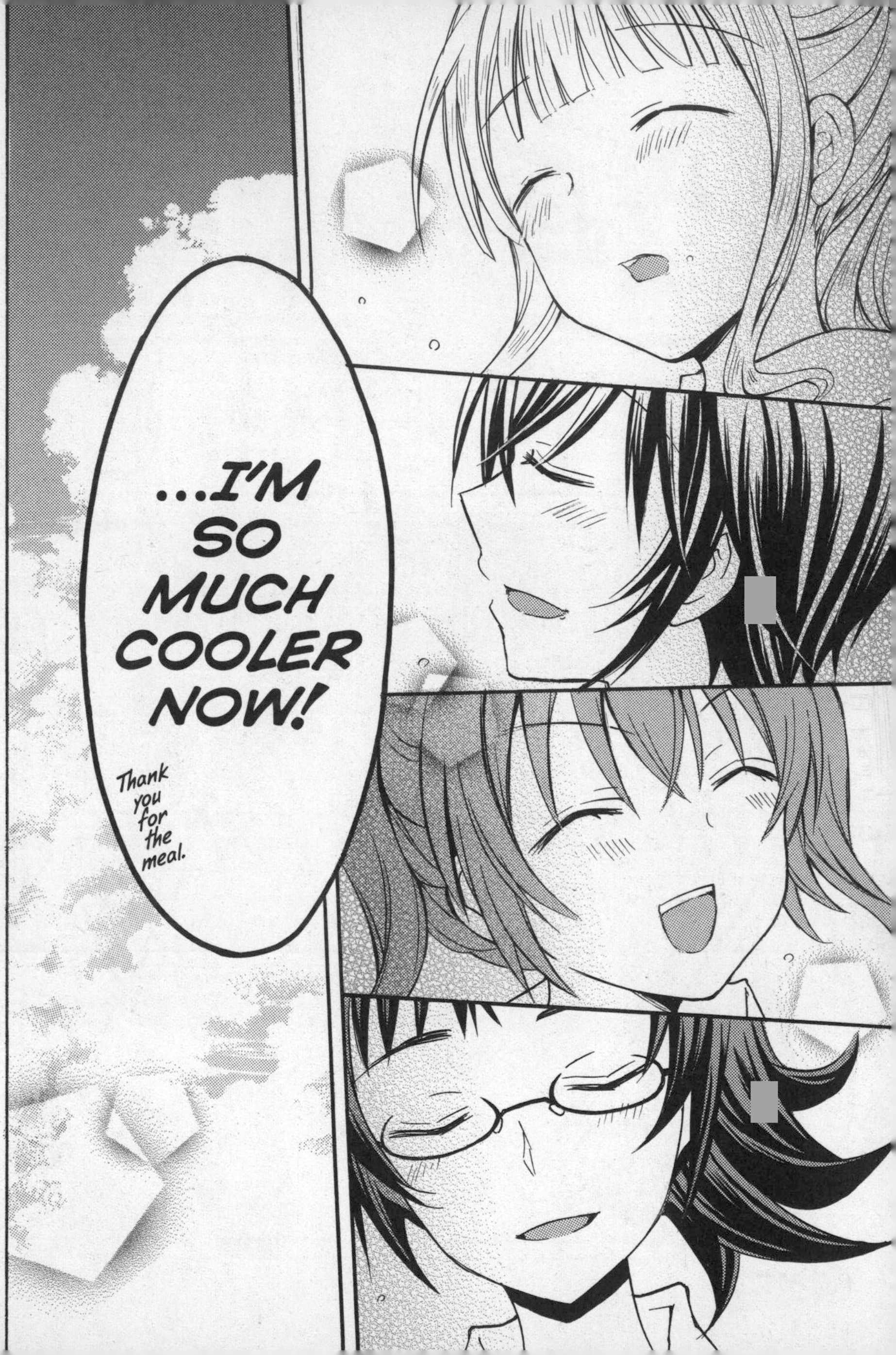
...I'M SO MUCH COOLER NOW!
Thank you for the meal.

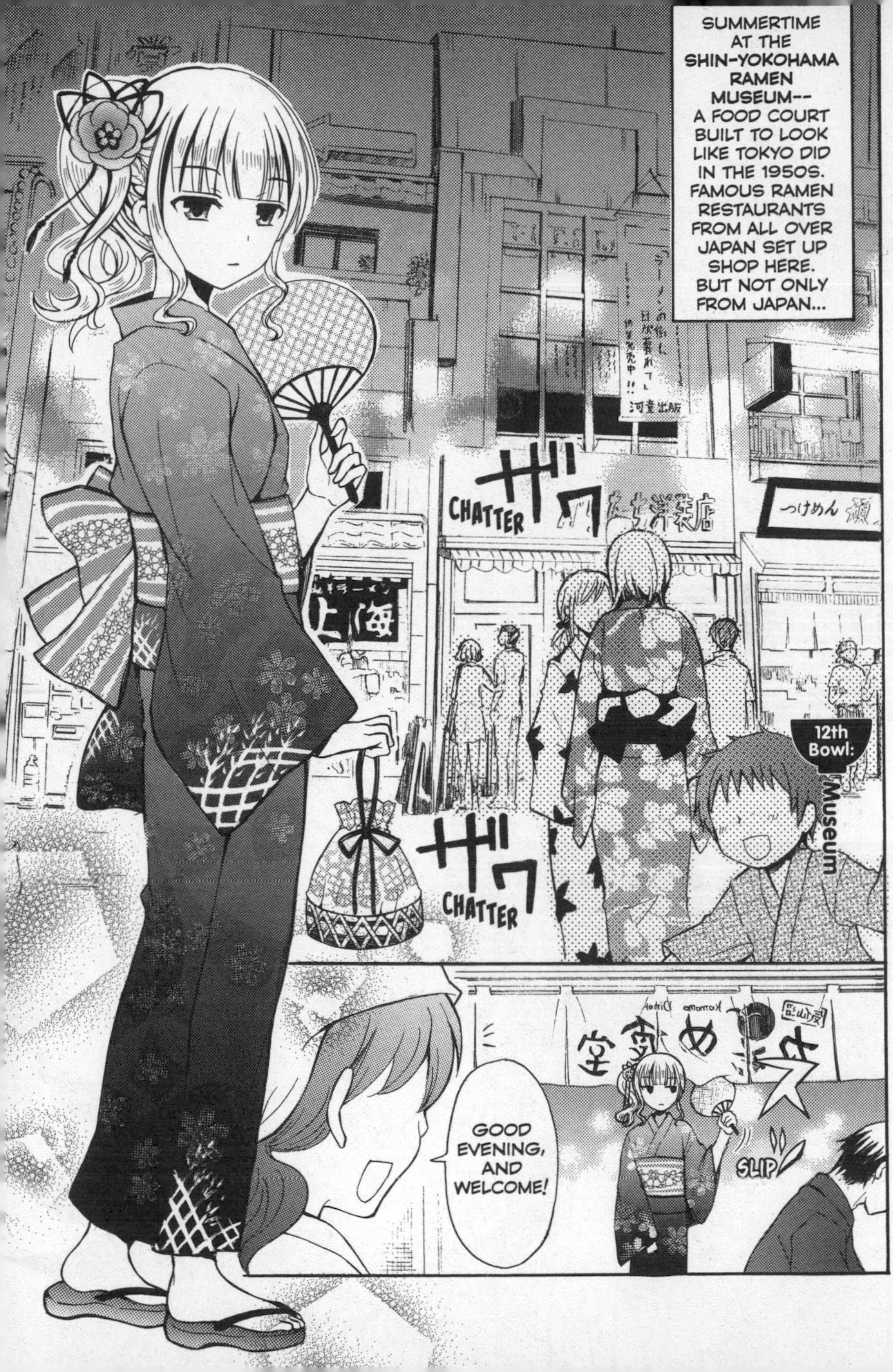
SUMMERTIME AT THE SHIN-YOKOHAMA RAMEN MUSEUM-- A FOOD COURT BUILT TO LOOK LIKE TOKYO DID IN THE 1950S. FAMOUS RAMEN RESTAURANTS FROM ALL OVER JAPAN SET UP SHOP HERE. BUT NOT ONLY FROM JAPAN...
ザワ CHATTER
12th Bowl: Museum
ザワ CHATTER
GOOD EVENING, AND WELCOME!
SLIP

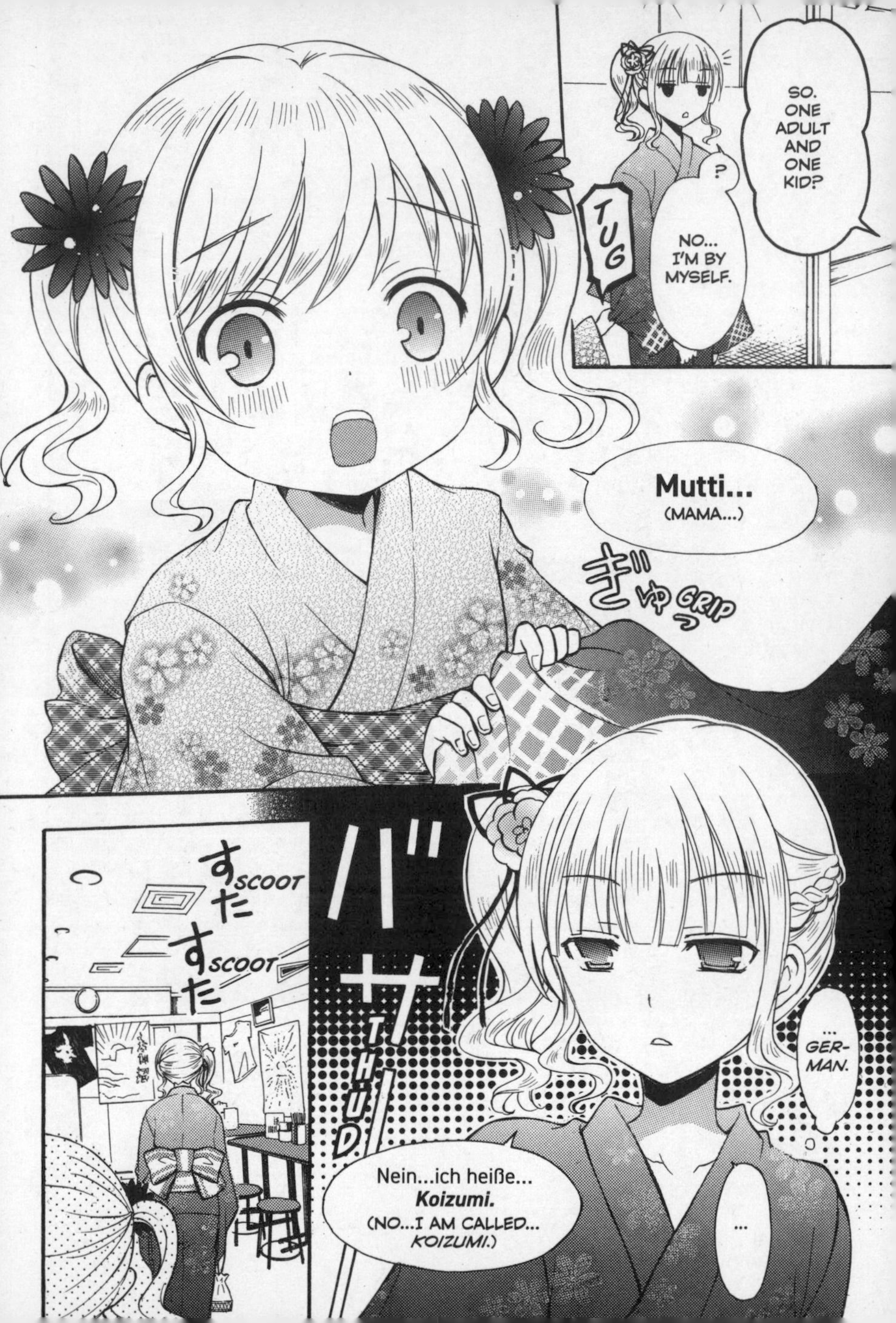
SO. ONE ADULT AND ONE KID?
?
TUG
NO... I'M BY MYSELF.
Mutti... (MAMA...)
ぎゅっ GRIP
... GER-MAN.
...
Nein...ich heiße... Koizumi. (NO...I AM CALLED... KOIZUMI.)
バサ THUD.
すた SCOOT
すた SCOOT

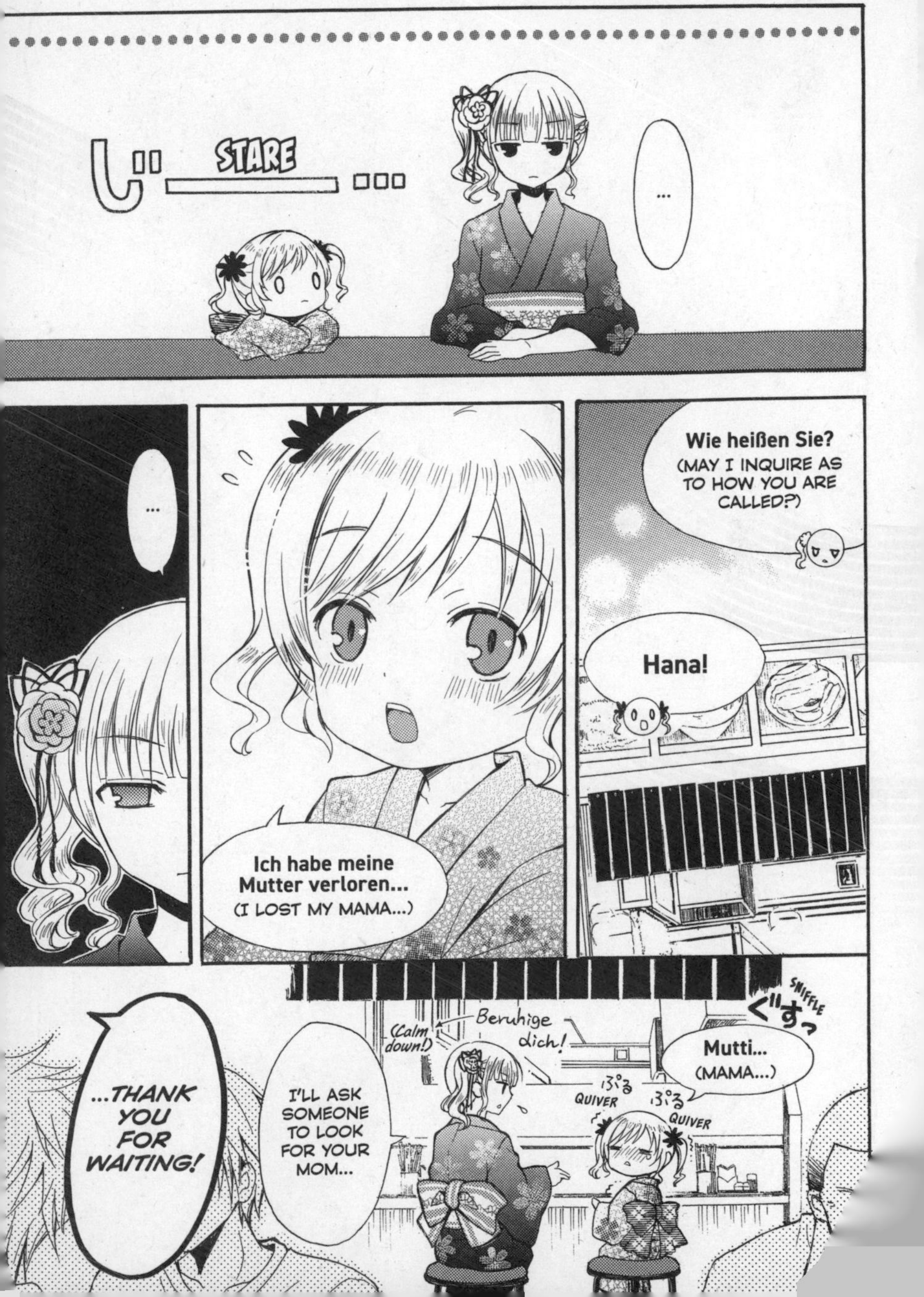
じ
STARE
...
Wie heißen Sie?
(MAY I INQUIRE AS TO HOW YOU ARE CALLED?)
Hana!
Ich habe meine Mutter verloren...
(I LOST MY MAMA...)
...
SNIFFLE
ぐすっ
Mutti...
(MAMA...)
ぷる
QUIVER
ぷる
QUIVER
Beruhige dich!
(Calm down!)
I'LL ASK SOMEONE TO LOOK FOR YOUR MOM...
...THANK YOU FOR WAITING!

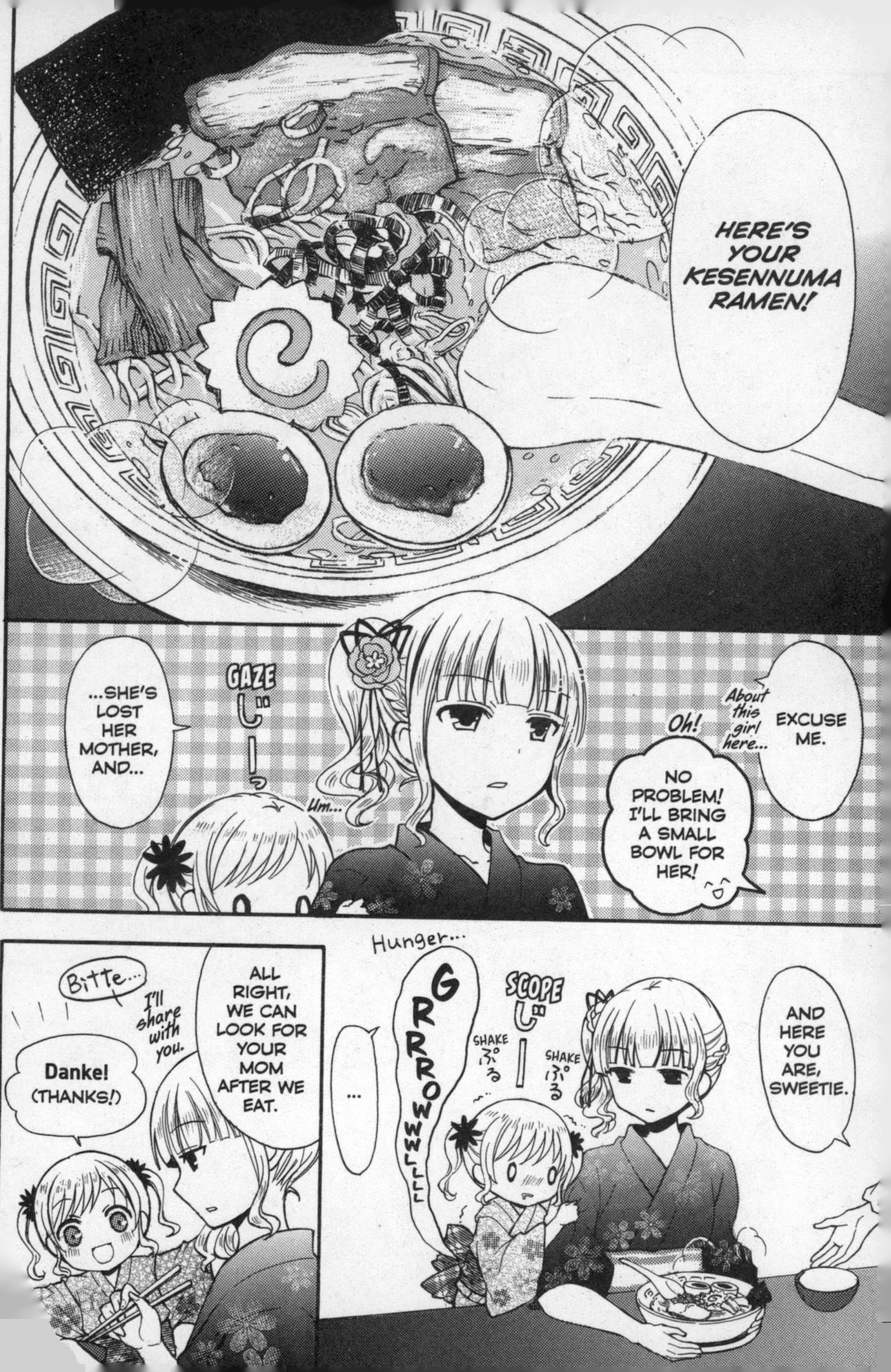
HERE'S YOUR KESENNUMA RAMEN!
EXCUSE ME.
About this girl here...
...SHE'S LOST HER MOTHER, AND...
GAZE
Oh!
NO PROBLEM! I'LL BRING A SMALL BOWL FOR HER!
Um...
AND HERE YOU ARE, SWEETIE.
SHAKE
SCOPE
SHAKE
Hunger...
GRRROWWWLLLL
...
ALL RIGHT, WE CAN LOOK FOR YOUR MOM AFTER WE EAT.
I'll share with you.
Bitte...
Danke! (THANKS!)

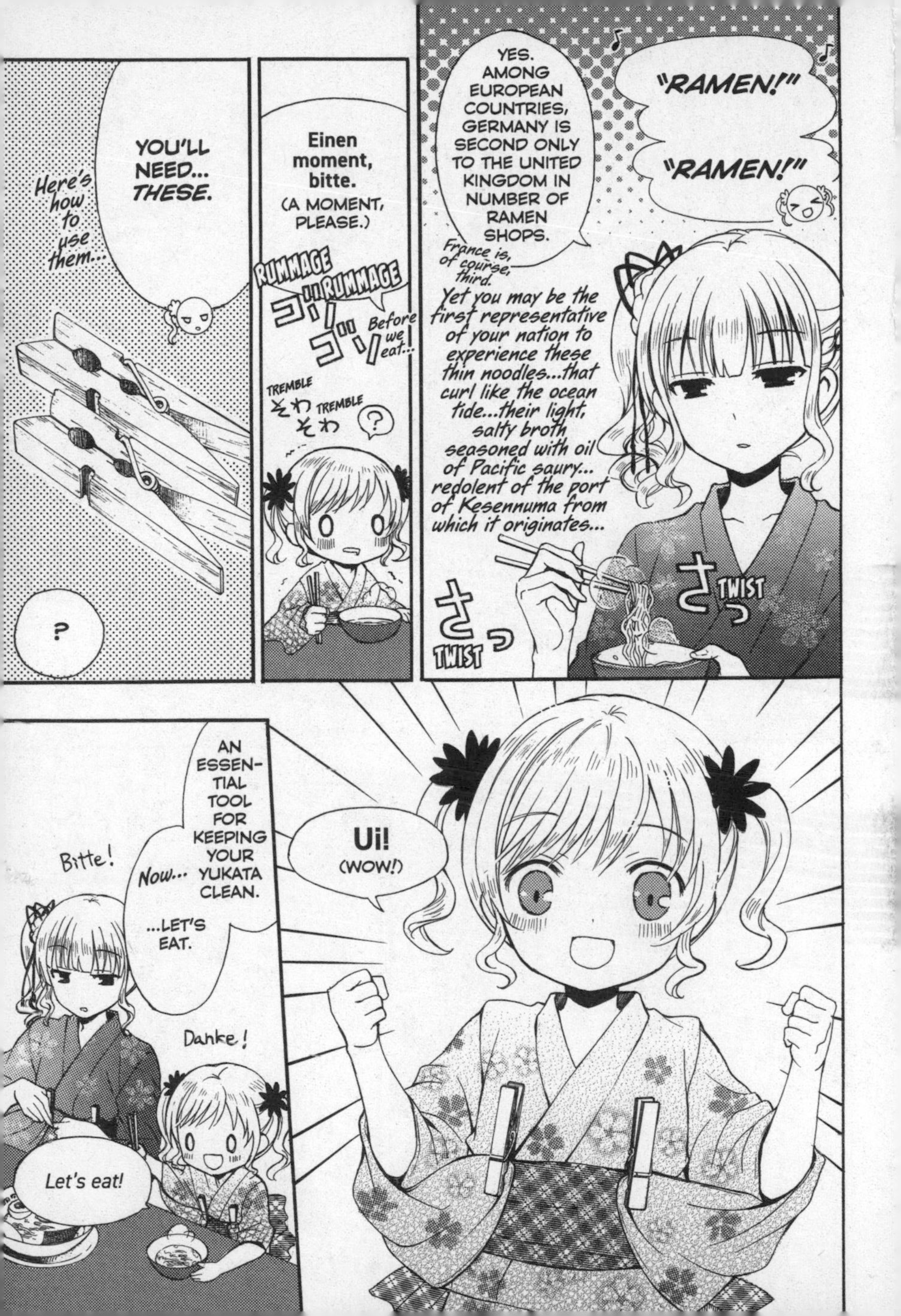
"RAMEN!"
"RAMEN!"
YES. AMONG EUROPEAN COUNTRIES, GERMANY IS SECOND ONLY TO THE UNITED KINGDOM IN NUMBER OF RAMEN SHOPS.
France is, of course, third.
Yet you may be the first representative of your nation to experience these thin noodles...that curl like the ocean tide...their light, salty broth seasoned with oil of Pacific saury... redolent of the port of Kesennuma from which it originates...
さっ TWIST
さっ TWIST
Einen moment, bitte.
(A MOMENT, PLEASE.)
RUMMAGE ゴソ RUMMAGE ゴソ
Before we eat...
TREMBLE そわ TREMBLE そわ
?
YOU'LL NEED... THESE.
Here's how to use them...
?
Ui!
(WOW!)
AN ESSENTIAL TOOL FOR KEEPING YOUR YUKATA CLEAN.
Now...
...LET'S EAT.
Bitte!
Danke!
Let's eat!

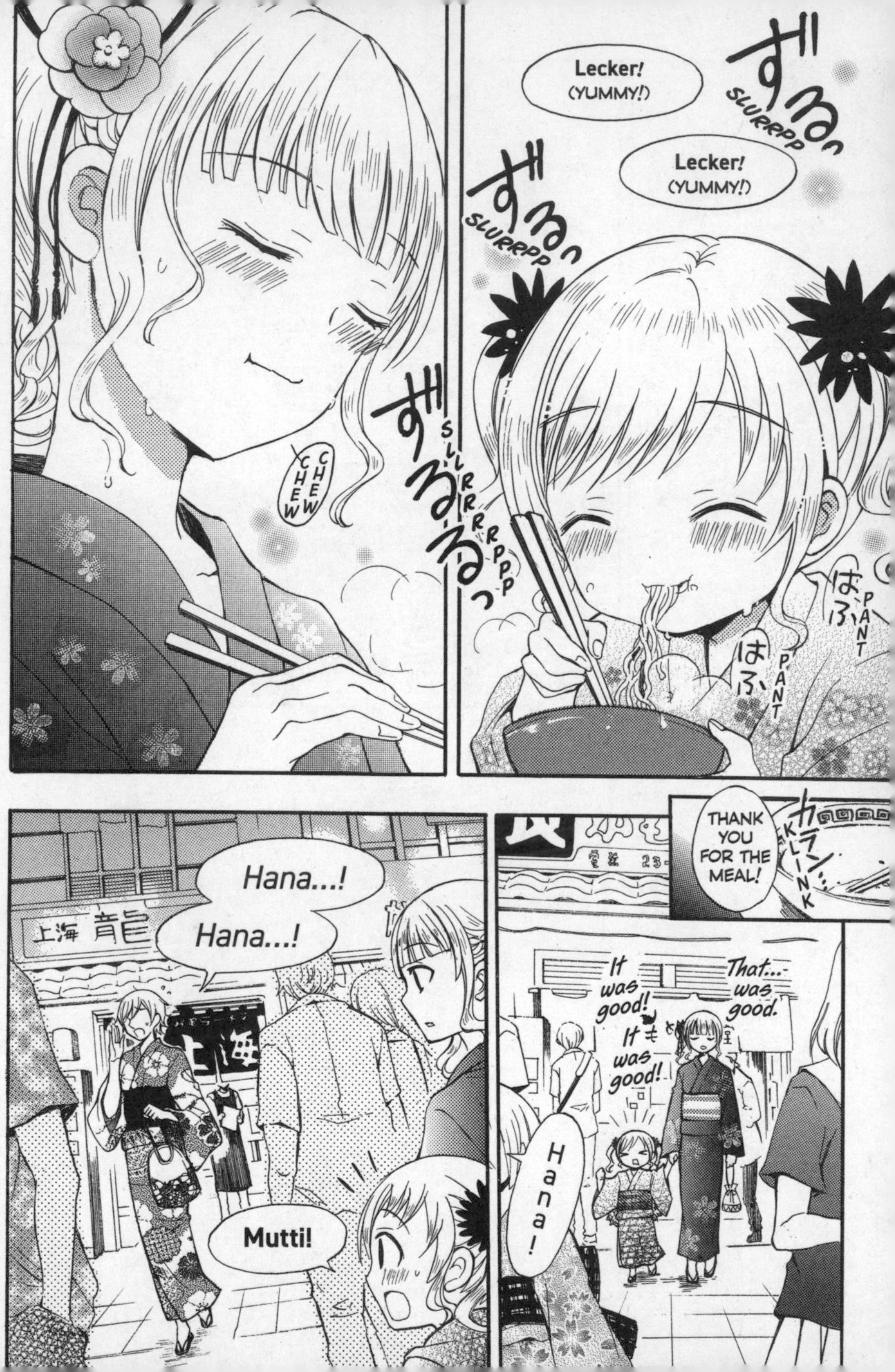
ずるっ
SLURRPPP
Lecker!
(YUMMY!)
Lecker!
(YUMMY!)
ずるっ
SLURRPPP
はふ
PANT
はふ
PANT
ずるるるっ
SLLRRRRPPP
CHEW CHEW
THANK YOU FOR THE MEAL!
カラン
KLINK
That... was good.
It was good!
It too was good!
Hana...!
Hana...!
Hana...!
Mutti!

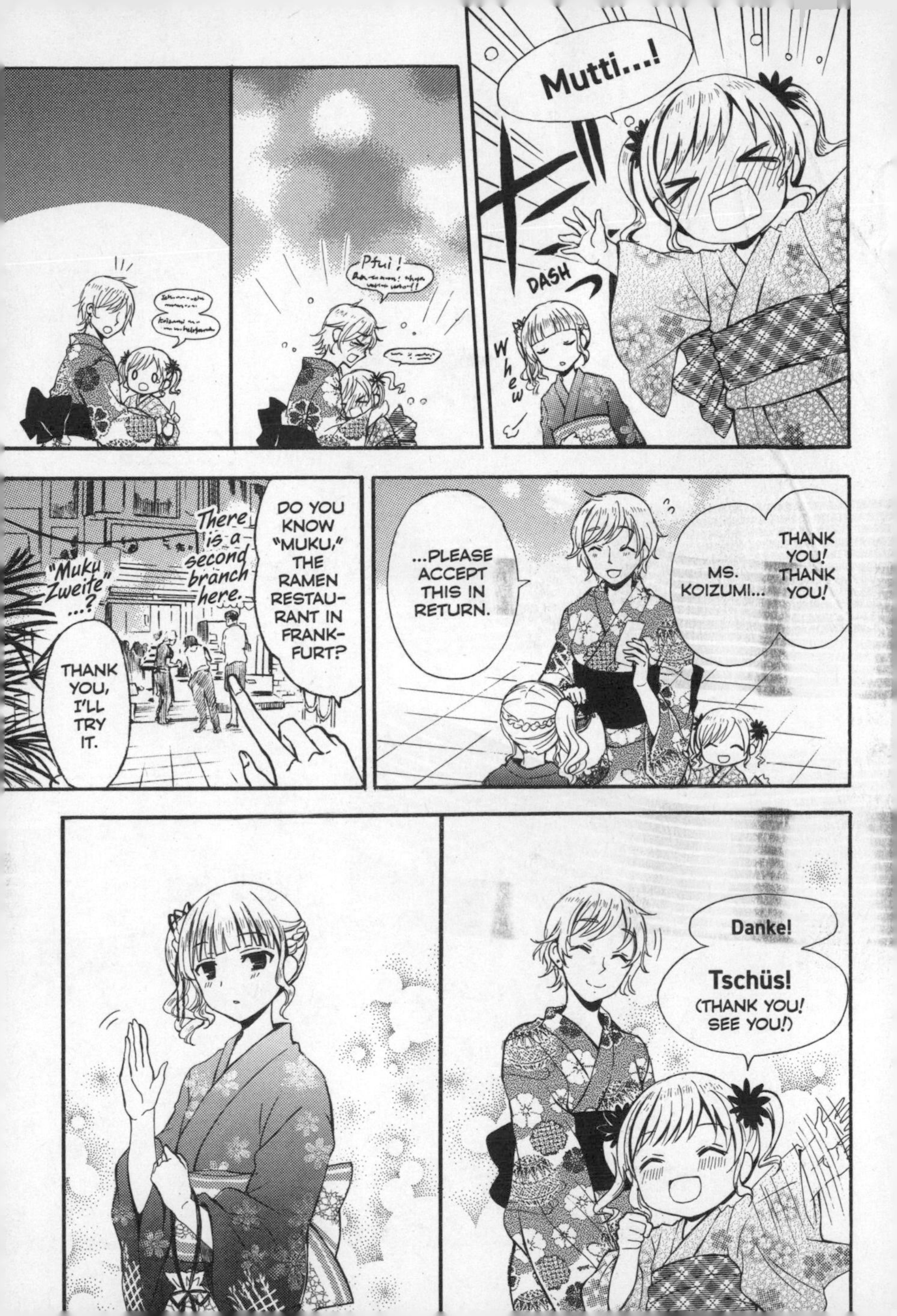
Mutti...!
DASH
Whew
Pfui!
THANK YOU! THANK YOU!
MS. KOIZUMI...
...PLEASE ACCEPT THIS IN RETURN.
DO YOU KNOW "MUKU," THE RAMEN RESTAURANT IN FRANKFURT?
There is a second branch here.
"Muku Zweite" ...?
THANK YOU, I'LL TRY IT.
Danke! Tschüs! (THANK YOU! SEE YOU!)

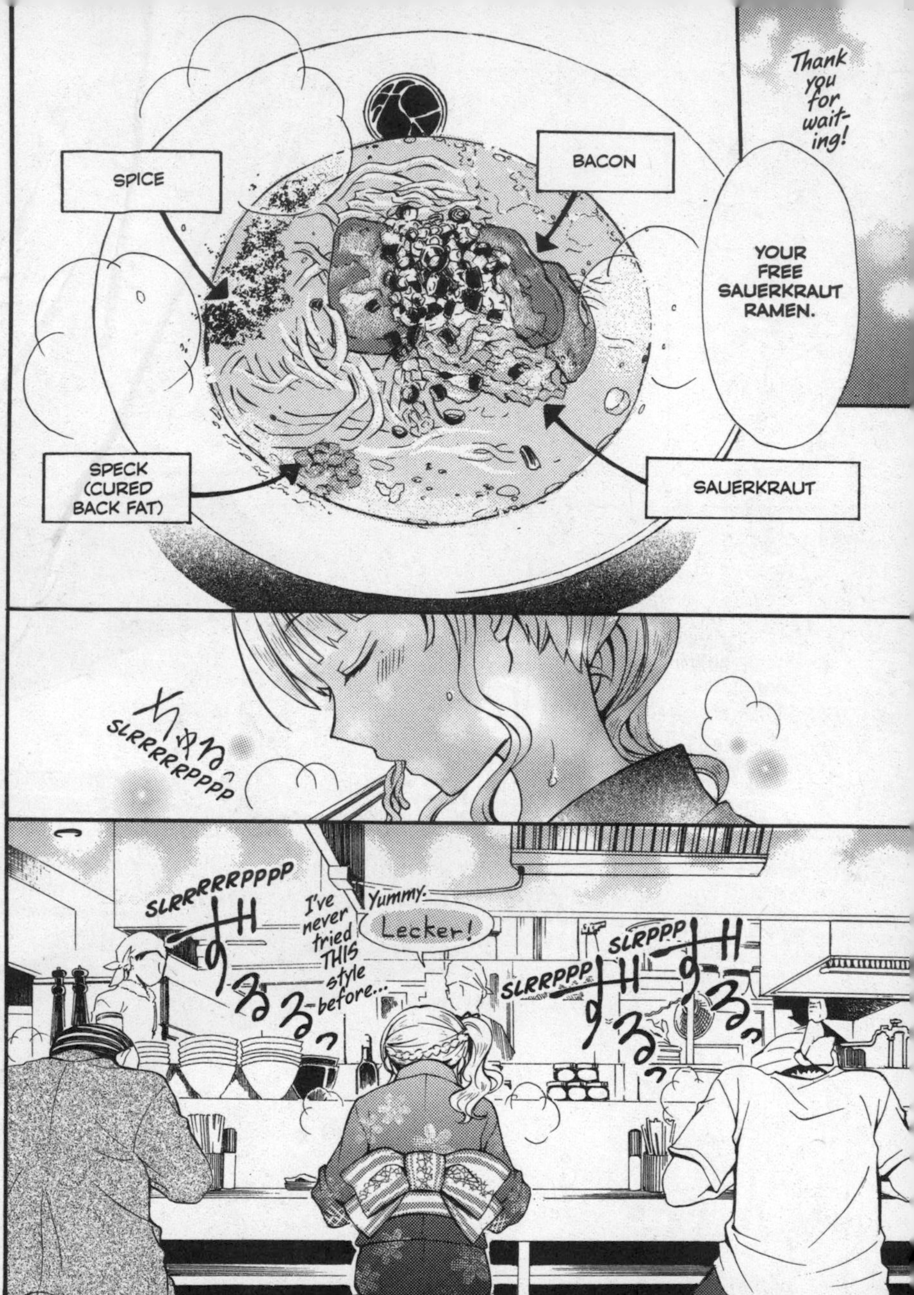
Thank you for waiting!
YOUR FREE SAUERKRAUT RAMEN.
BACON
SPICE
SAUERKRAUT
SPECK (CURED BACK FAT)
SLRRRRRPPPP
SLRPPP
SLRPPP
Yummy.
Lecker!
I've never tried THIS style before...
SLRRRRRPPPP

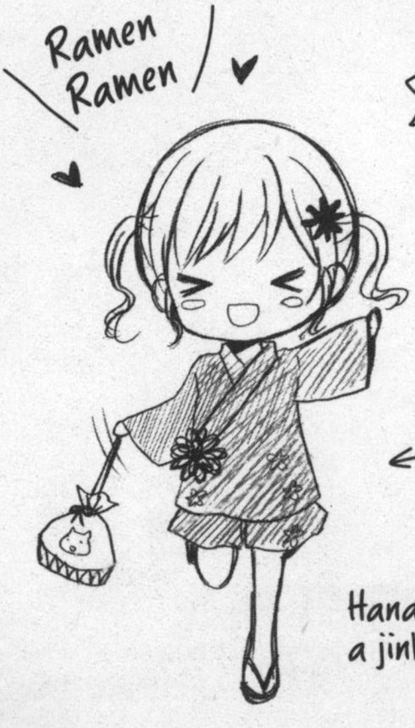
Ramen
Ramen

Summer special deal!

Some museums offer a free pass if you wear traditional Japanese summer clothes such as yukata, jinbei, or samue.

Second time for me!

Hana is wearing a jinbei.

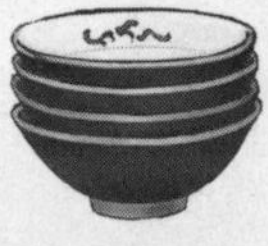

Ms. Koizumi loves ramen noodles

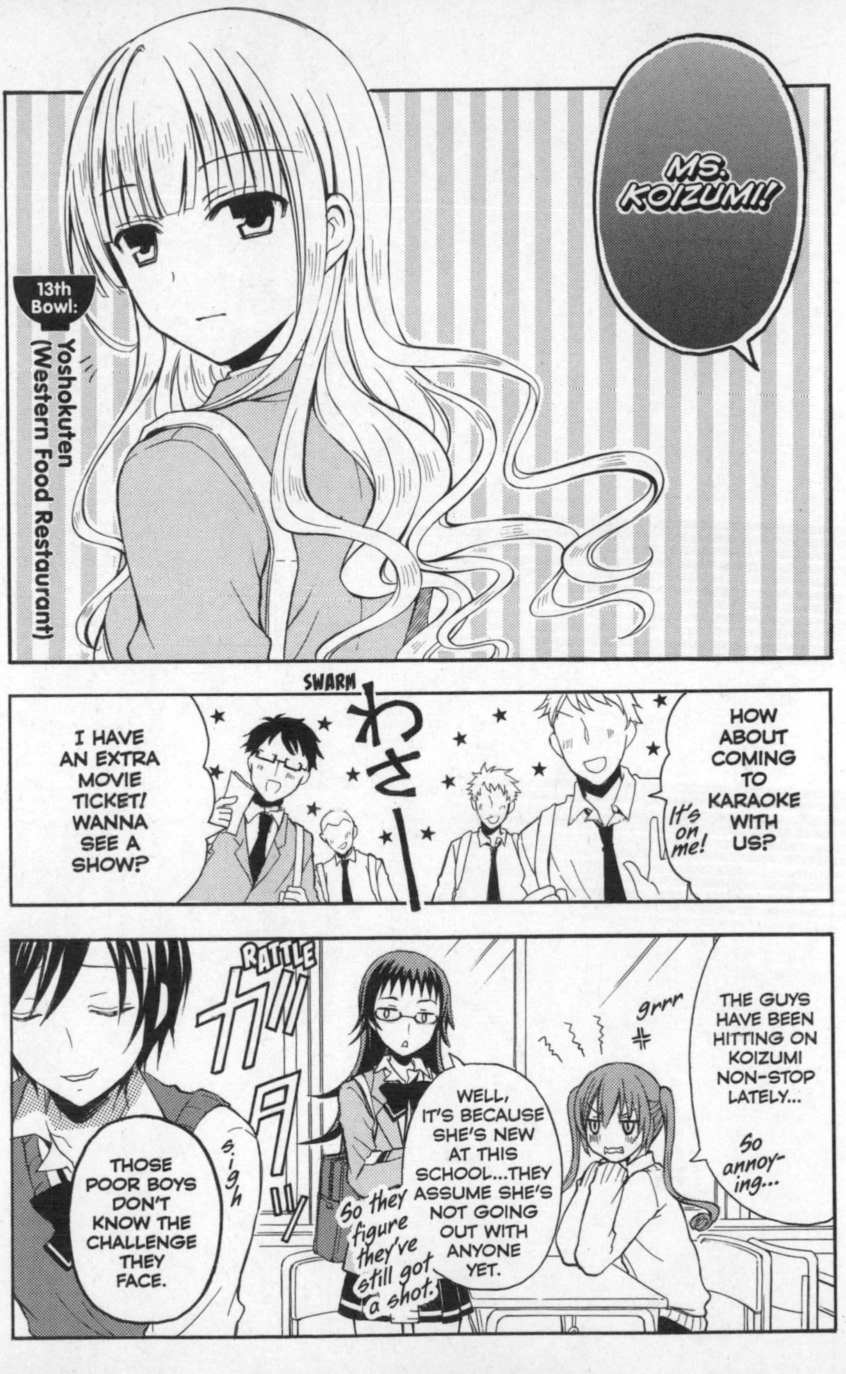
MS. KOIZUMI!
13th Bowl: Yoshokuten (Western Food Restaurant)
SWARM
わさー
HOW ABOUT COMING TO KARAOKE WITH US?
It's on me!
I HAVE AN EXTRA MOVIE TICKET! WANNA SEE A SHOW?
THE GUYS HAVE BEEN HITTING ON KOIZUMI NON-STOP LATELY...
So annoy-ing...
grrr
WELL, IT'S BECAUSE SHE'S NEW AT THIS SCHOOL...THEY ASSUME SHE'S NOT GOING OUT WITH ANYONE YET.
So they figure they've still got a shot.
sigh
RATTLE
ガタッ
THOSE POOR BOYS DON'T KNOW THE CHALLENGE THEY FACE.

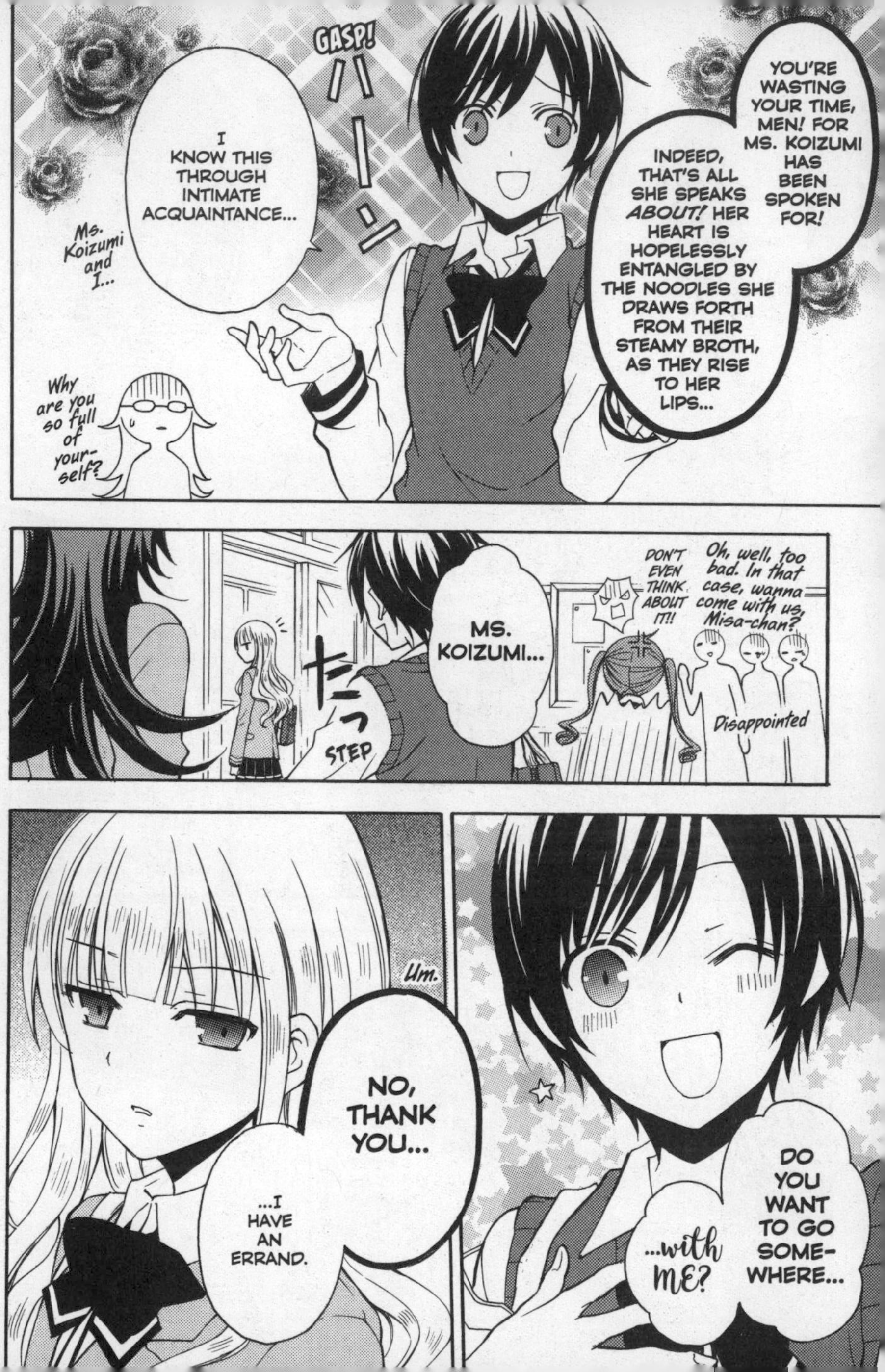
YOU'RE WASTING YOUR TIME, MEN! FOR MS. KOIZUMI HAS BEEN SPOKEN FOR!
INDEED, THAT'S ALL SHE SPEAKS *ABOUT!* HER HEART IS HOPELESSLY ENTANGLED BY THE NOODLES SHE DRAWS FORTH FROM THEIR STEAMY BROTH, AS THEY RISE TO HER LIPS...
GASP!
I KNOW THIS THROUGH INTIMATE ACQUAINTANCE...
Ms. Koizumi and I...
Why are you so full of your-self?
Oh, well, too bad. In that case, wanna come with us, Misa-chan?
DON'T EVEN THINK ABOUT IT!!
Disappointed
MS. KOIZUMI...
STEP
DO YOU WANT TO GO SOME-WHERE...
...with ME?
Um.
NO, THANK YOU...
...I HAVE AN ERRAND.

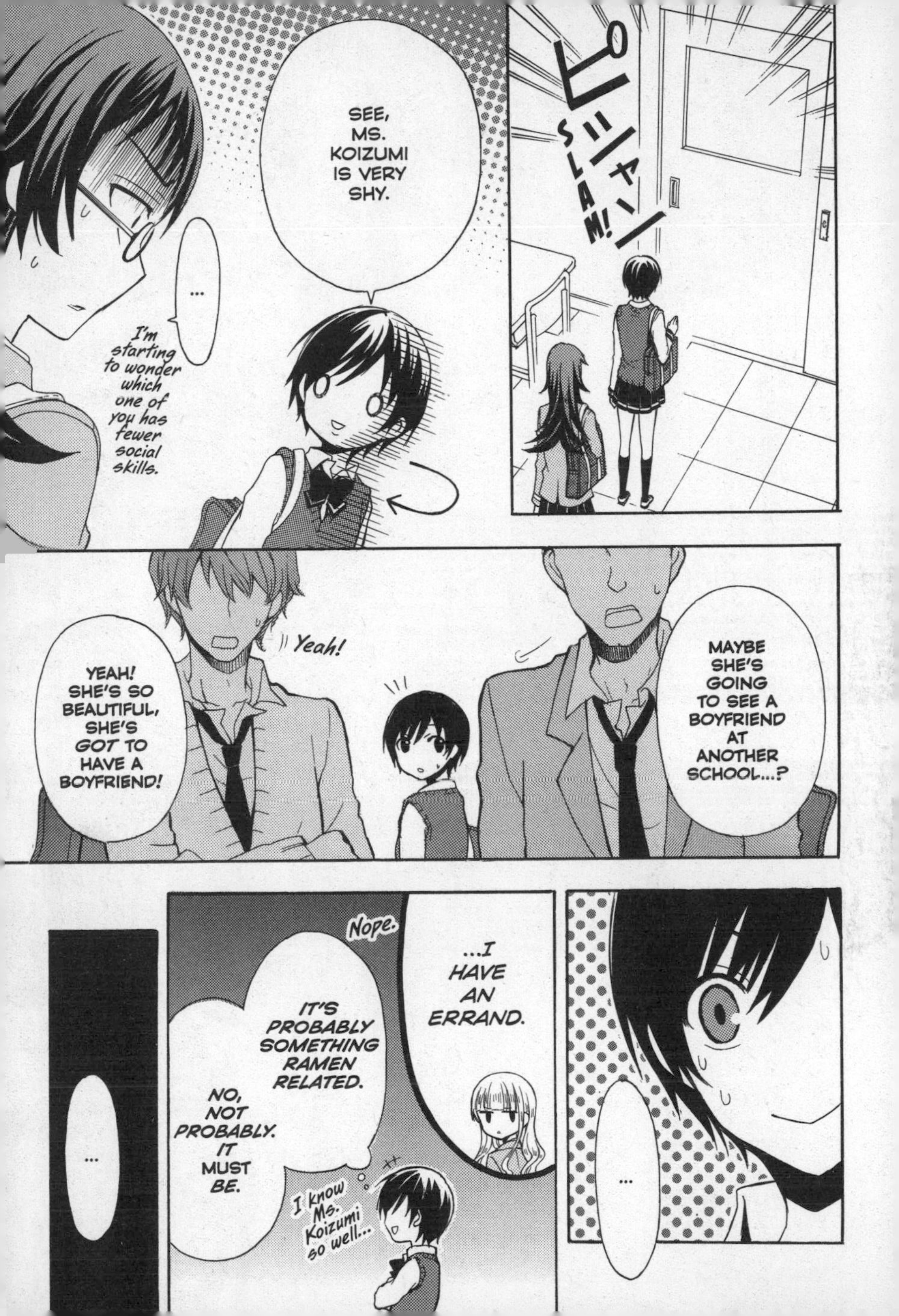
ピシャン
SLAM!
SEE, MS. KOIZUMI IS VERY SHY.
...
I'm starting to wonder which one of you has fewer social skills.
MAYBE SHE'S GOING TO SEE A BOYFRIEND AT ANOTHER SCHOOL...?
Yeah!
YEAH! SHE'S SO BEAUTIFUL, SHE'S *GOT* TO HAVE A BOYFRIEND!
...
...I HAVE AN ERRAND.
Nope.
IT'S PROBABLY SOMETHING RAMEN RELATED.
NO, NOT PROBABLY. IT MUST *BE*.
I know Ms. Koizumi so well...
...

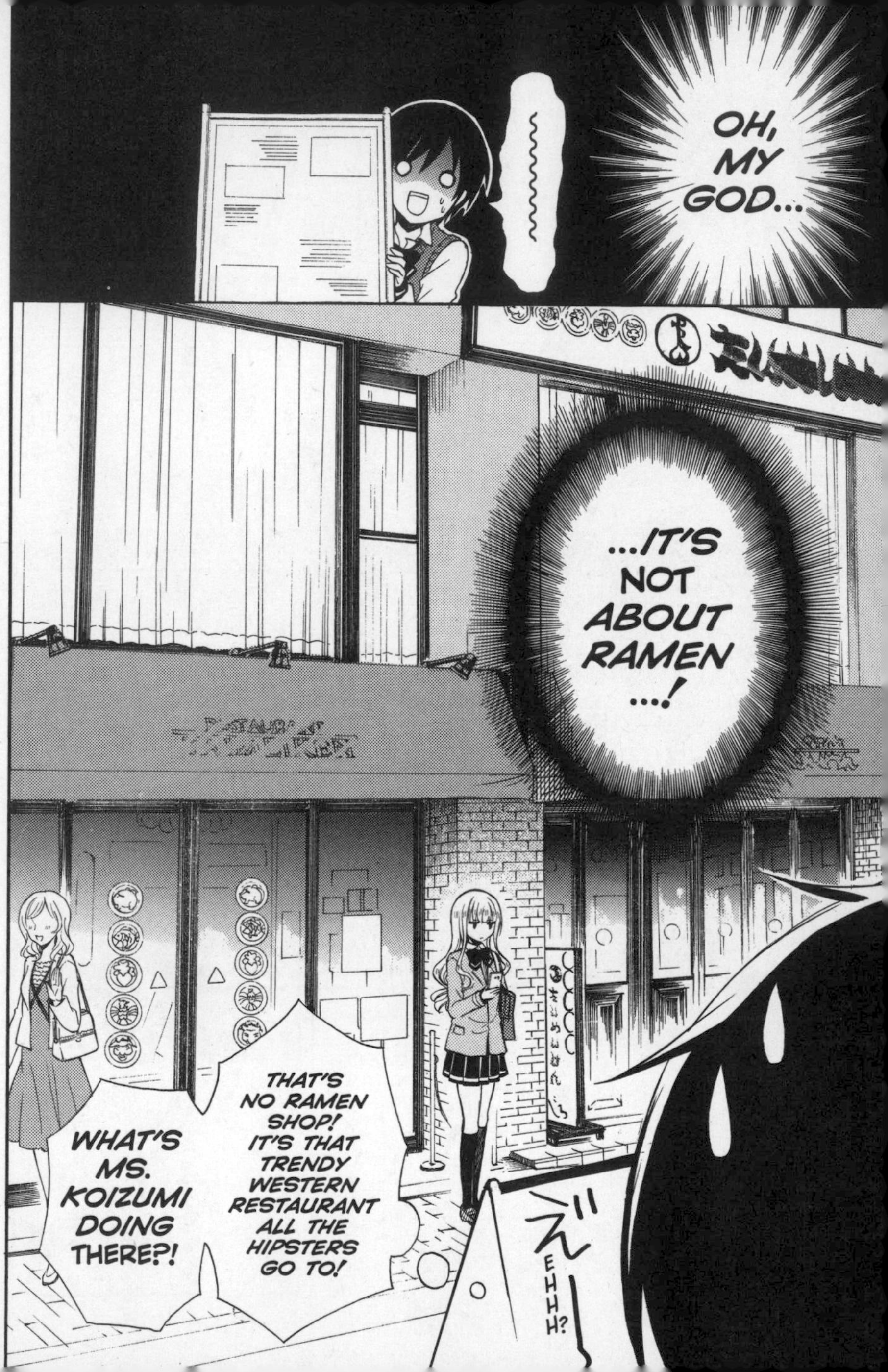
OH, MY GOD...
...IT'S NOT ABOUT RAMEN...!
EHHH?
THAT'S NO RAMEN SHOP! IT'S THAT TRENDY WESTERN RESTAURANT ALL THE HIPSTERS GO TO!
WHAT'S MS. KOIZUMI DOING THERE?!

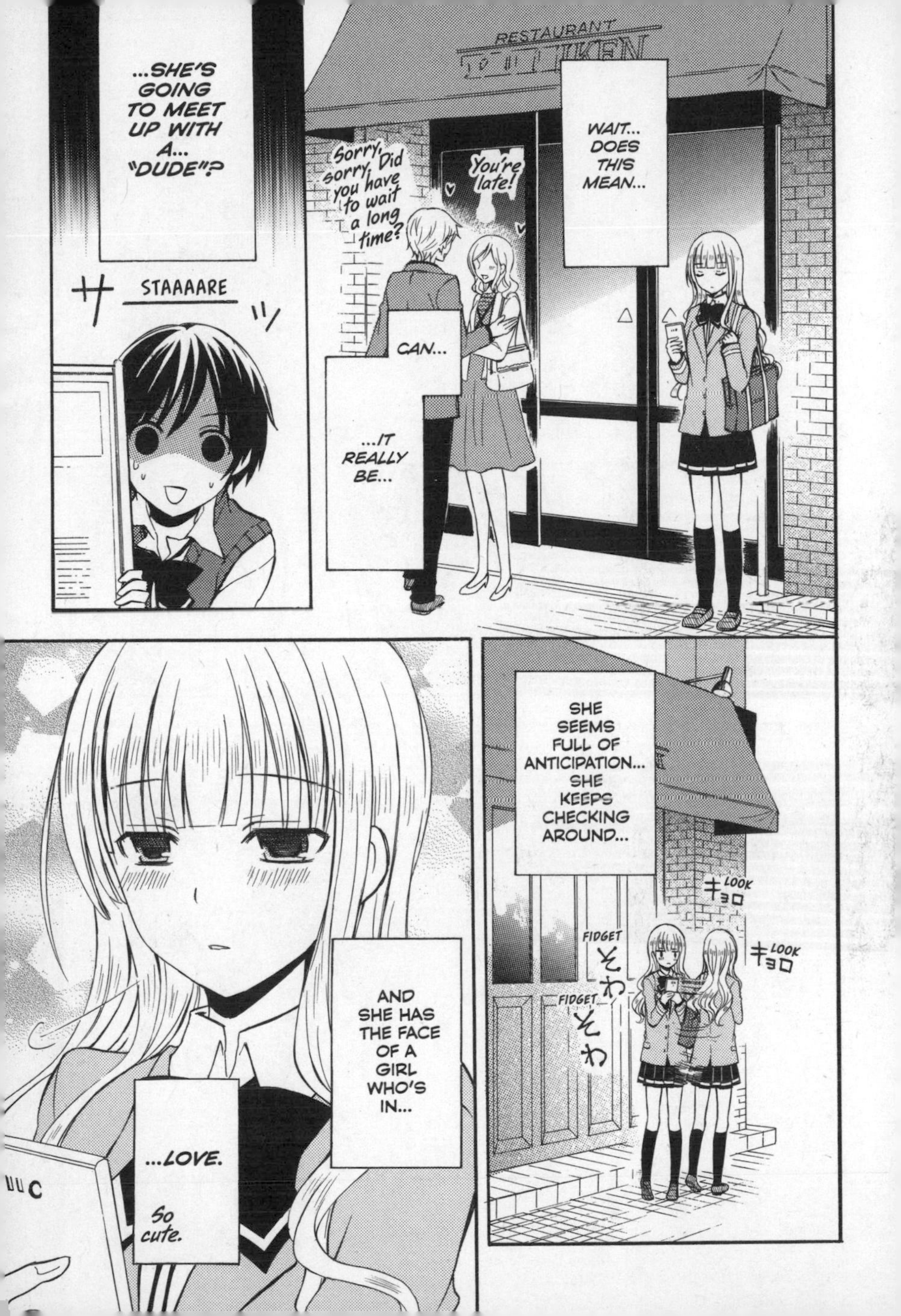
RESTAURANT
WAIT... DOES THIS MEAN...
You're late!
Sorry, sorry. Did you have to wait a long time?
CAN...
...IT REALLY BE...
...SHE'S GOING TO MEET UP WITH A... "DUDE"?
STAAAARE
SHE SEEMS FULL OF ANTICIPATION... SHE KEEPS CHECKING AROUND...
LOOK キョロ
FIDGET そわ
FIDGET そわ
LOOK キョロ
AND SHE HAS THE FACE OF A GIRL WHO'S IN...
...LOVE.
So cute.

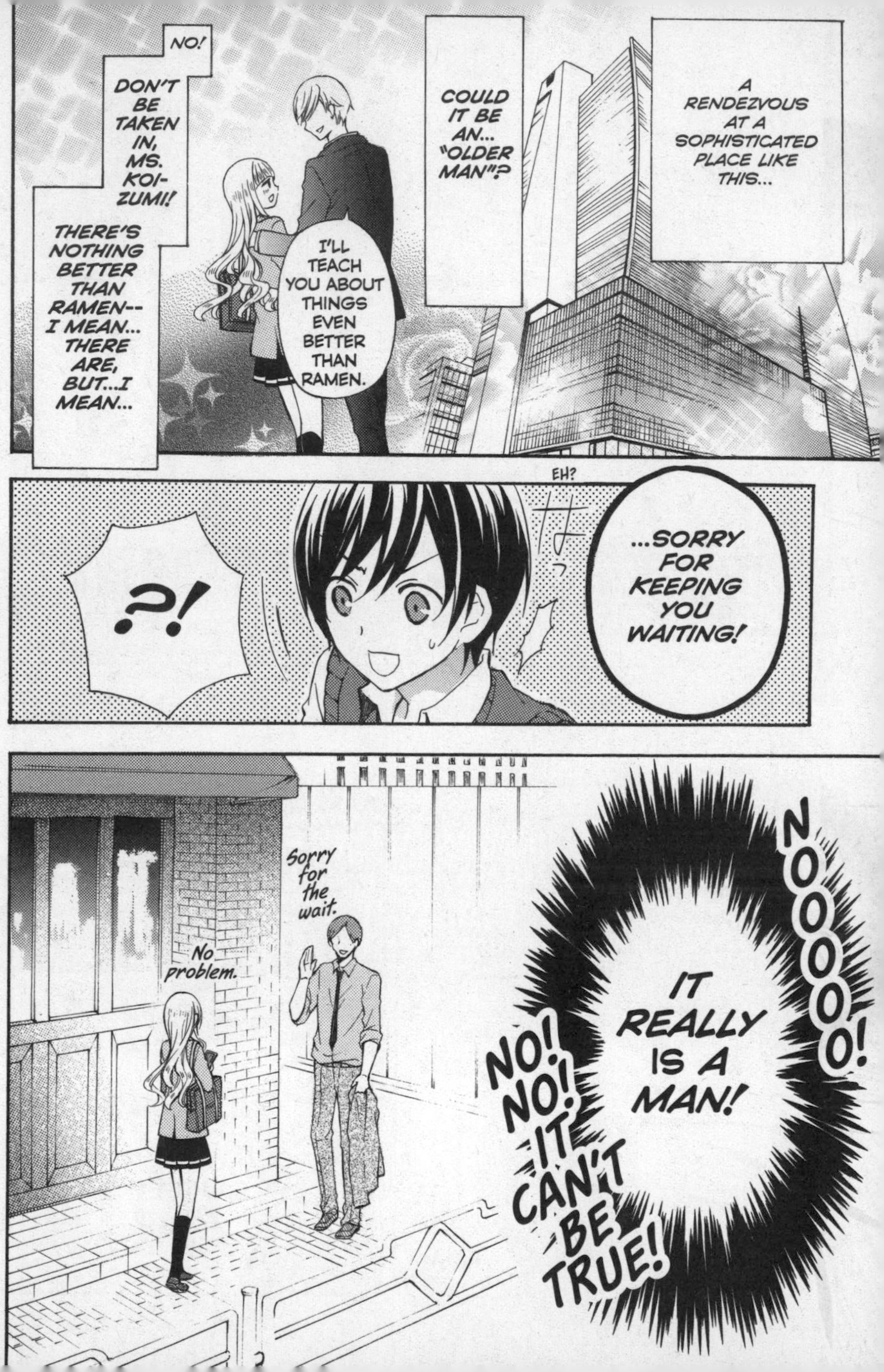
A RENDEZVOUS AT A SOPHISTICATED PLACE LIKE THIS...
COULD IT BE AN... "OLDER MAN"?
I'LL TEACH YOU ABOUT THINGS EVEN BETTER THAN RAMEN.
NO!
DON'T BE TAKEN IN, MS. KOI-ZUMI!
THERE'S NOTHING BETTER THAN RAMEN-- I MEAN... THERE ARE, BUT...I MEAN...
EH?
...SORRY FOR KEEPING YOU WAITING!
?!
NOOOOO!
IT REALLY IS A MAN!
NO! NO! IT CAN'T BE TRUE!
Sorry for the wait.
No problem.

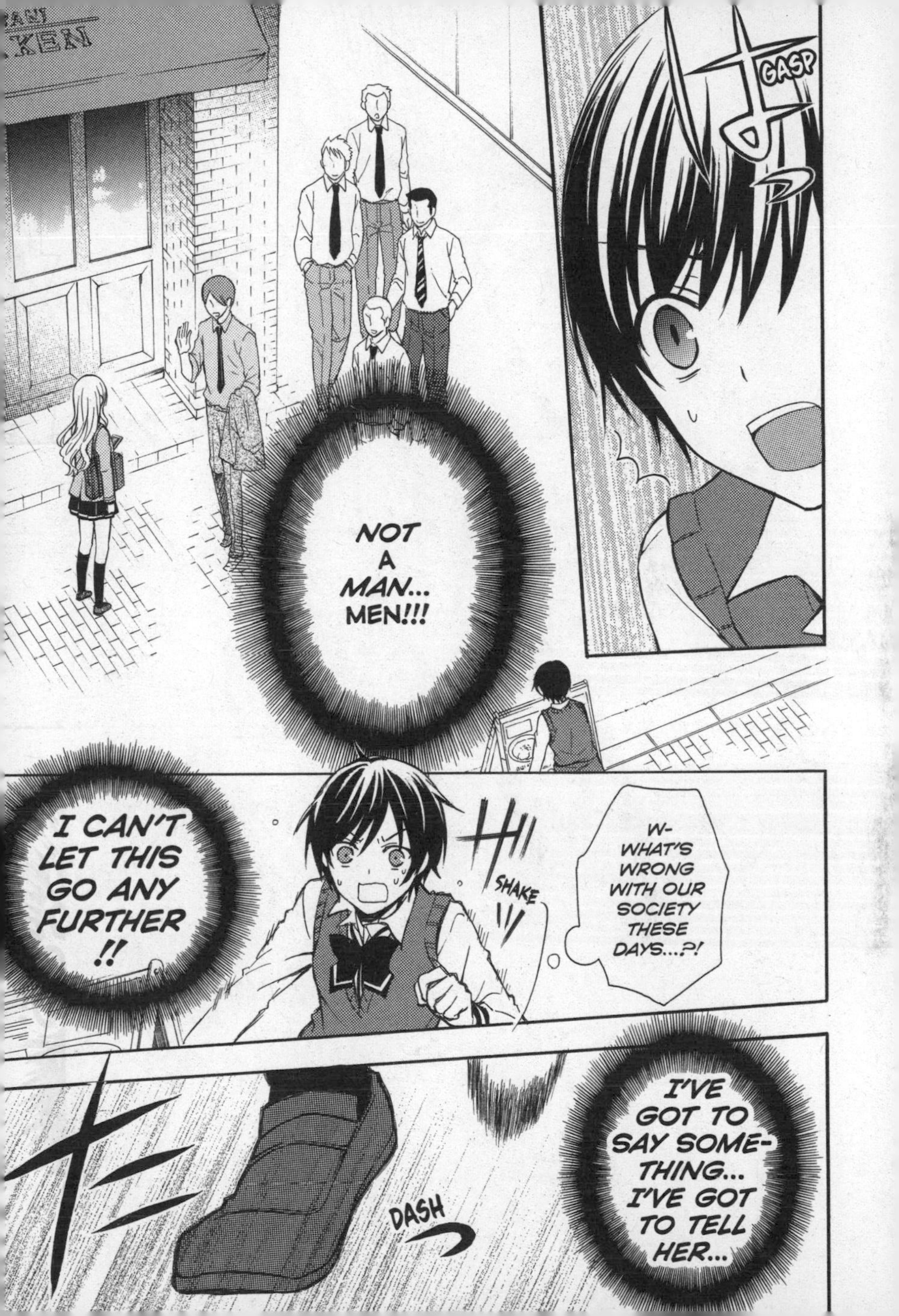
GASP
NOT A MAN... MEN!!!
W-WHAT'S WRONG WITH OUR SOCIETY THESE DAYS...?!
SHAKE
I CAN'T LET THIS GO ANY FURTHER!!
I'VE GOT TO SAY SOME-THING... I'VE GOT TO TELL HER...
DASH

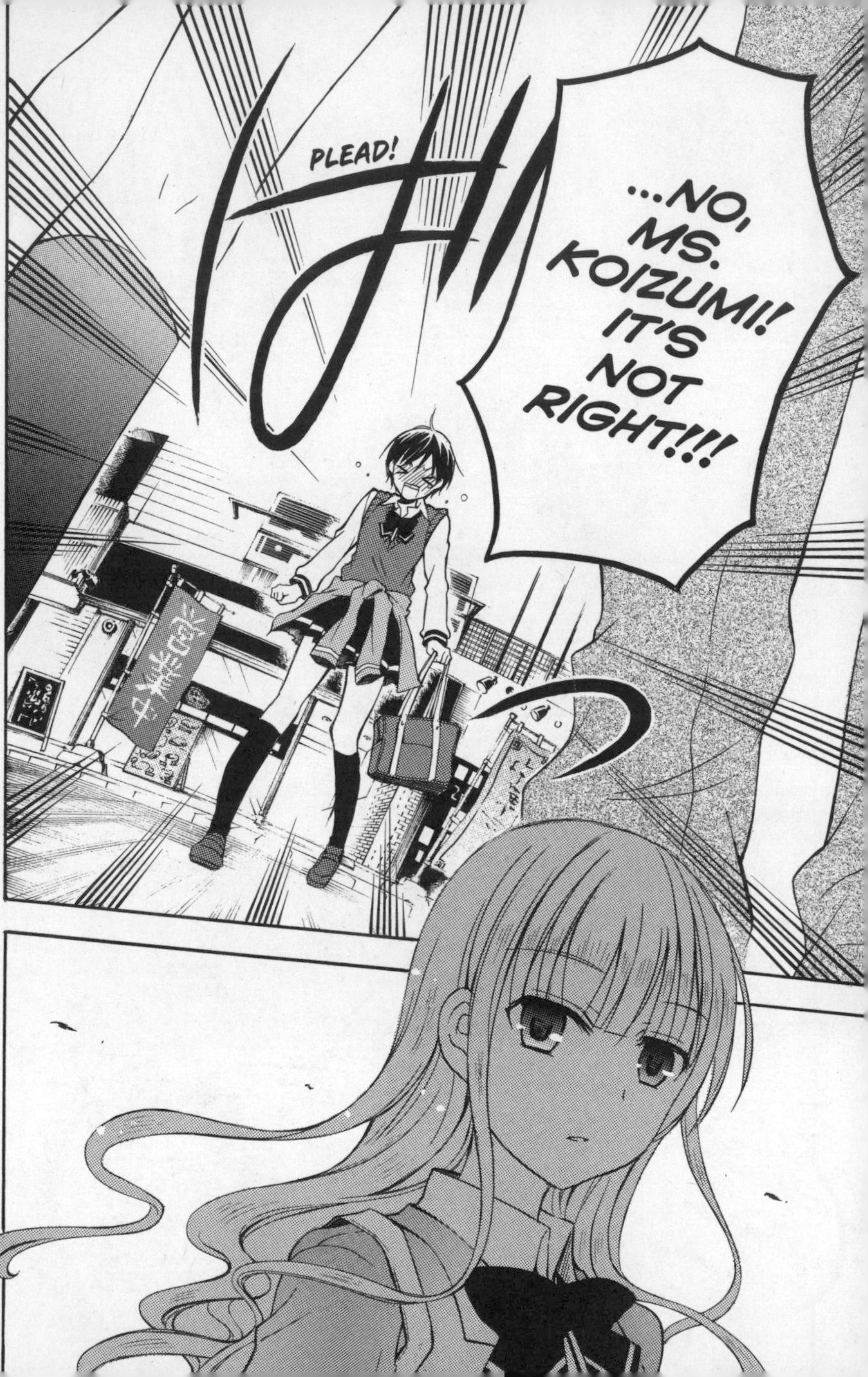
...NO, MS. KOIZUMI! IT'S NOT RIGHT!!!
PLEAD!

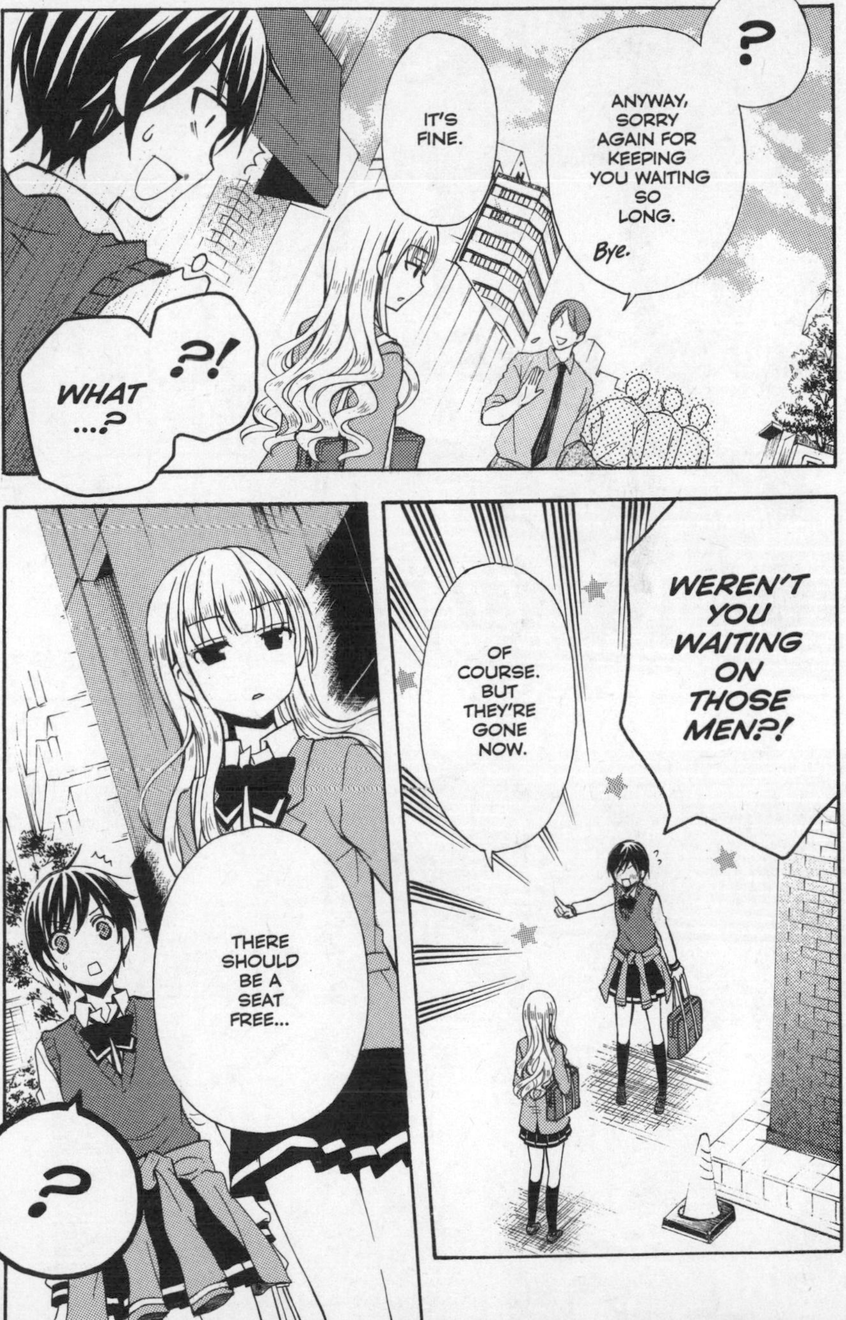
?
ANYWAY, SORRY AGAIN FOR KEEPING YOU WAITING SO LONG.
Bye.
IT'S FINE.
?!
WHAT ...?
WEREN'T YOU WAITING ON THOSE MEN?!
OF COURSE. BUT THEY'RE GONE NOW.
THERE SHOULD BE A SEAT FREE...
?

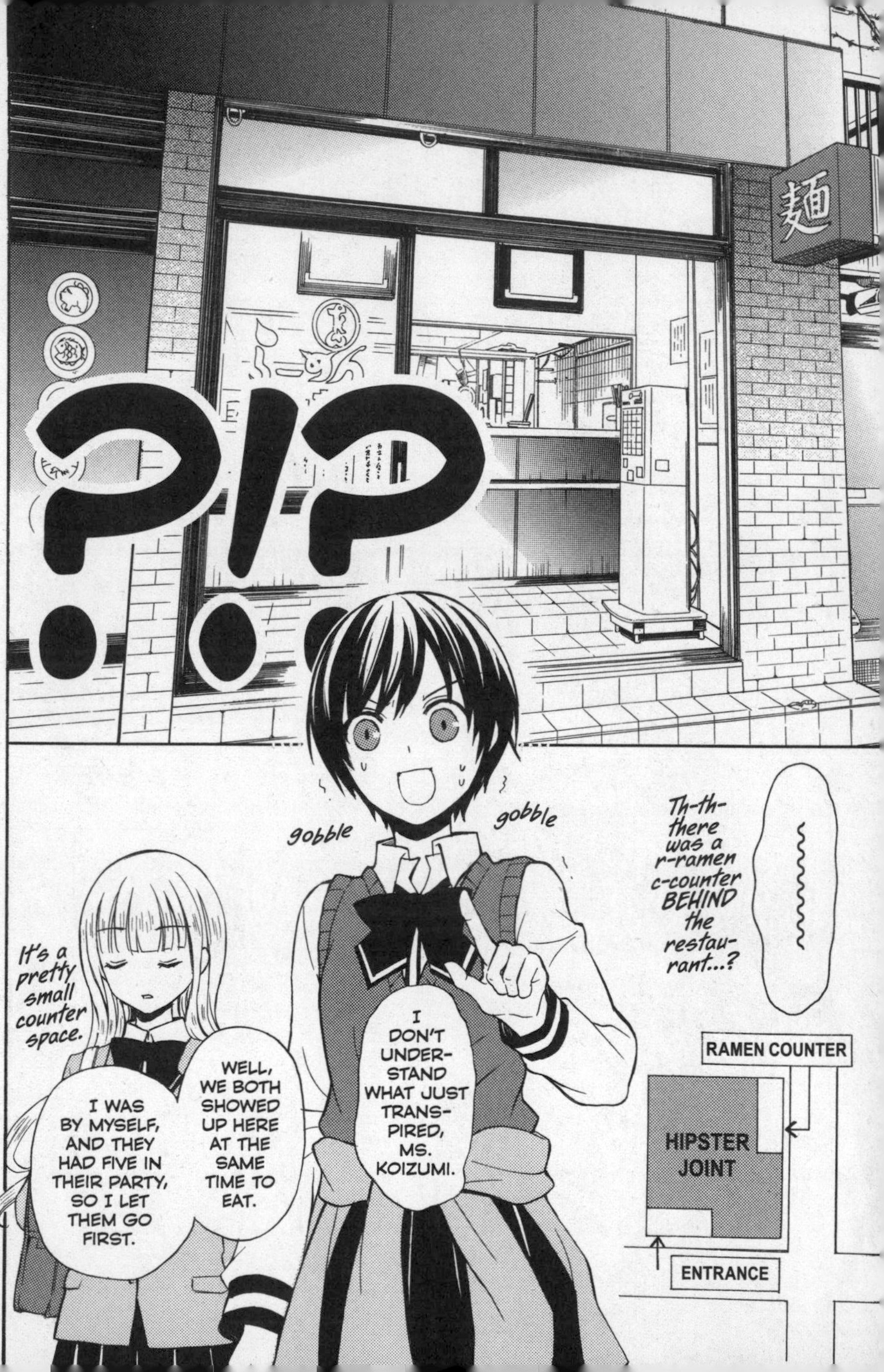
麺
?!?
Th-th-there was a r-ramen c-counter BEHIND the restau-rant...?
RAMEN COUNTER
HIPSTER JOINT
ENTRANCE
gobble gobble
I DON'T UNDER-STAND WHAT JUST TRANS-PIRED, MS. KOIZUMI.
WELL, WE BOTH SHOWED UP HERE AT THE SAME TIME TO EAT.
I WAS BY MYSELF, AND THEY HAD FIVE IN THEIR PARTY, SO I LET THEM GO FIRST.
It's a pretty small counter space.

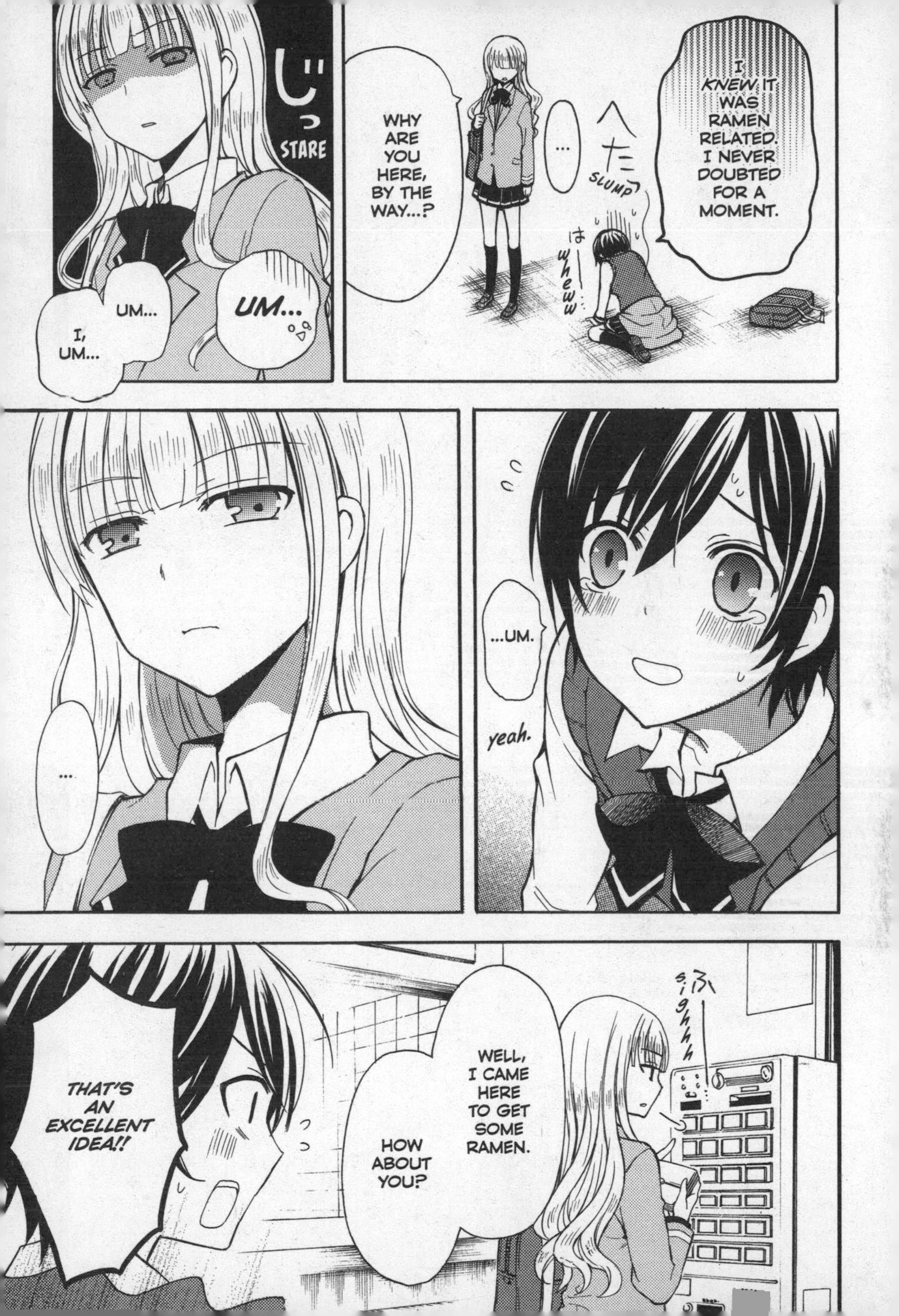
I KNEW IT WAS RAMEN RELATED. I NEVER DOUBTED FOR A MOMENT.
へた SLUMP
は WHEWW
...
WHY ARE YOU HERE, BY THE WAY...?
じっ STARE
UM...
UM...
I, UM...
...UM.
yeah.
...
ふ SIGHHH
WELL, I CAME HERE TO GET SOME RAMEN.
HOW ABOUT YOU?
THAT'S AN EXCELLENT IDEA!!

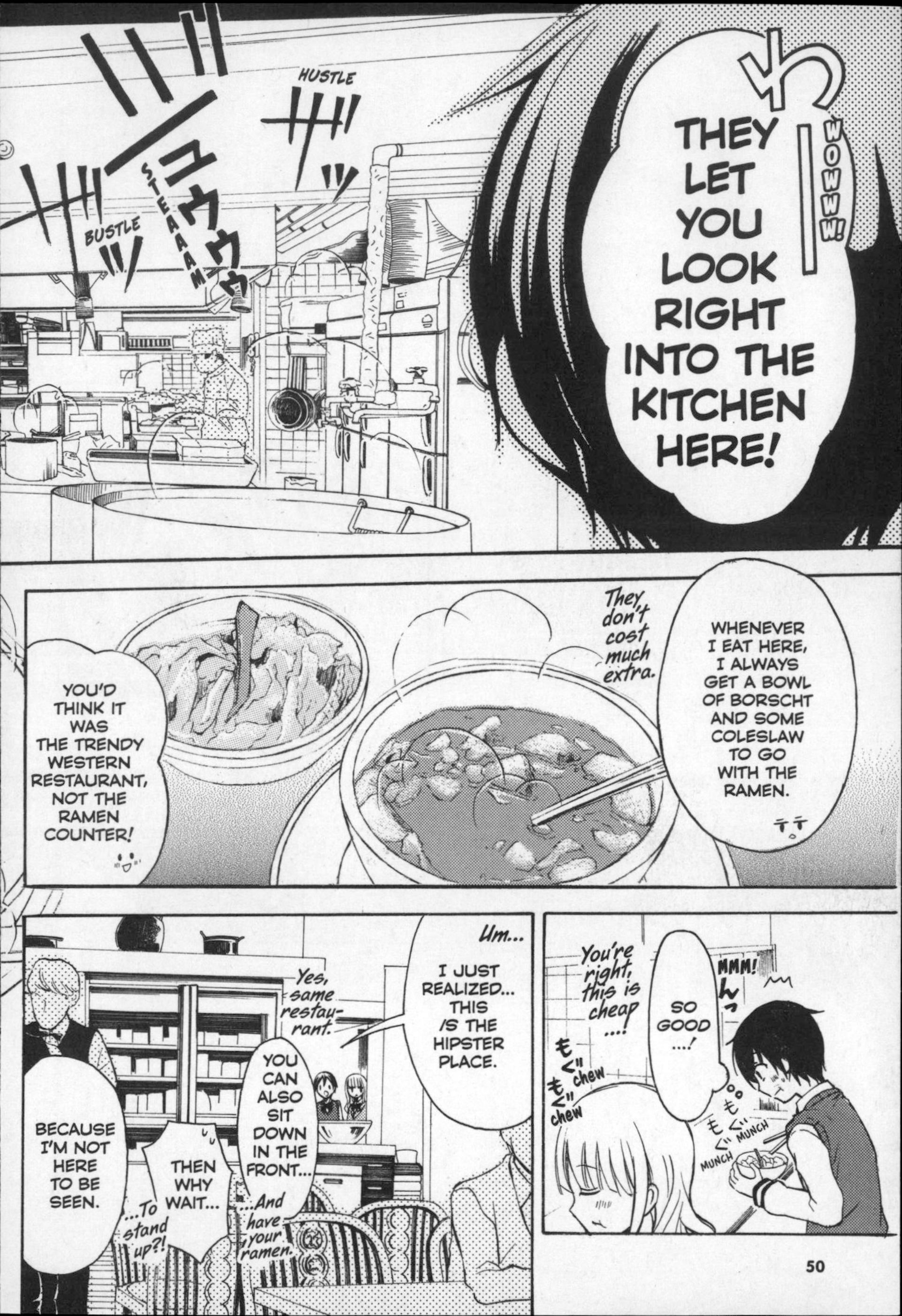
WOWWWW!
THEY LET YOU LOOK RIGHT INTO THE KITCHEN HERE!
HUSTLE
STEAAAAM
BUSTLE
WHENEVER I EAT HERE, I ALWAYS GET A BOWL OF BORSCHT AND SOME COLESLAW TO GO WITH THE RAMEN.
They don't cost much extra.
YOU'D THINK IT WAS THE TRENDY WESTERN RESTAURANT, NOT THE RAMEN COUNTER!
MMM!
SO GOOD ...!
You're right, this is cheap ....
chew
chew
MUNCH
MUNCH
Um...
I JUST REALIZED... THIS IS THE HIPSTER PLACE.
Yes, same restaurant.
YOU CAN ALSO SIT DOWN IN THE FRONT...
...And have your ramen.
THEN WHY WAIT...
...To stand up?!
BECAUSE I'M NOT HERE TO BE SEEN.

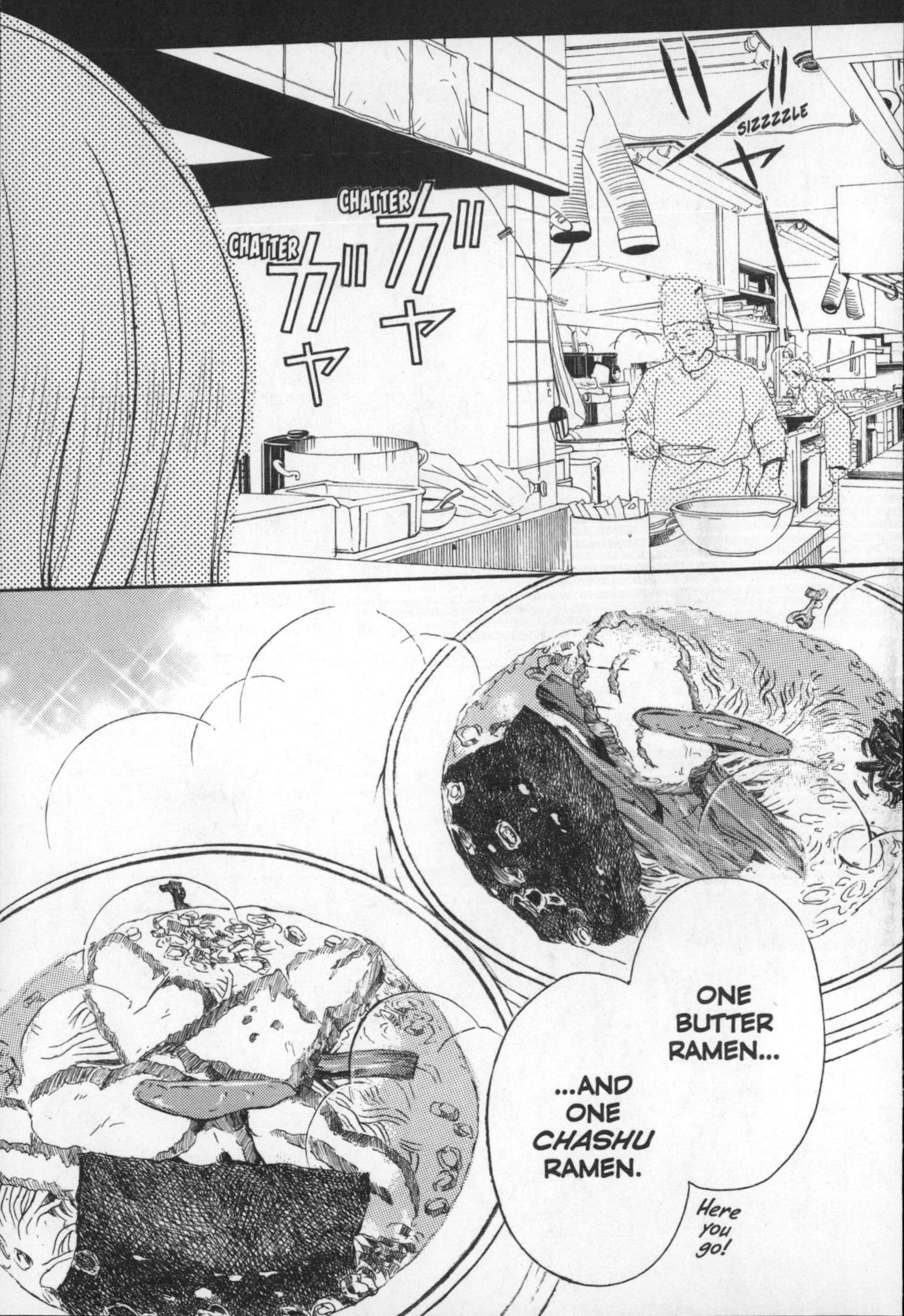
SIZZZZLE
CHATTER
ガヤ
CHATTER
ガヤ
ONE BUTTER RAMEN...
...AND ONE *CHASHU* RAMEN.
Here you go!

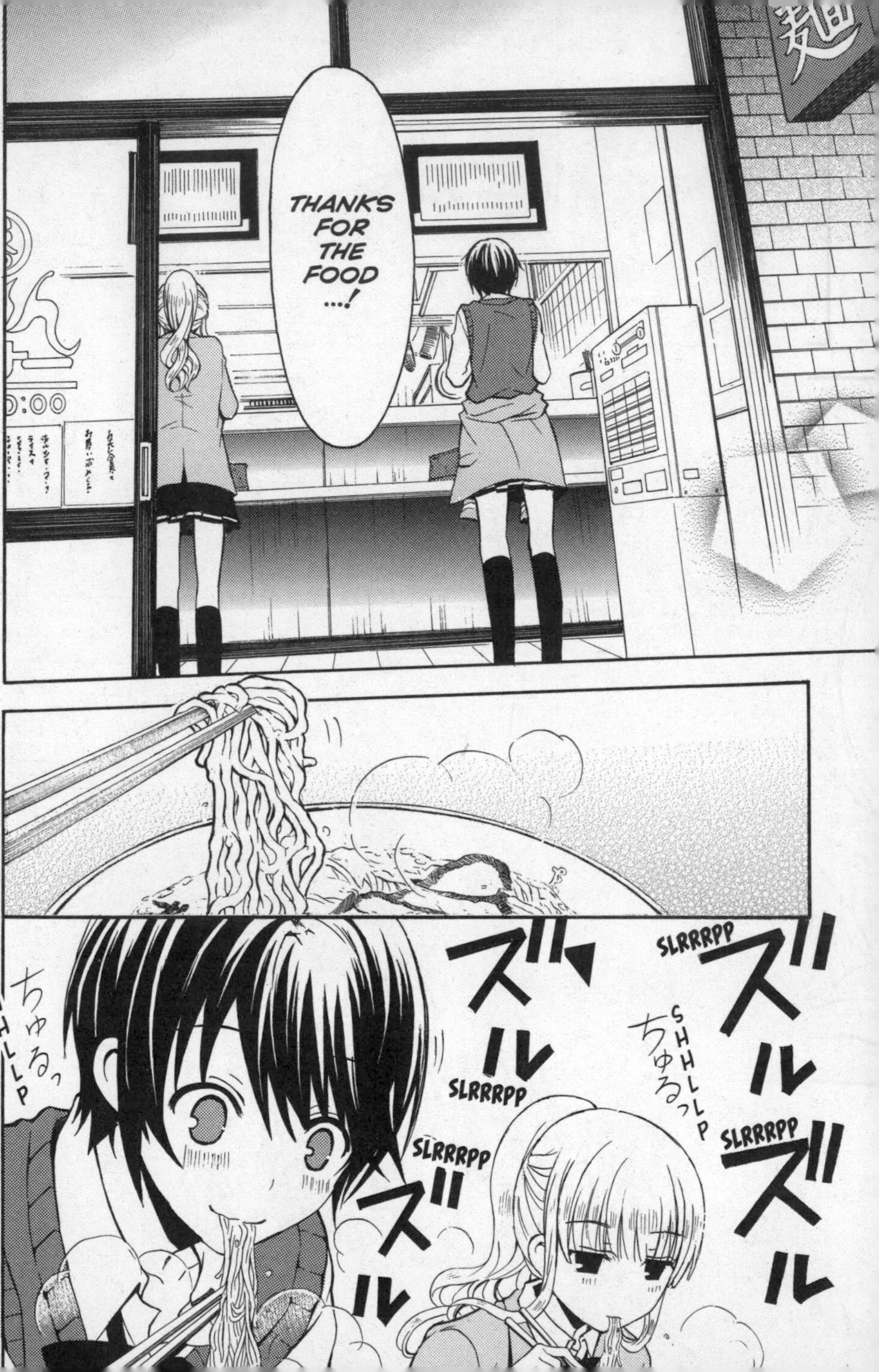

麺
THANKS FOR THE FOOD ...!
SLRRRPP
ズル
SLRRRPP
ズル
SHHLLP
ちゅるっ
ズル
SLRRRPP
ズル
SLRRRPP
ちゅるっ
SHHLLP

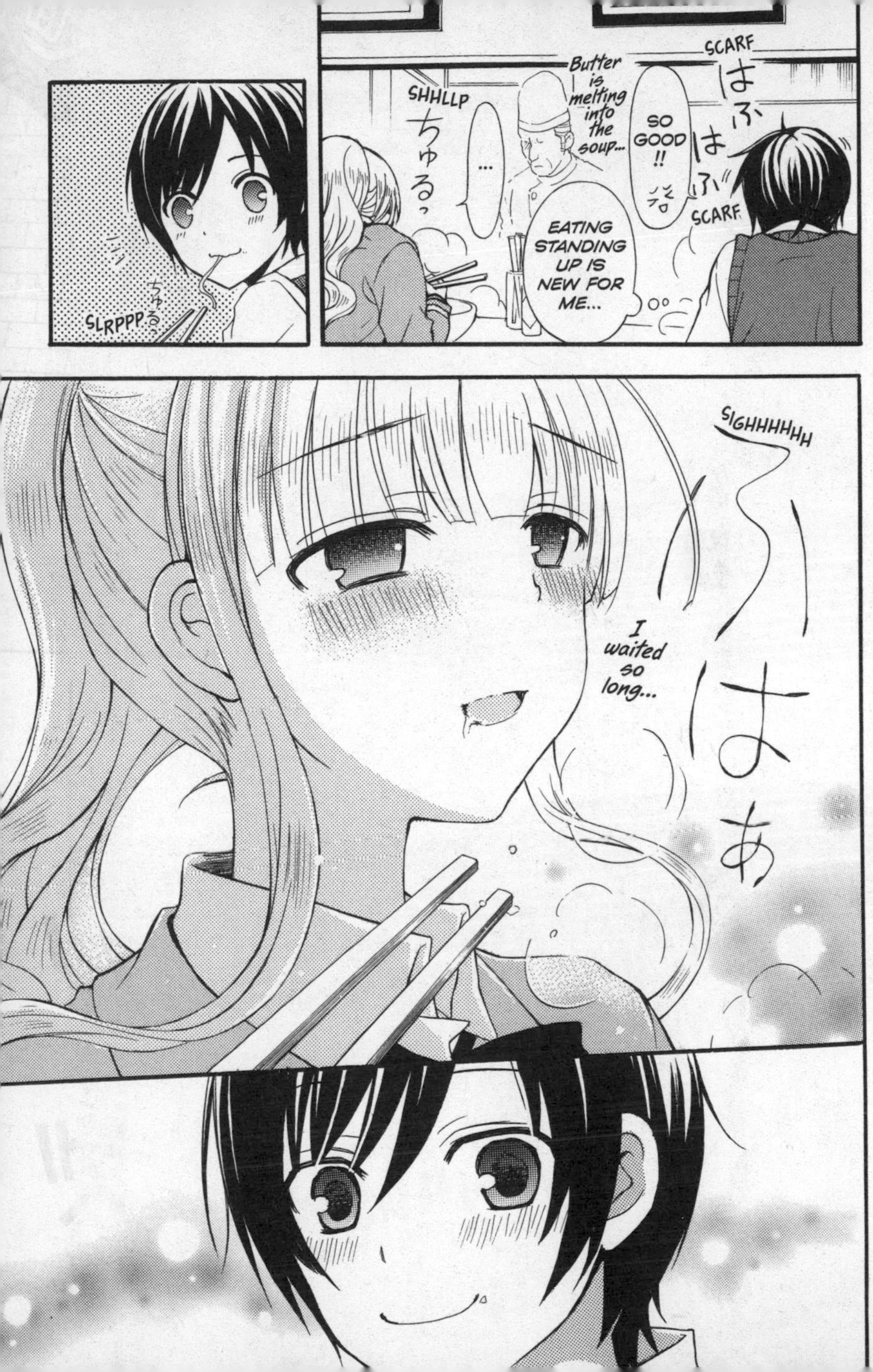
SCARF
はふはふ
SO GOOD!!
Butter is melting into the soup...
SCARF
EATING STANDING UP IS NEW FOR ME...
...
SHHLLP
ちゅるっ
SLRPPP
ちゅる
SIGHHHHHH
ふはぁ
I waited so long...

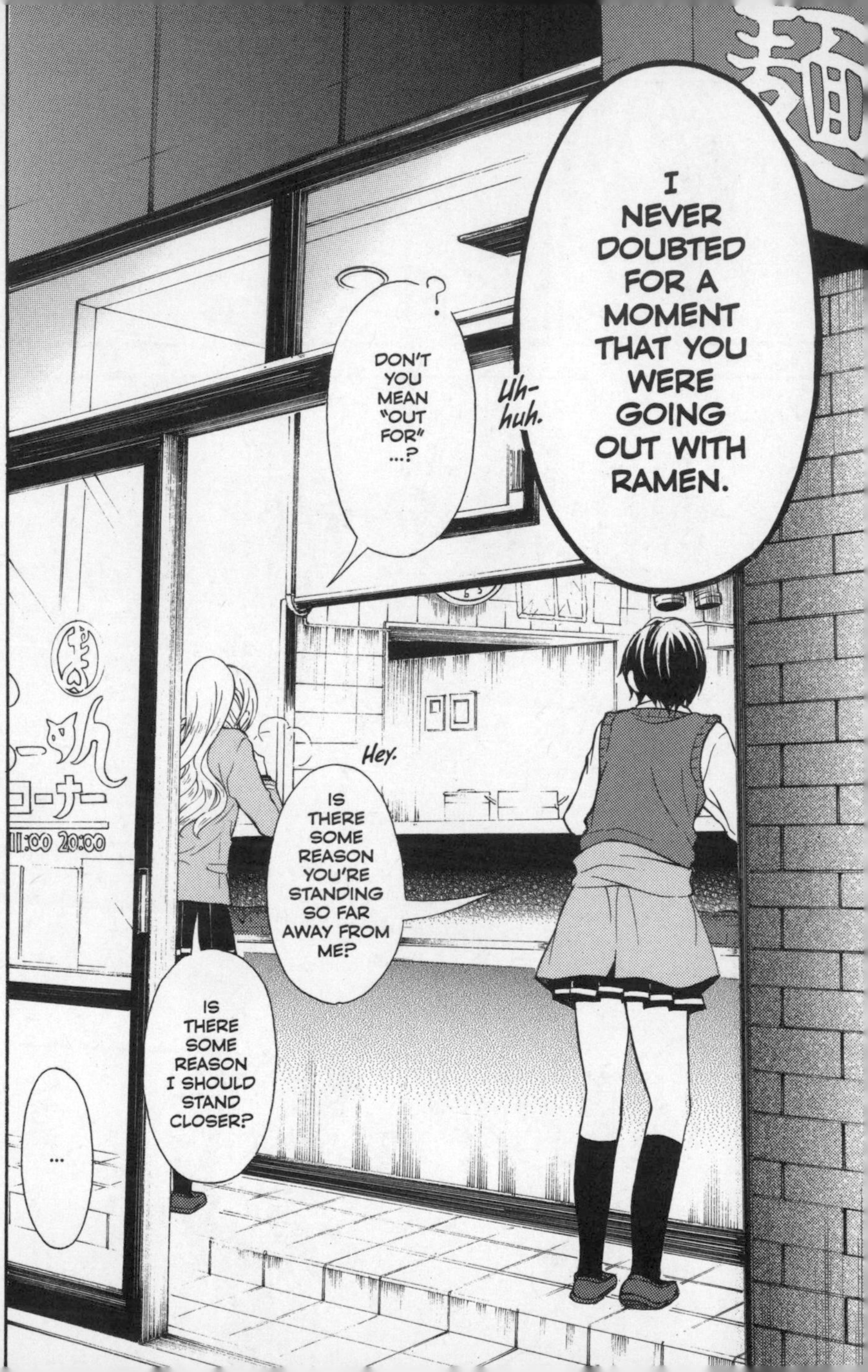
I NEVER DOUBTED FOR A MOMENT THAT YOU WERE GOING OUT WITH RAMEN.
Uh-huh.
DON'T YOU MEAN "OUT FOR" ...?
Hey.
IS THERE SOME REASON YOU'RE STANDING SO FAR AWAY FROM ME?
IS THERE SOME REASON I SHOULD STAND CLOSER?
...

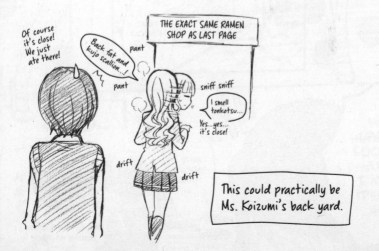

THE EXACT SAME RAMEN SHOP AS LAST PAGE
sniff sniff
I smell tonkotsu...
Yes...yes... it's close!
Back fat and kujo scallion...!
pant
pant
Of course it's close! We just ate there!
drift
drift
This could practically be Ms. Koizumi's back yard.

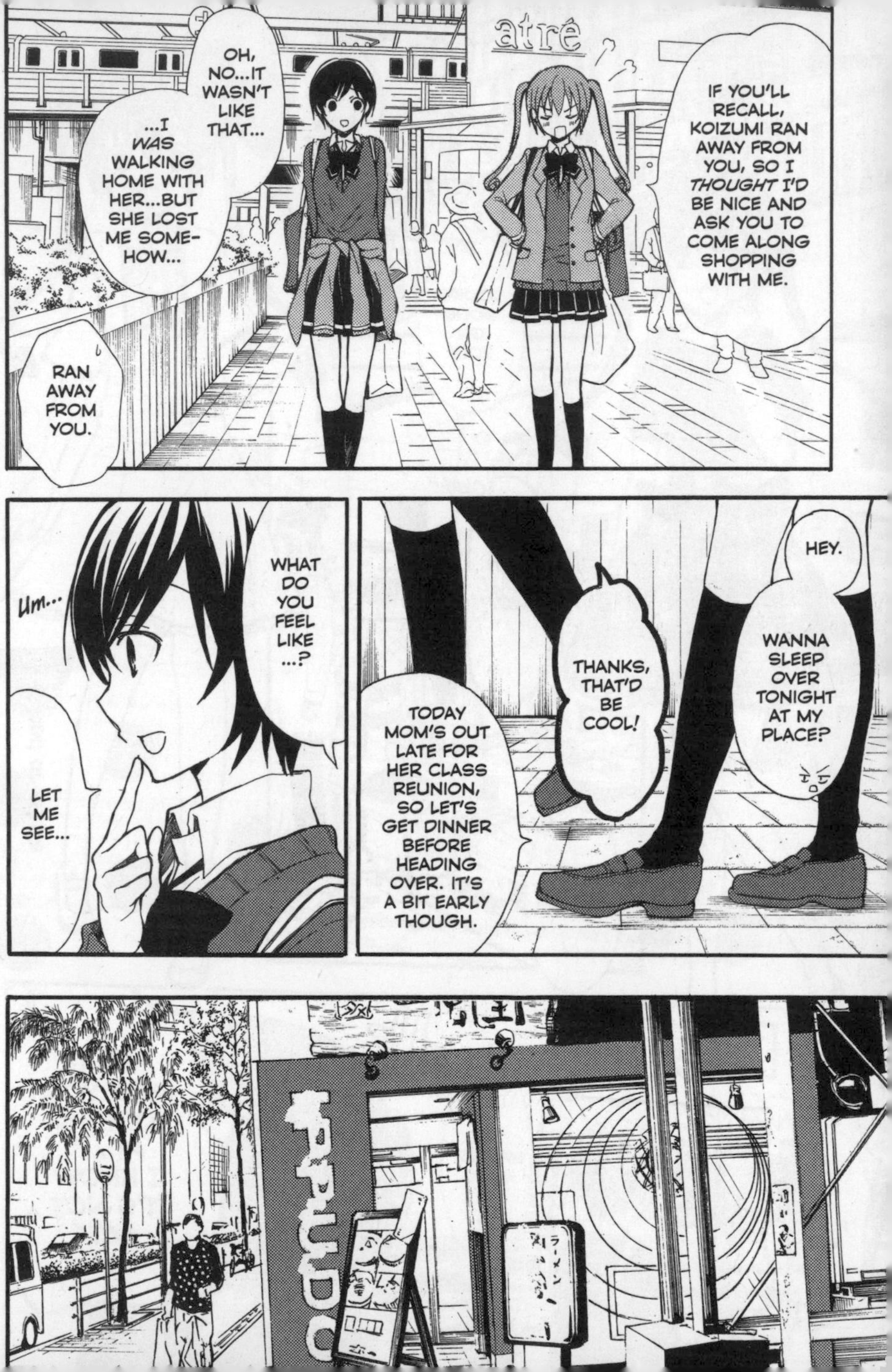
atré
IF YOU'LL RECALL, KOIZUMI RAN AWAY FROM YOU, SO I *THOUGHT* I'D BE NICE AND ASK YOU TO COME ALONG SHOPPING WITH ME.
OH, NO...IT WASN'T LIKE THAT...
...I *WAS* WALKING HOME WITH HER...BUT SHE LOST ME SOME-HOW...
RAN AWAY FROM YOU.
HEY.
WANNA SLEEP OVER TONIGHT AT MY PLACE?
THANKS, THAT'D BE COOL!
TODAY MOM'S OUT LATE FOR HER CLASS REUNION, SO LET'S GET DINNER BEFORE HEADING OVER. IT'S A BIT EARLY THOUGH.
WHAT DO YOU FEEL LIKE ...?
Um...
LET ME SEE...

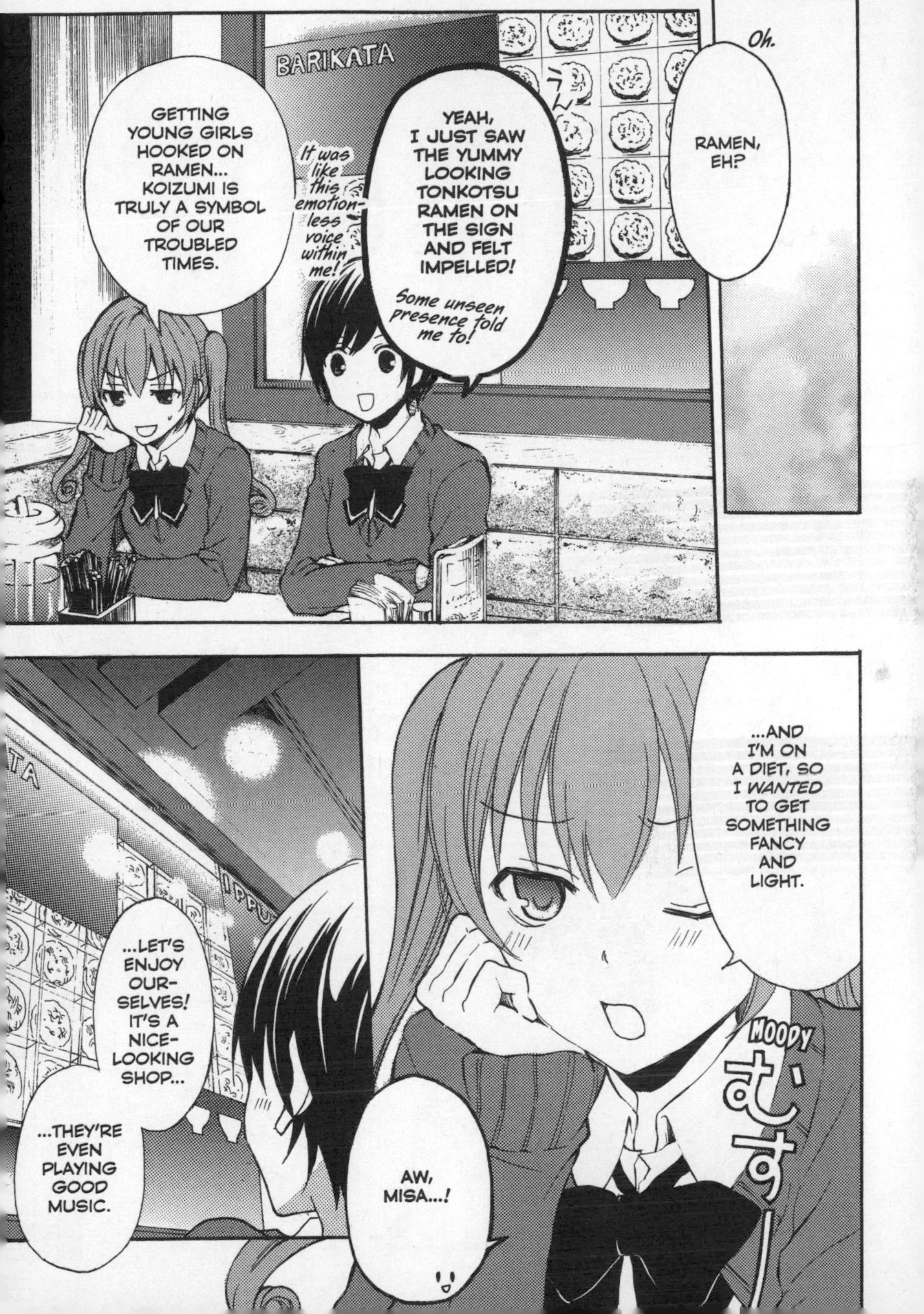
Oh.
RAMEN, EH?
YEAH, I JUST SAW THE YUMMY LOOKING TONKOTSU RAMEN ON THE SIGN AND FELT IMPELLED!
Some unseen presence told me to!
It was like this emotion-less voice within me!
BARIKATA
GETTING YOUNG GIRLS HOOKED ON RAMEN... KOIZUMI IS TRULY A SYMBOL OF OUR TROUBLED TIMES.
...AND I'M ON A DIET, SO I WANTED TO GET SOMETHING FANCY AND LIGHT.
MOODY むす
AW, MISA...!
...LET'S ENJOY OUR-SELVES! IT'S A NICE-LOOKING SHOP...
...THEY'RE EVEN PLAYING GOOD MUSIC.

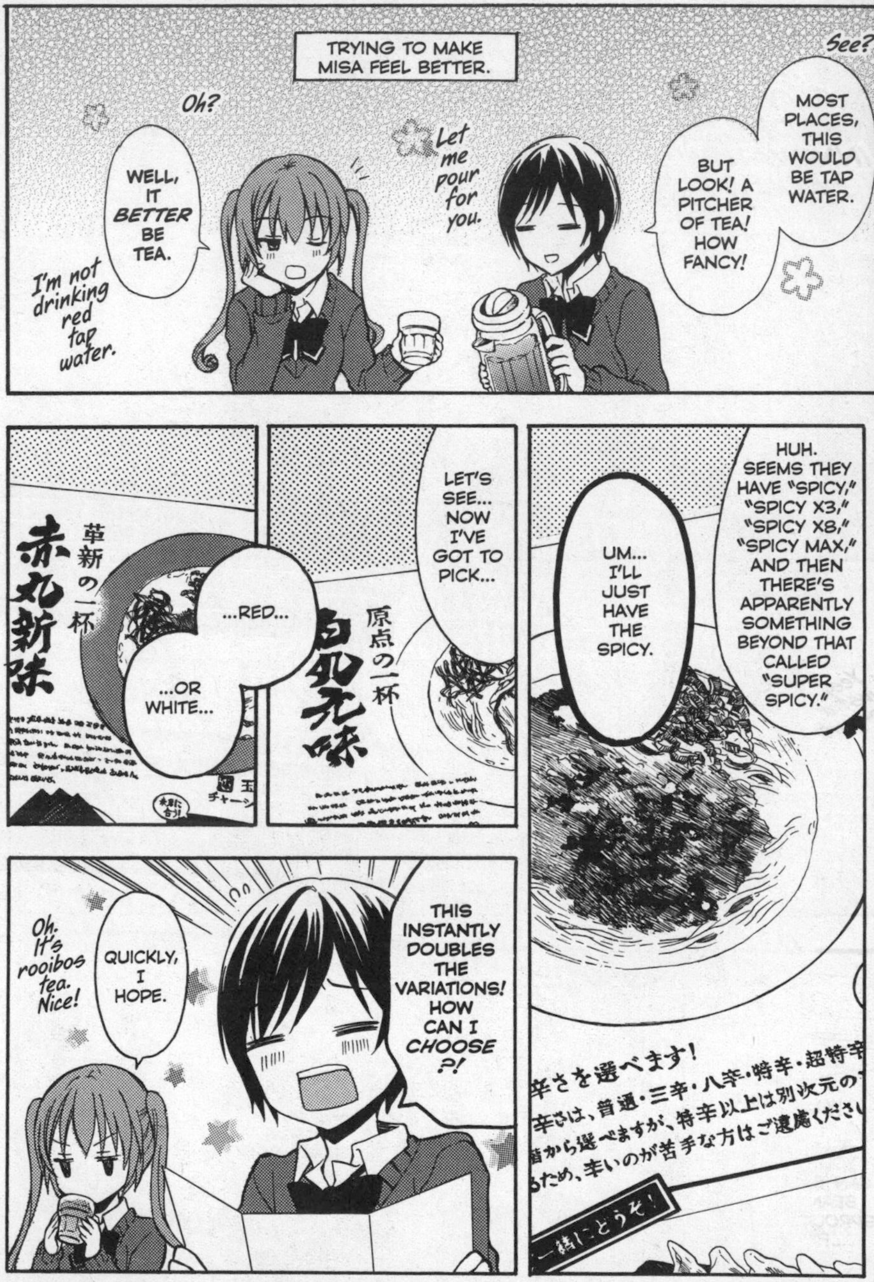
TRYING TO MAKE MISA FEEL BETTER.
See?
MOST PLACES, THIS WOULD BE TAP WATER.
BUT LOOK! A PITCHER OF TEA! HOW FANCY!
Let me pour for you.
Oh?
WELL, IT BETTER BE TEA.
I'm not drinking red tap water.
HUH. SEEMS THEY HAVE "SPICY," "SPICY X3," "SPICY X8," "SPICY MAX," AND THEN THERE'S APPARENTLY SOMETHING BEYOND THAT CALLED "SUPER SPICY."
UM... I'LL JUST HAVE THE SPICY.
辛さを選べます!
LET'S SEE... NOW I'VE GOT TO PICK...
原点の一杯
白丸元味
...RED...
...OR WHITE...
革新の一杯
赤丸新味
THIS INSTANTLY DOUBLES THE VARIATIONS! HOW CAN I CHOOSE?!
QUICKLY, I HOPE.
Oh. It's rooibos tea. Nice!

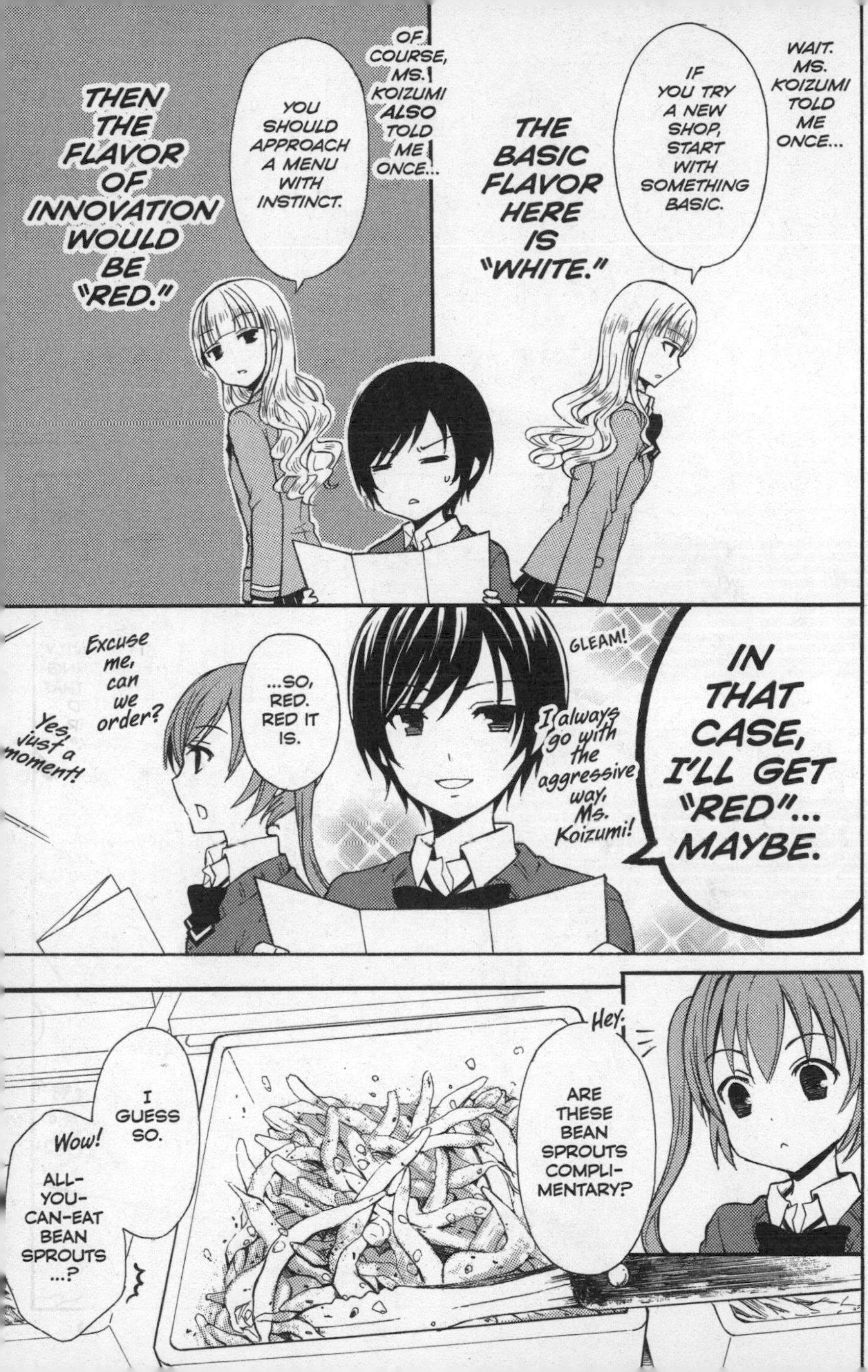
WAIT. MS. KOIZUMI TOLD ME ONCE...
IF YOU TRY A NEW SHOP, START WITH SOMETHING BASIC.
THE BASIC FLAVOR HERE IS "WHITE."
OF COURSE, MS. KOIZUMI ALSO TOLD ME ONCE...
YOU SHOULD APPROACH A MENU WITH INSTINCT.
THEN THE FLAVOR OF INNOVATION WOULD BE "RED."
IN THAT CASE, I'LL GET "RED"... MAYBE.
GLEAM!
I always go with the aggressive way, Ms. Koizumi!
...SO, RED. RED IT IS.
Excuse me, can we order?
Yes, just a moment!
Hey:
ARE THESE BEAN SPROUTS COMPLIMENTARY?
I GUESS SO.
Wow!
ALL-YOU-CAN-EAT BEAN SPROUTS ...?

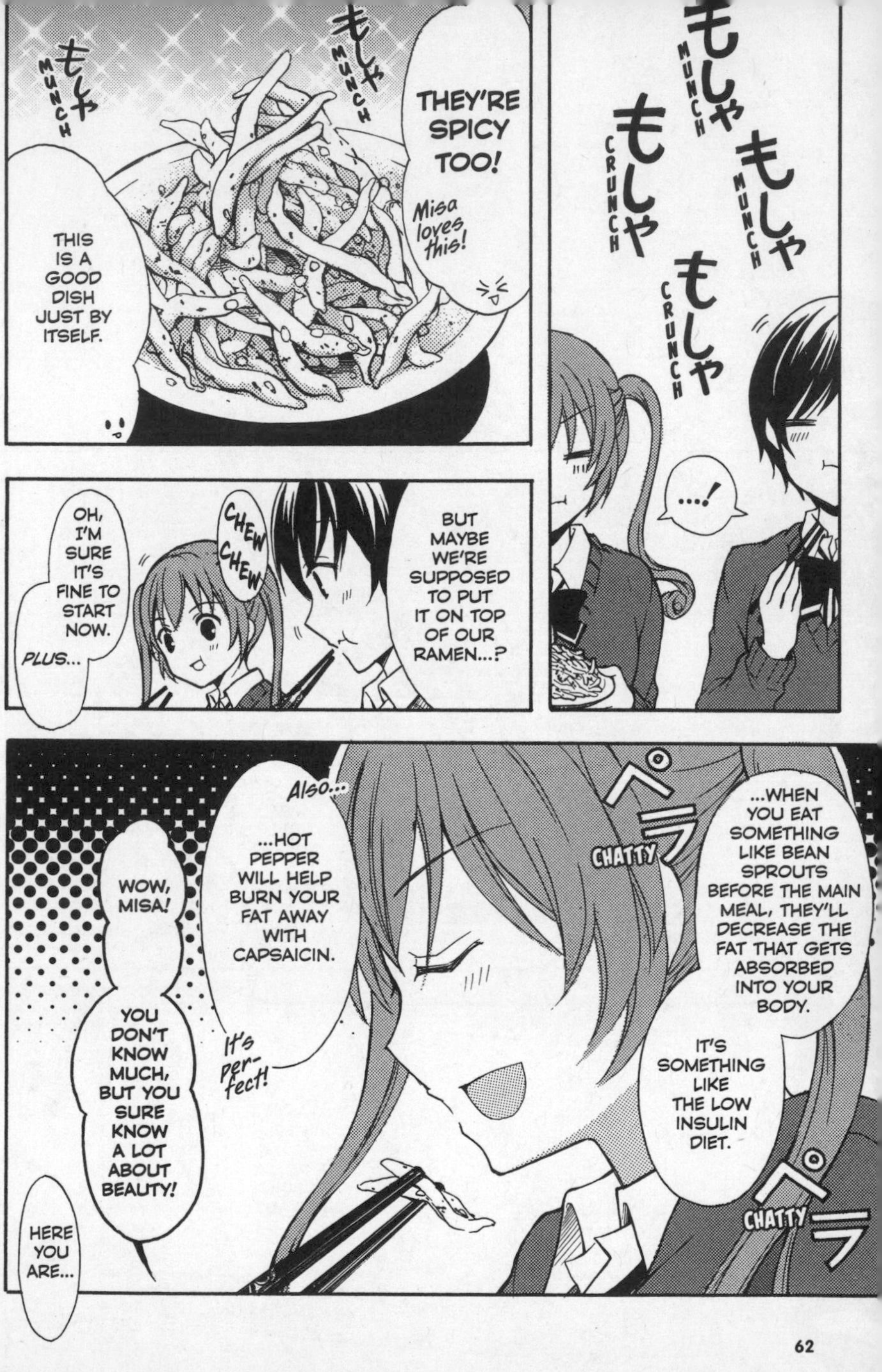

もしゃ MUNCH
もしゃ CRUNCH
もしゃ MUNCH
もしゃ CRUNCH
もしゃ CRUNCH
....!
もしゃ MUNCH
THEY'RE SPICY TOO!
Misa loves this!
もしゃ MUNCH
THIS IS A GOOD DISH JUST BY ITSELF.
BUT MAYBE WE'RE SUPPOSED TO PUT IT ON TOP OF OUR RAMEN...?
CHEW CHEW
OH, I'M SURE IT'S FINE TO START NOW.
PLUS...
ペラ CHATTY
...WHEN YOU EAT SOMETHING LIKE BEAN SPROUTS BEFORE THE MAIN MEAL, THEY'LL DECREASE THE FAT THAT GETS ABSORBED INTO YOUR BODY.
IT'S SOMETHING LIKE THE LOW INSULIN DIET.
ペラ CHATTY
Also...
...HOT PEPPER WILL HELP BURN YOUR FAT AWAY WITH CAPSAICIN.
It's perfect!
WOW, MISA!
YOU DON'T KNOW MUCH, BUT YOU SURE KNOW A LOT ABOUT BEAUTY!
HERE YOU ARE...

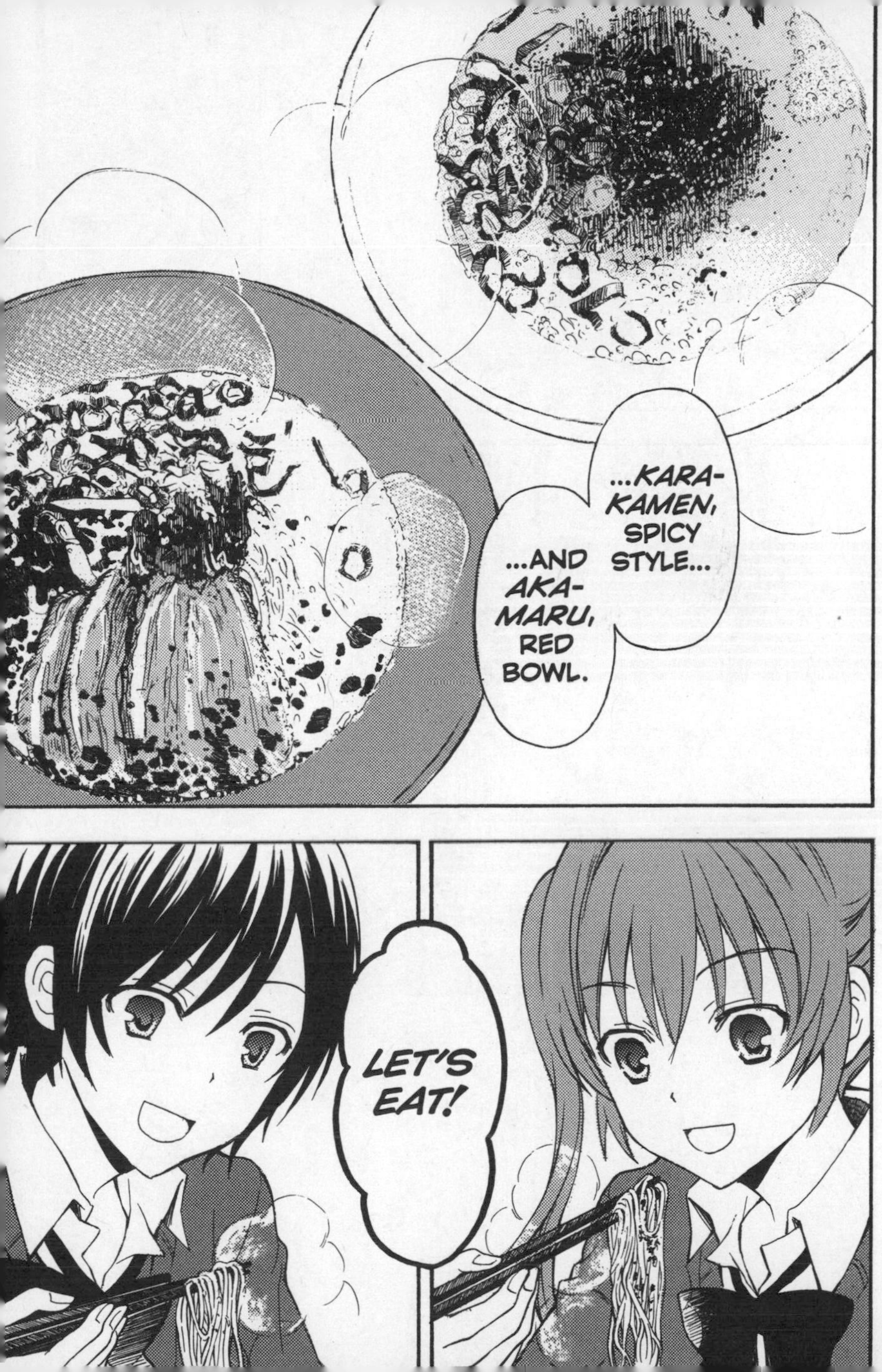
...KARA-KAMEN, SPICY STYLE...
...AND AKA-MARU, RED BOWL.
LET'S EAT!

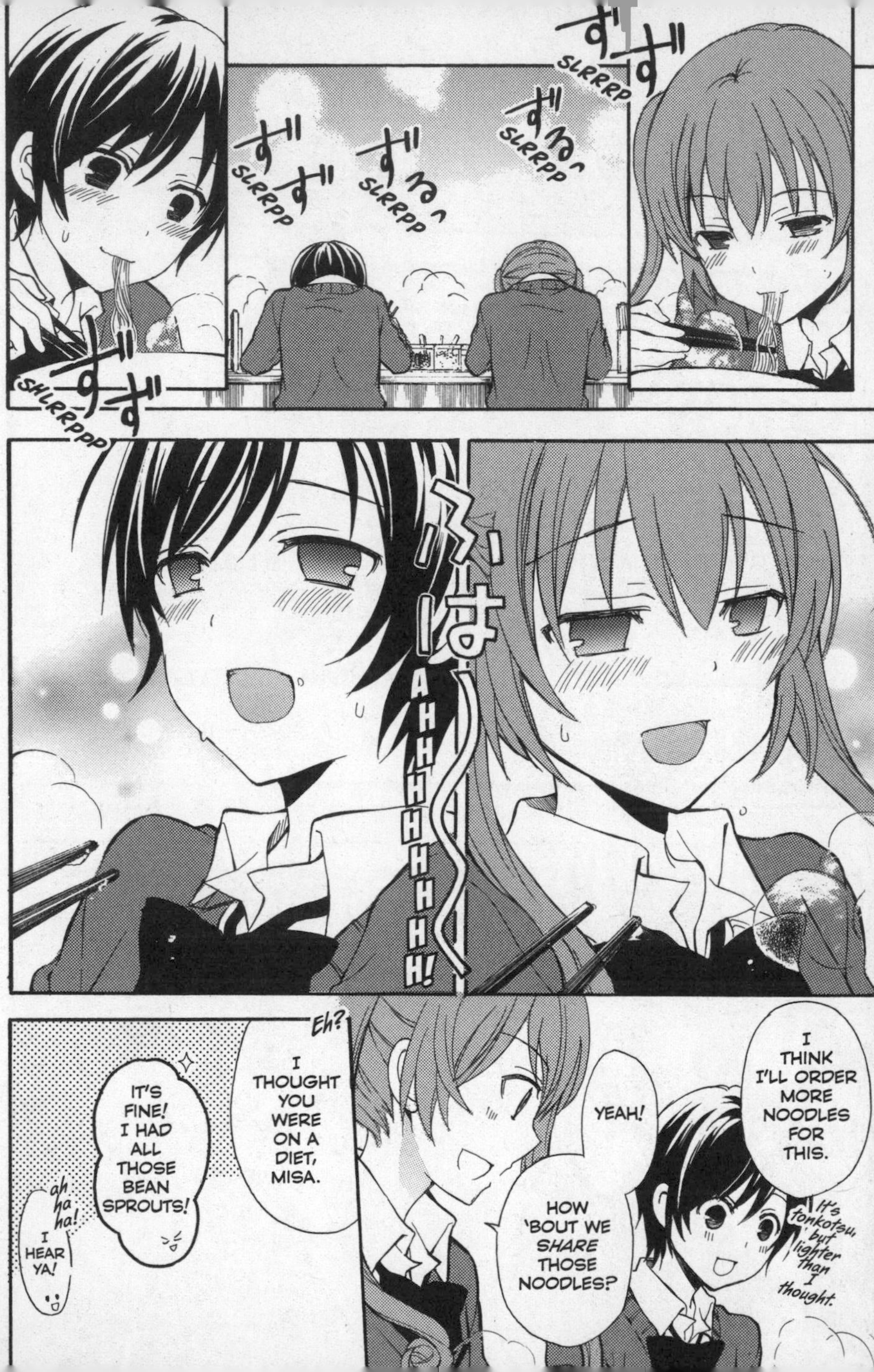
ずず
SLRRRP
ずる
SLRRPP
ずる
SLRRPP
ずず
SLRRPP
ずず
SHLRRPPP
ふは〜
AHHHHHHHHH!
I THINK I'LL ORDER MORE NOODLES FOR THIS.
It's tonkotsu, but lighter than I thought.
YEAH!
HOW 'BOUT WE SHARE THOSE NOODLES?
Eh?
I THOUGHT YOU WERE ON A DIET, MISA.
IT'S FINE! I HAD ALL THOSE BEAN SPROUTS!
ah ha ha!
I HEAR YA!

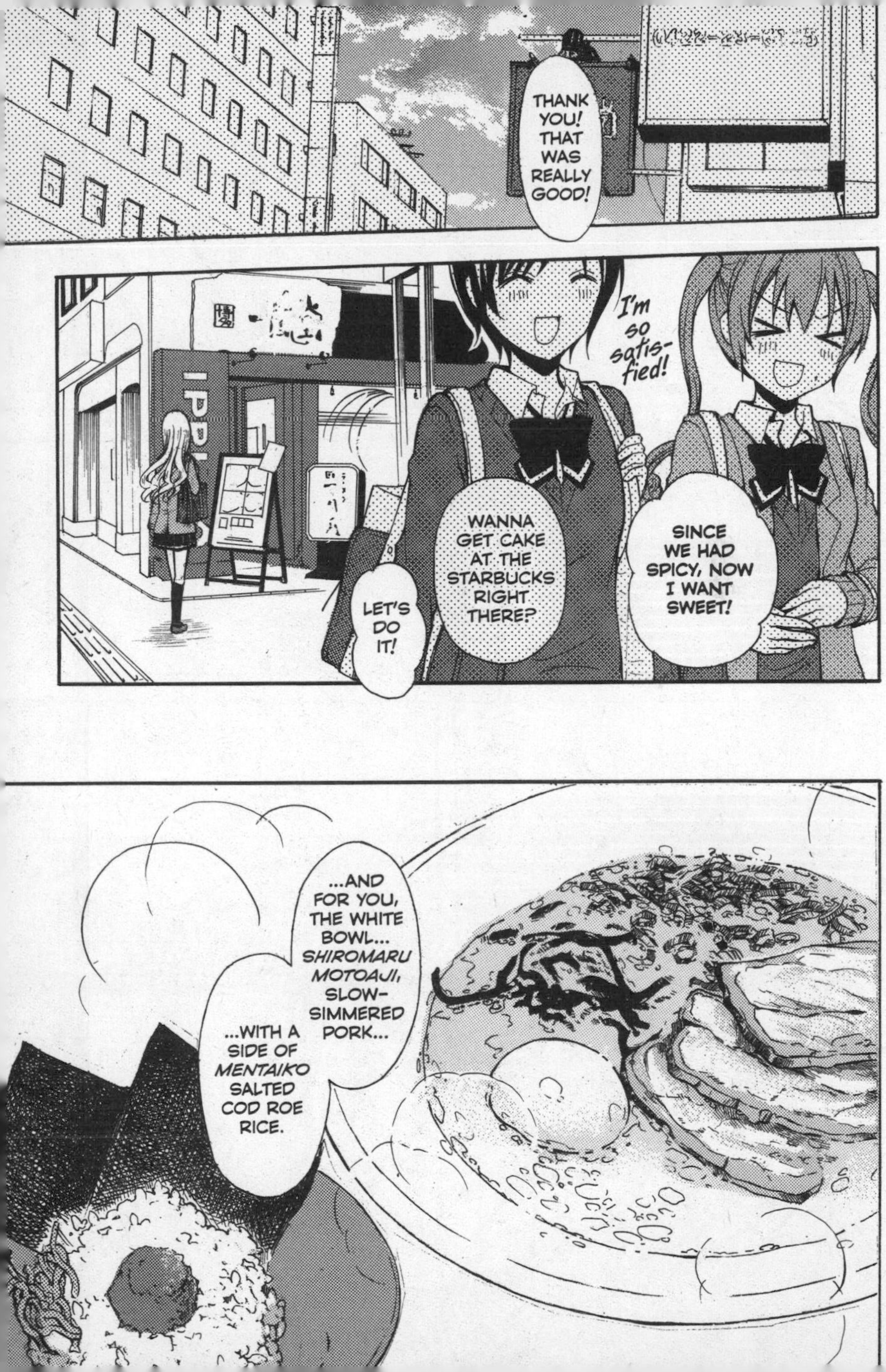
THANK YOU! THAT WAS REALLY GOOD!
I'm so satis-fied!
SINCE WE HAD SPICY, NOW I WANT SWEET!
WANNA GET CAKE AT THE STARBUCKS RIGHT THERE?
LET'S DO IT!
...AND FOR YOU, THE WHITE BOWL... *SHIROMARU MOTOAJI*, SLOW-SIMMERED PORK...
...WITH A SIDE OF *MENTAIKO* SALTED COD ROE RICE.

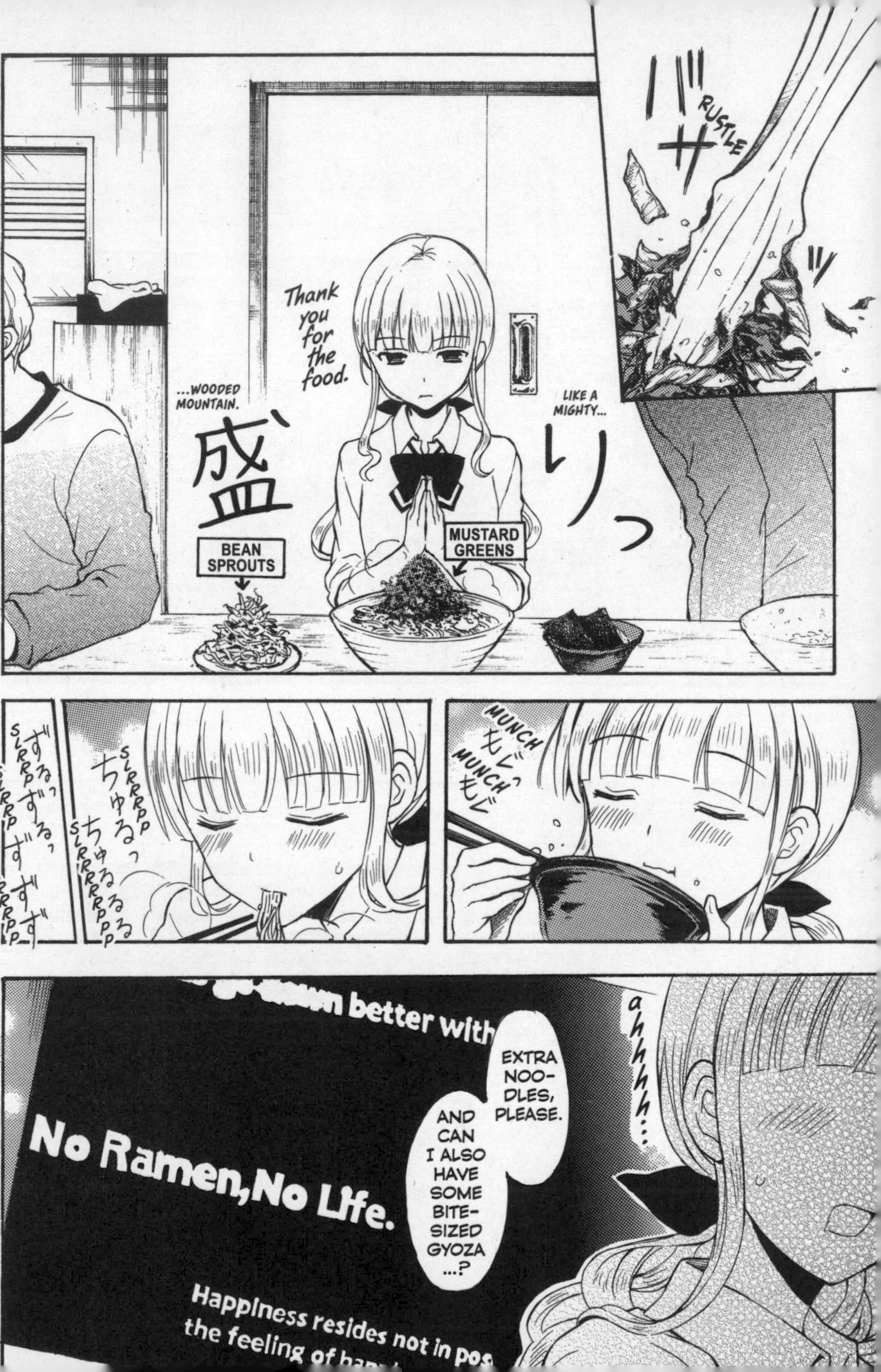
RUSTLE
LIKE A MIGHTY...
Thank you for the food.
...WOODED MOUNTAIN.
MUSTARD GREENS
BEAN SPROUTS
MUNCH MUNCH
SLRRP SLRRP SLRRRPP
SLRRPP SLRRRRPPP
ahhhhh...
EXTRA NOODLES, PLEASE.
AND CAN I ALSO HAVE SOME BITE-SIZED GYOZA...?
better with
No Ramen,No Life.
Happiness resides not in pos
the feeling of hap

On All Nippon Airways,
you can* slurp noodles
at 35,000 ft.!

Have a wonderful
flight...with two
choices of ramen.

☆ Rich miso "Daichi," a
meatless option. It's in
partnership with the
Ippudo chain!

☆ "Soraton," tonkotsu
above the clouds. Pigs
don't fly. But pork
broth does.

* In a premium cabin.

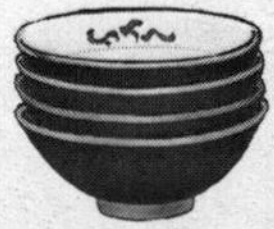
らーめん

Ms. Koizumi loves ramen noodles

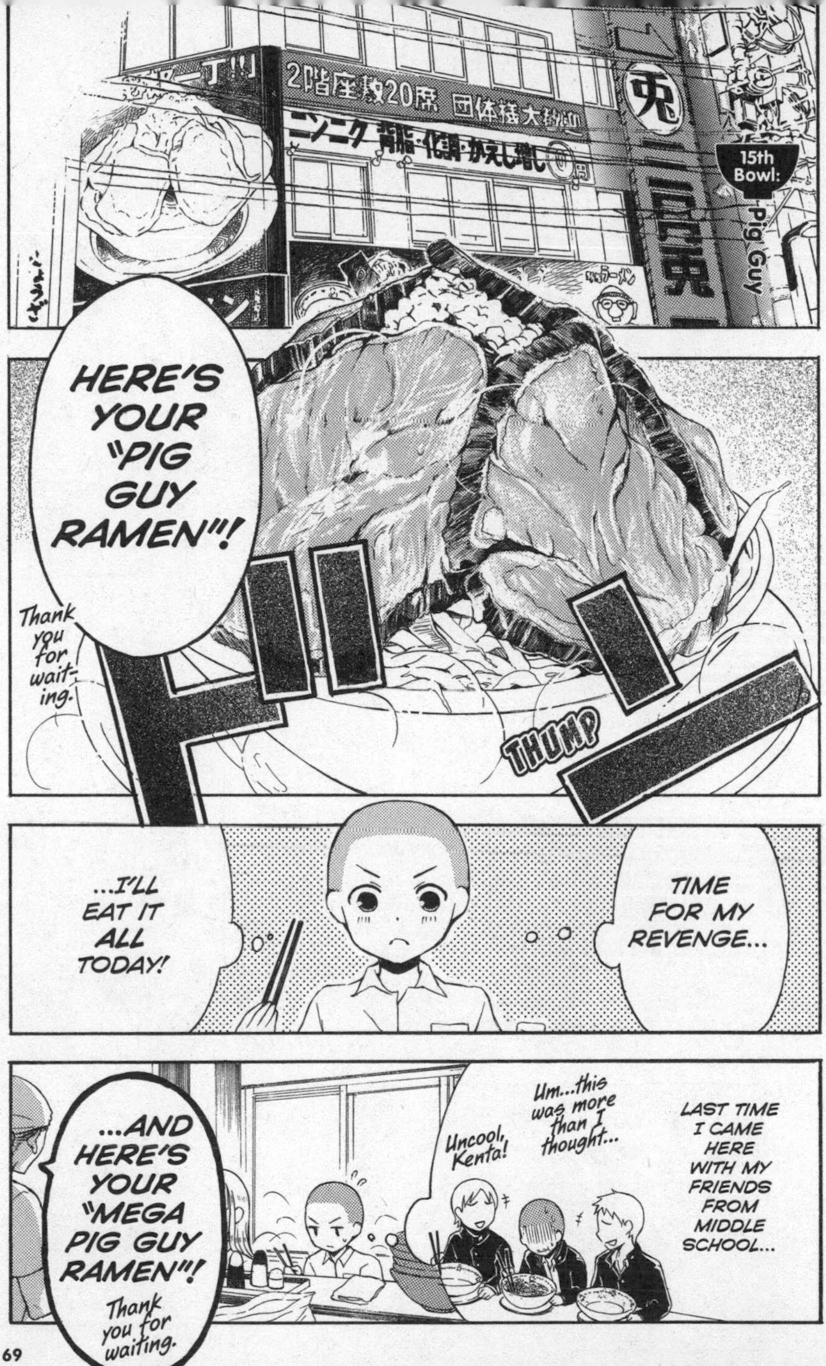
15th Bowl: Pig Guy
2階座敷20席 団体様大歓迎
HERE'S YOUR "PIG GUY RAMEN"!
Thank you for waiting.
THUMP
TIME FOR MY REVENGE...
...I'LL EAT IT ALL TODAY!
LAST TIME I CAME HERE WITH MY FRIENDS FROM MIDDLE SCHOOL...
Um...this was more than I thought...
Uncool, Kenta!
...AND HERE'S YOUR "MEGA PIG GUY RAMEN"!
Thank you for waiting.

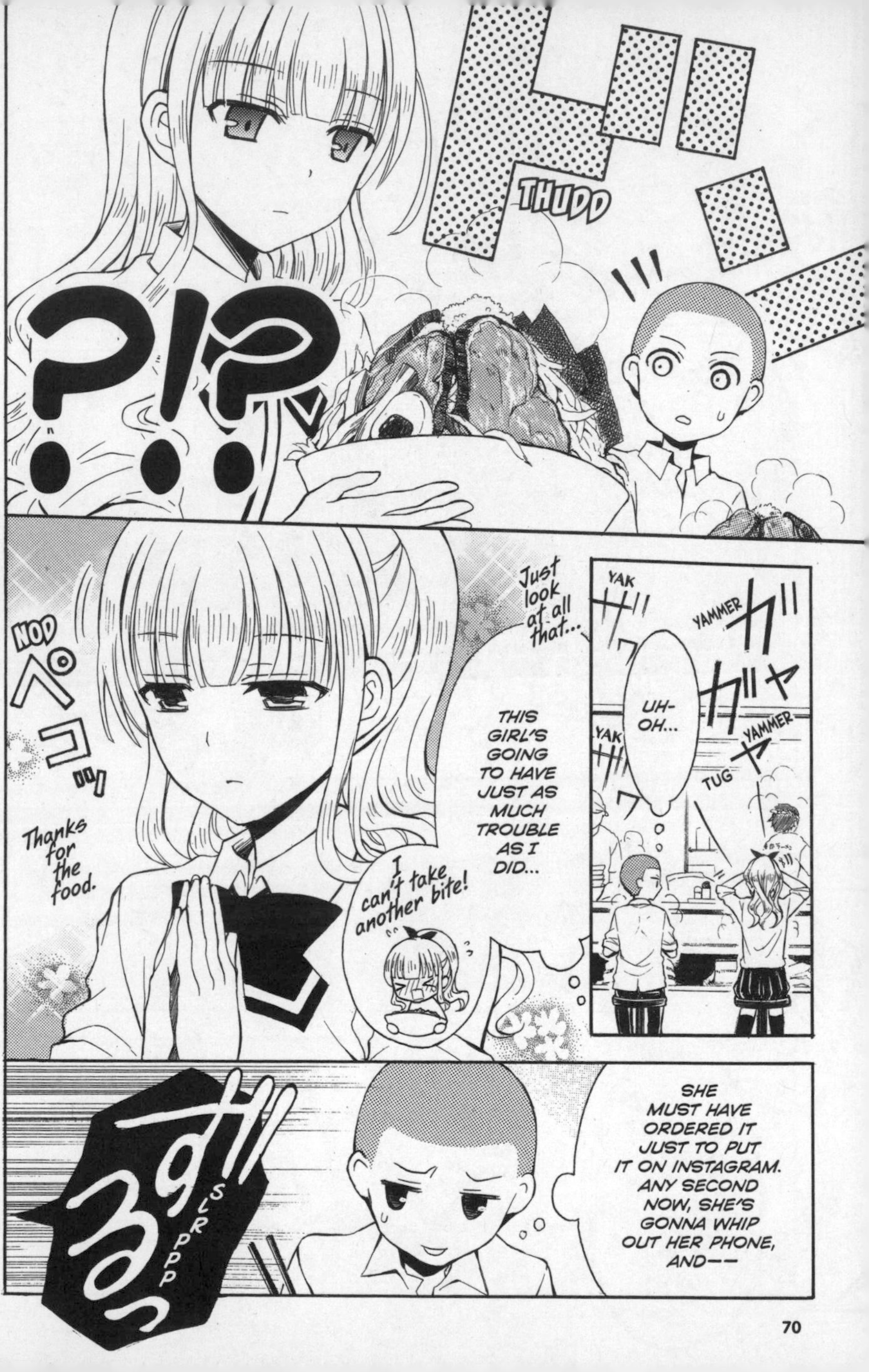
THUDD
?!?
YAK
YAMMER
UH-OH...
YAK
YAMMER
TUG
Just look at all that...
THIS GIRL'S GOING TO HAVE JUST AS MUCH TROUBLE AS I DID...
I can't take another bite!
NOD
Thanks for the food.
SHE MUST HAVE ORDERED IT JUST TO PUT IT ON INSTAGRAM. ANY SECOND NOW, SHE'S GONNA WHIP OUT HER PHONE, AND--
SLRPPP

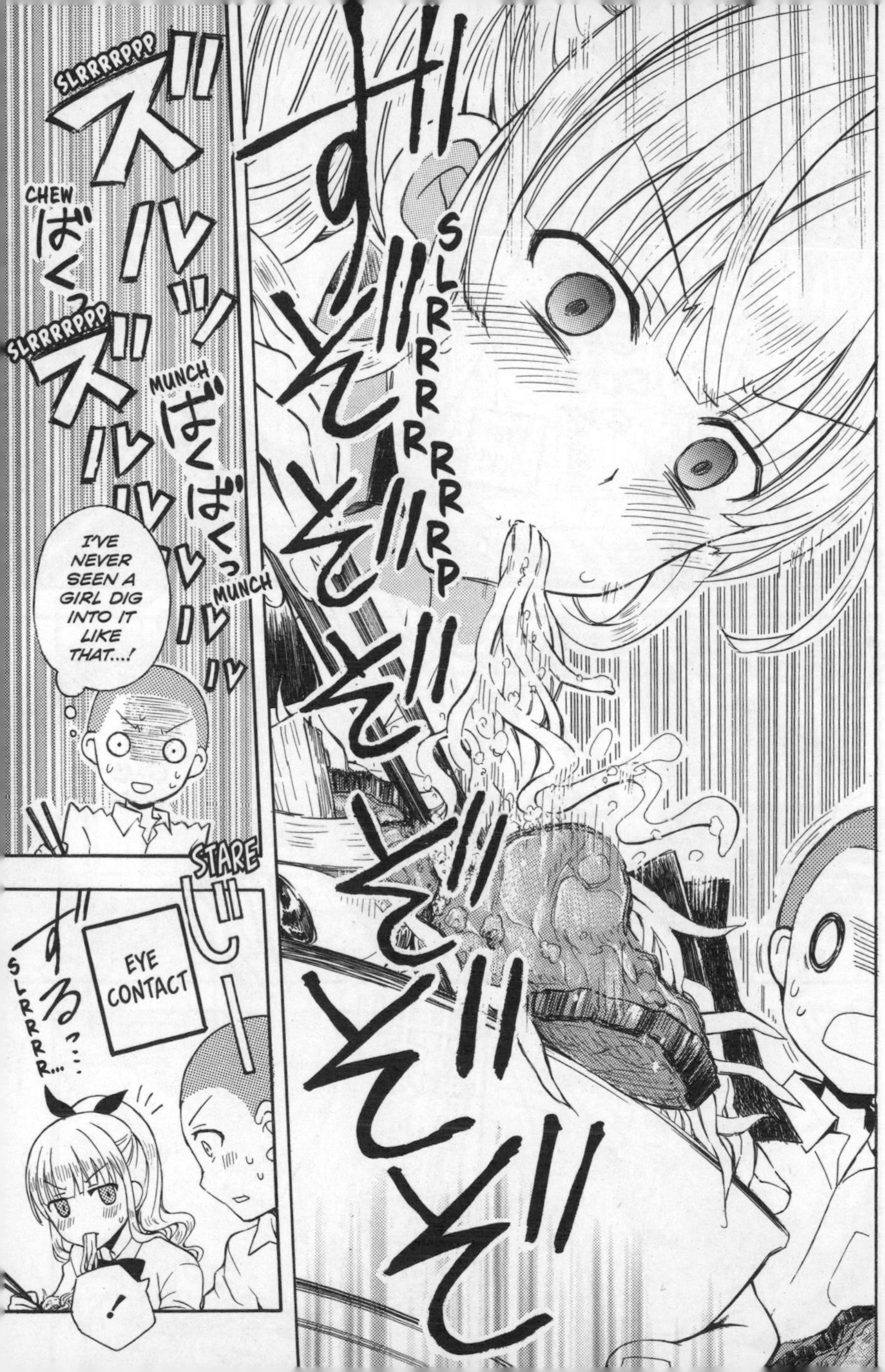
SLRRRRRRRRRP
SLRRRRPPP
ズルッ
CHEW
ばくっ
SLRRRRPPP
ズルルルル
MUNCH
ばくばくっ
MUNCH
I'VE NEVER SEEN A GIRL DIG INTO IT LIKE THAT...!
STARE
じーー
EYE CONTACT
SLRRRRR...
するっ
!

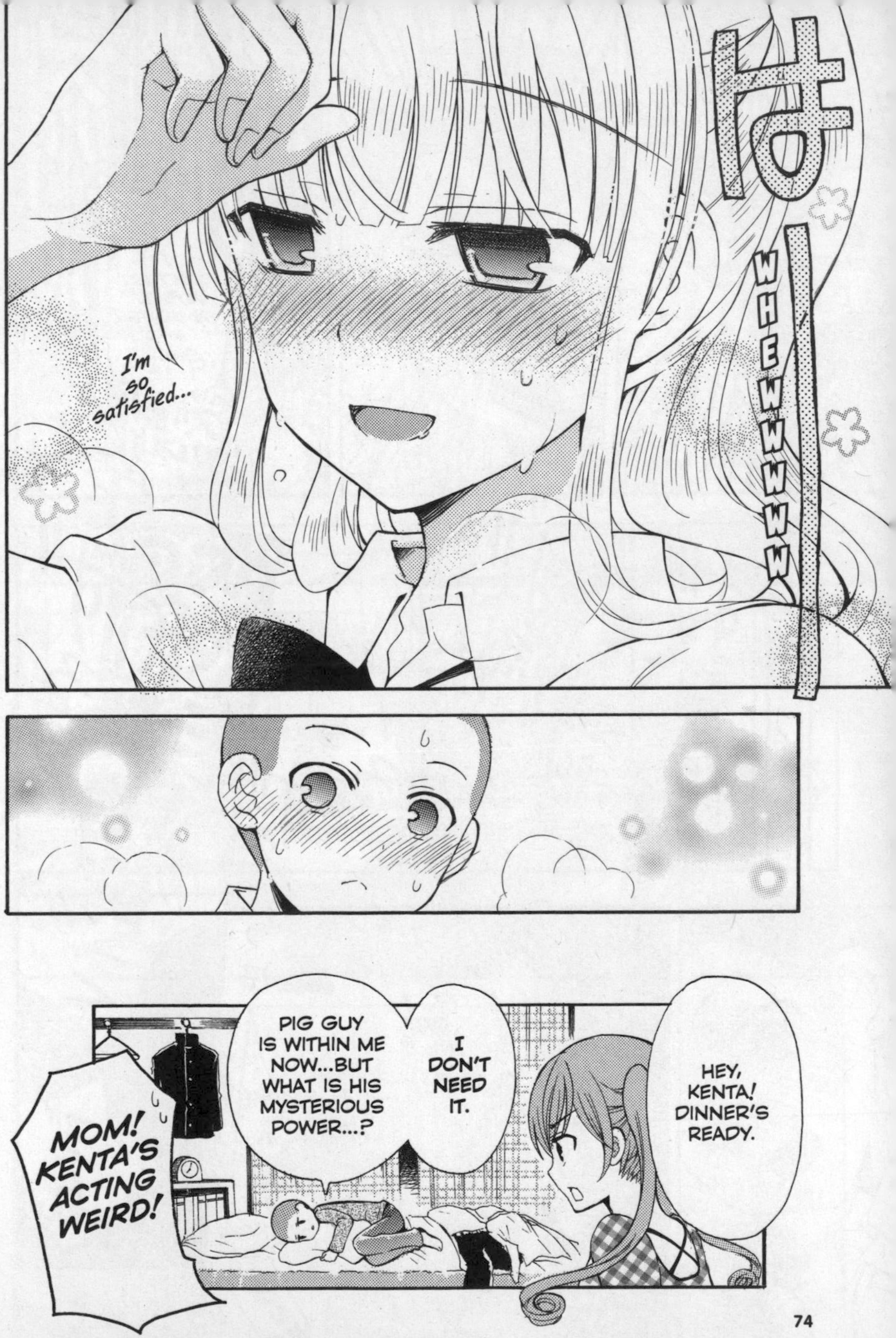
は
WHEWWWWW
I'm so satisfied...
HEY, KENTA! DINNER'S READY.
I DON'T NEED IT.
PIG GUY IS WITHIN ME NOW...BUT WHAT IS HIS MYSTERIOUS POWER...?
MOM! KENTA'S ACTING WEIRD!

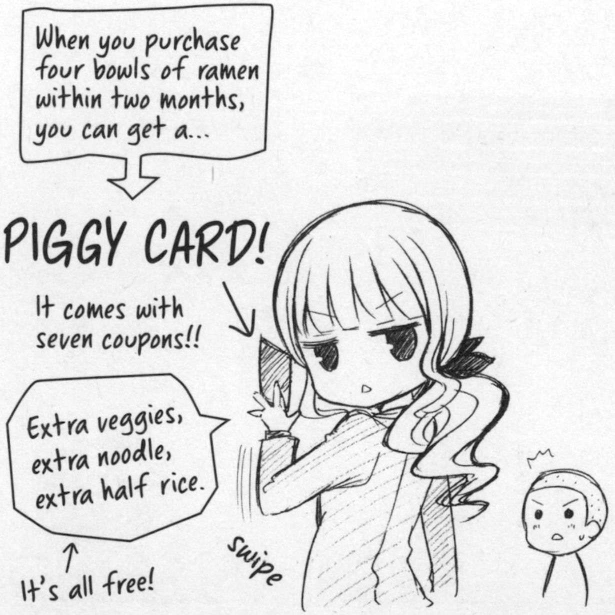
When you purchase four bowls of ramen within two months, you can get a...
PIGGY CARD!
It comes with seven coupons!!
Extra veggies, extra noodle, extra half rice.
It's all free!
swipe

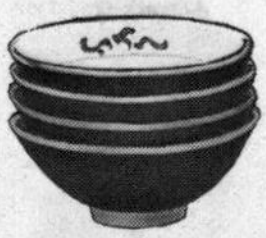

Ms. Koizumi loves ramen noodles

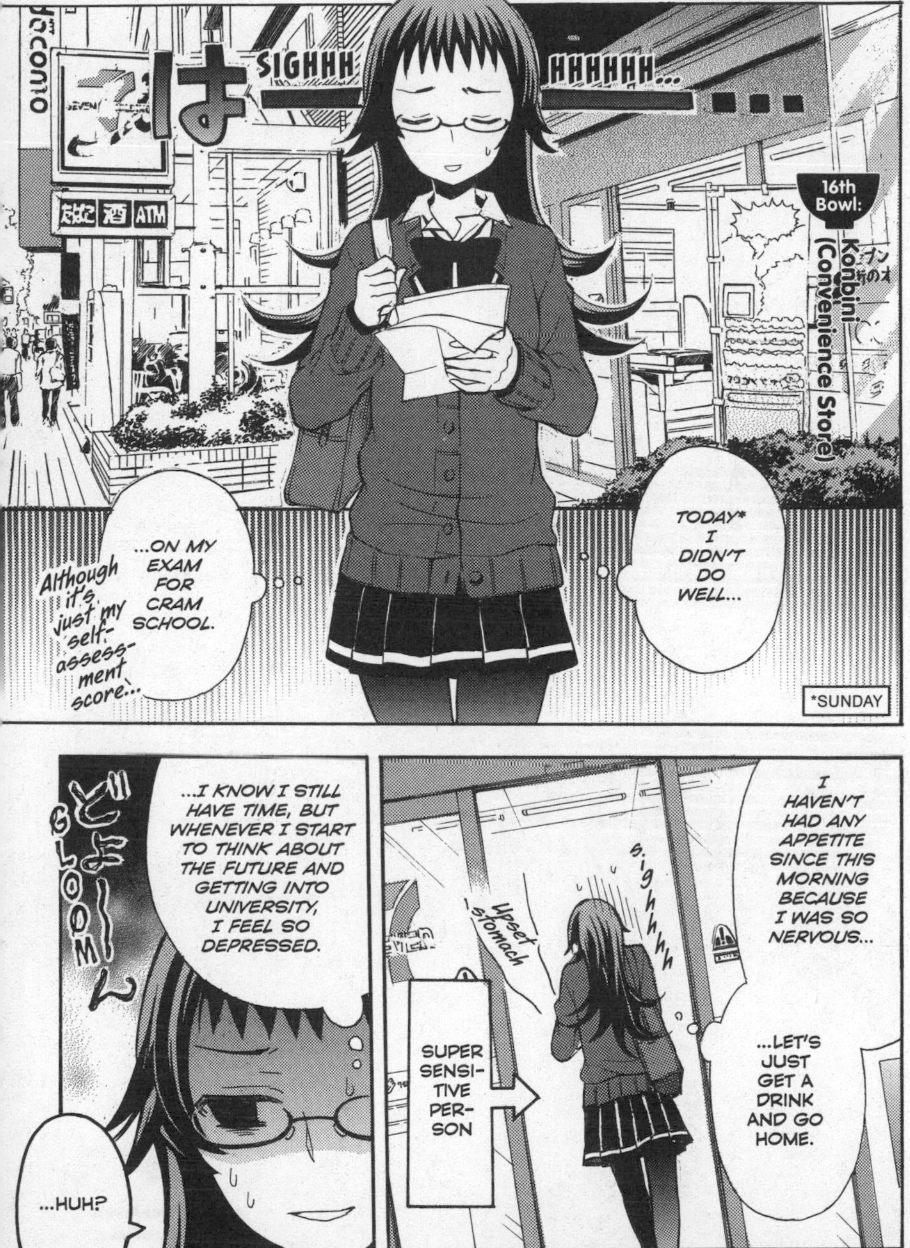
16th Bowl:
Konbini (Convenience Store)
はーーー...
SIGHHHHHHHHHH...
TODAY* I DIDN'T DO WELL...
...ON MY EXAM FOR CRAM SCHOOL.
Although it's just my self-assessment score...
*SUNDAY
I HAVEN'T HAD ANY APPETITE SINCE THIS MORNING BECAUSE I WAS SO NERVOUS...
sighhhh
Upset stomach
SUPER SENSITIVE PERSON
...LET'S JUST GET A DRINK AND GO HOME.
...I KNOW I STILL HAVE TIME, BUT WHENEVER I START TO THINK ABOUT THE FUTURE AND GETTING INTO UNIVERSITY, I FEEL SO DEPRESSED.
どよーーん
GLOOM
...HUH?

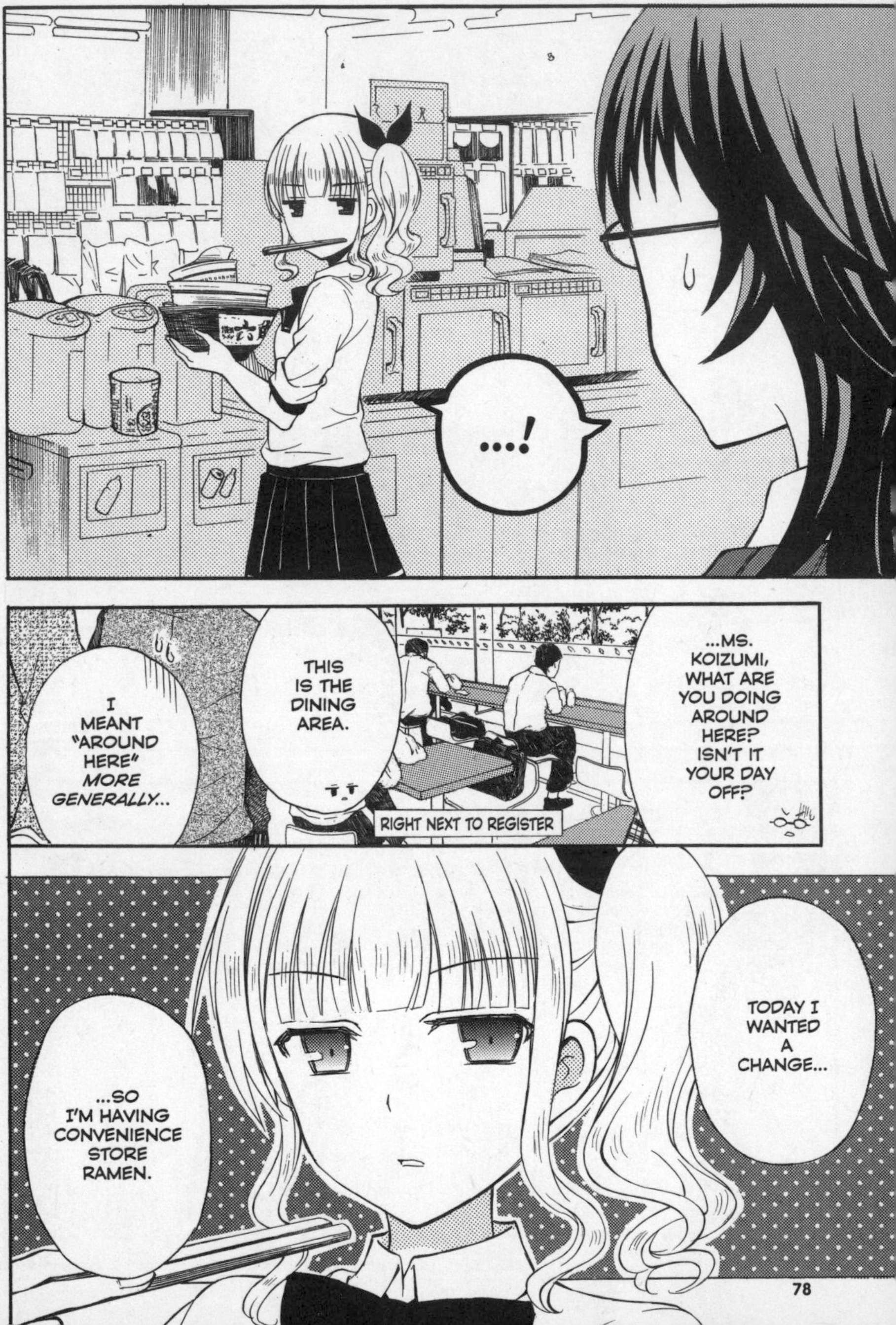
...!
...MS. KOIZUMI, WHAT ARE YOU DOING AROUND HERE? ISN'T IT YOUR DAY OFF?
THIS IS THE DINING AREA.
RIGHT NEXT TO REGISTER
I MEANT "AROUND HERE" MORE GENERALLY...
TODAY I WANTED A CHANGE...
...SO I'M HAVING CONVENIENCE STORE RAMEN.

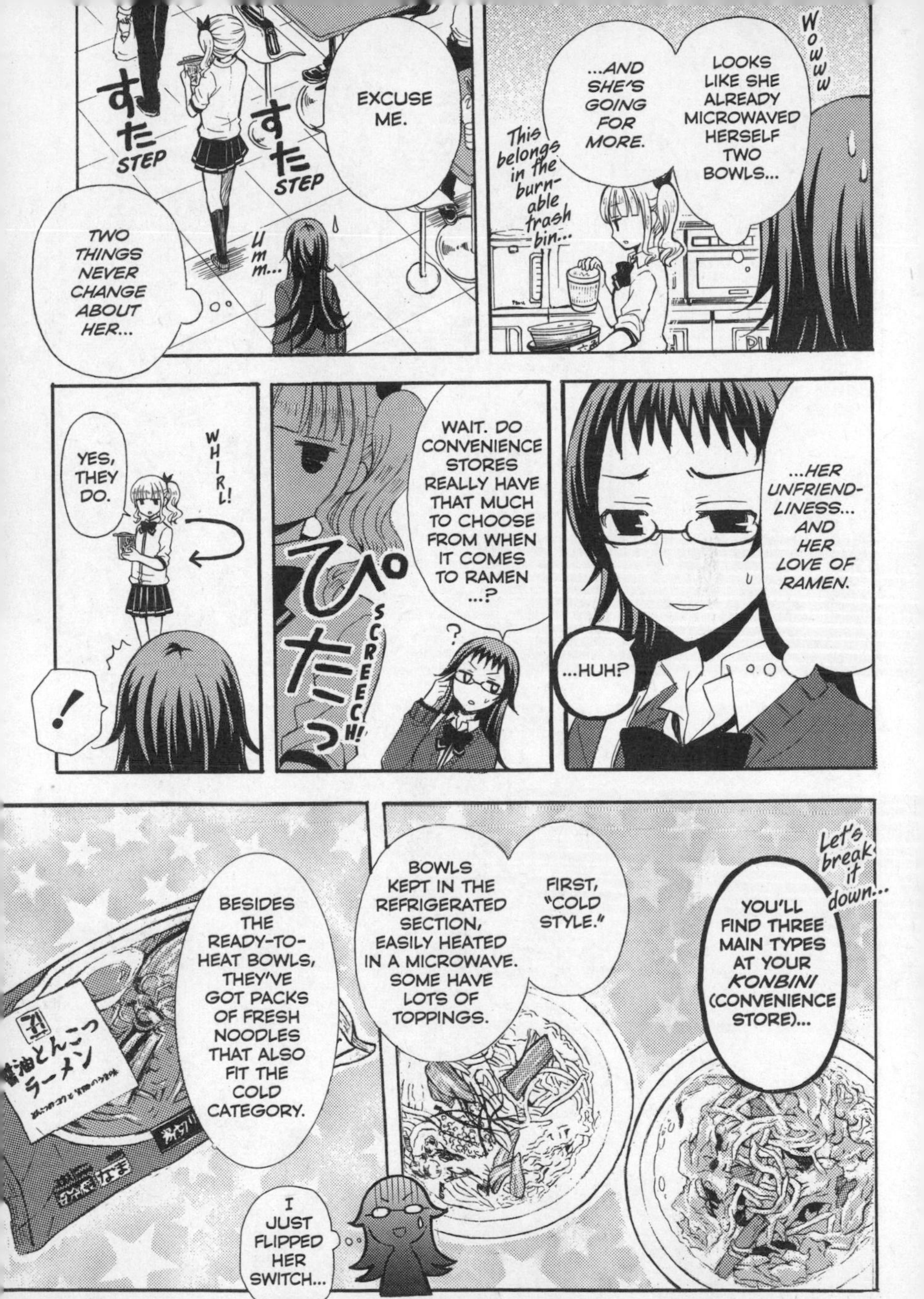
Wowww
LOOKS LIKE SHE ALREADY MICROWAVED HERSELF TWO BOWLS...
...AND SHE'S GOING FOR MORE.
This belongs in the burnable trash bin...
EXCUSE ME.
すた STEP
すた STEP
Umm...
TWO THINGS NEVER CHANGE ABOUT HER...
...HER UNFRIENDLINESS... AND HER LOVE OF RAMEN.
...HUH?
WAIT. DO CONVENIENCE STORES REALLY HAVE THAT MUCH TO CHOOSE FROM WHEN IT COMES TO RAMEN...?
?
ぴたっ SCREECH!
YES, THEY DO.
WHIRL!
!
Let's break it down...
YOU'LL FIND THREE MAIN TYPES AT YOUR *KONBINI* (CONVENIENCE STORE)...
FIRST, "COLD STYLE."
BOWLS KEPT IN THE REFRIGERATED SECTION, EASILY HEATED IN A MICROWAVE. SOME HAVE LOTS OF TOPPINGS.
BESIDES THE READY-TO-HEAT BOWLS, THEY'VE GOT PACKS OF FRESH NOODLES THAT ALSO FIT THE COLD CATEGORY.
醤油とんこつラーメン
I JUST FLIPPED HER SWITCH...

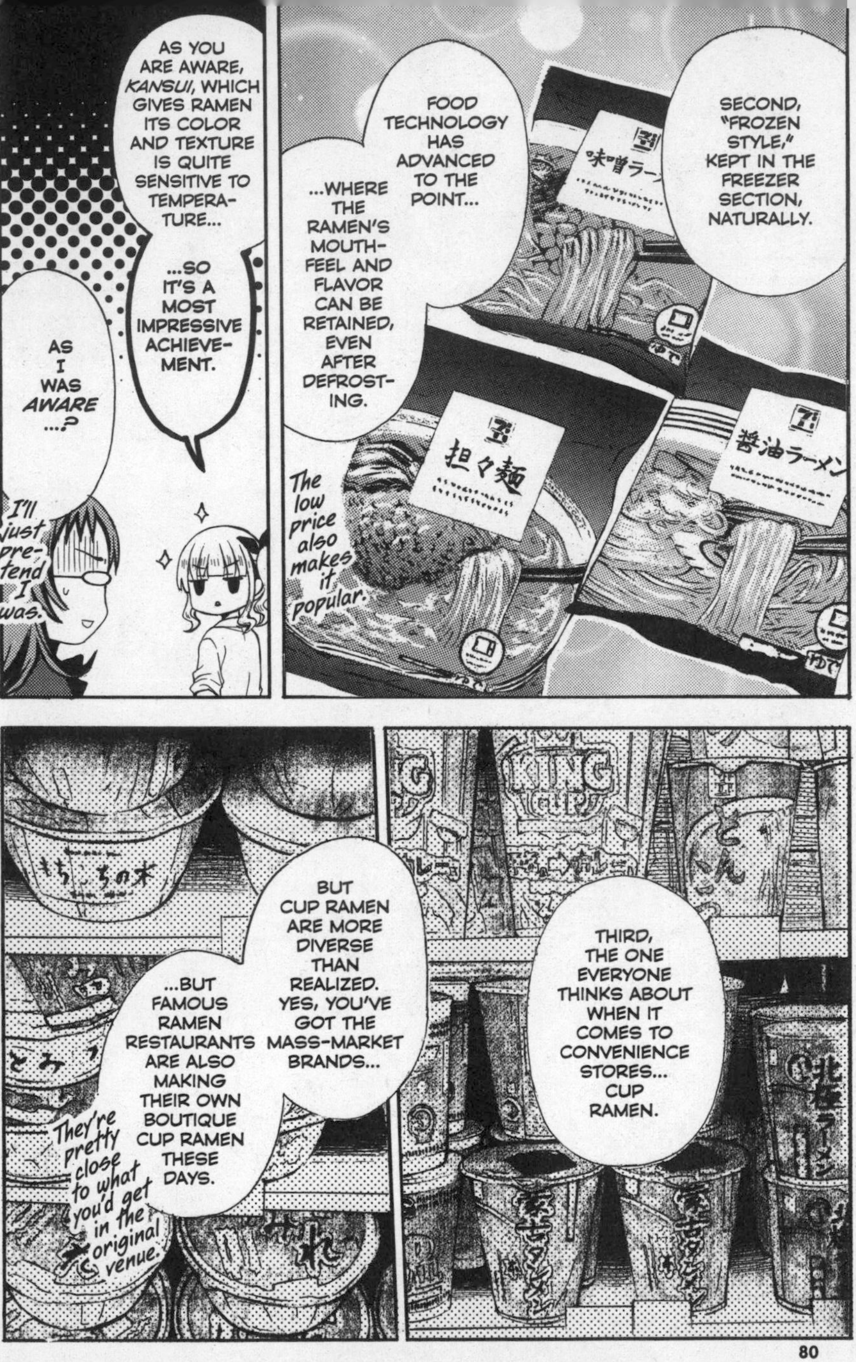
SECOND, "FROZEN STYLE," KEPT IN THE FREEZER SECTION, NATURALLY.
FOOD TECHNOLOGY HAS ADVANCED TO THE POINT...
...WHERE THE RAMEN'S MOUTH-FEEL AND FLAVOR CAN BE RETAINED, EVEN AFTER DEFROST-ING.
担々麺
醤油ラーメン
The low price also makes it popular.
AS YOU ARE AWARE, *KANSUI*, WHICH GIVES RAMEN ITS COLOR AND TEXTURE IS QUITE SENSITIVE TO TEMPERA-TURE...
...SO IT'S A MOST IMPRESSIVE ACHIEVE-MENT.
AS I WAS *AWARE* ...?
I'll just pre-tend I was.
THIRD, THE ONE EVERYONE THINKS ABOUT WHEN IT COMES TO CONVENIENCE STORES... CUP RAMEN.
BUT CUP RAMEN ARE MORE DIVERSE THAN REALIZED. YES, YOU'VE GOT THE MASS-MARKET BRANDS...
...BUT FAMOUS RAMEN RESTAURANTS ARE ALSO MAKING THEIR OWN BOUTIQUE CUP RAMEN THESE DAYS.
They're pretty close to what you'd get in the original venue.

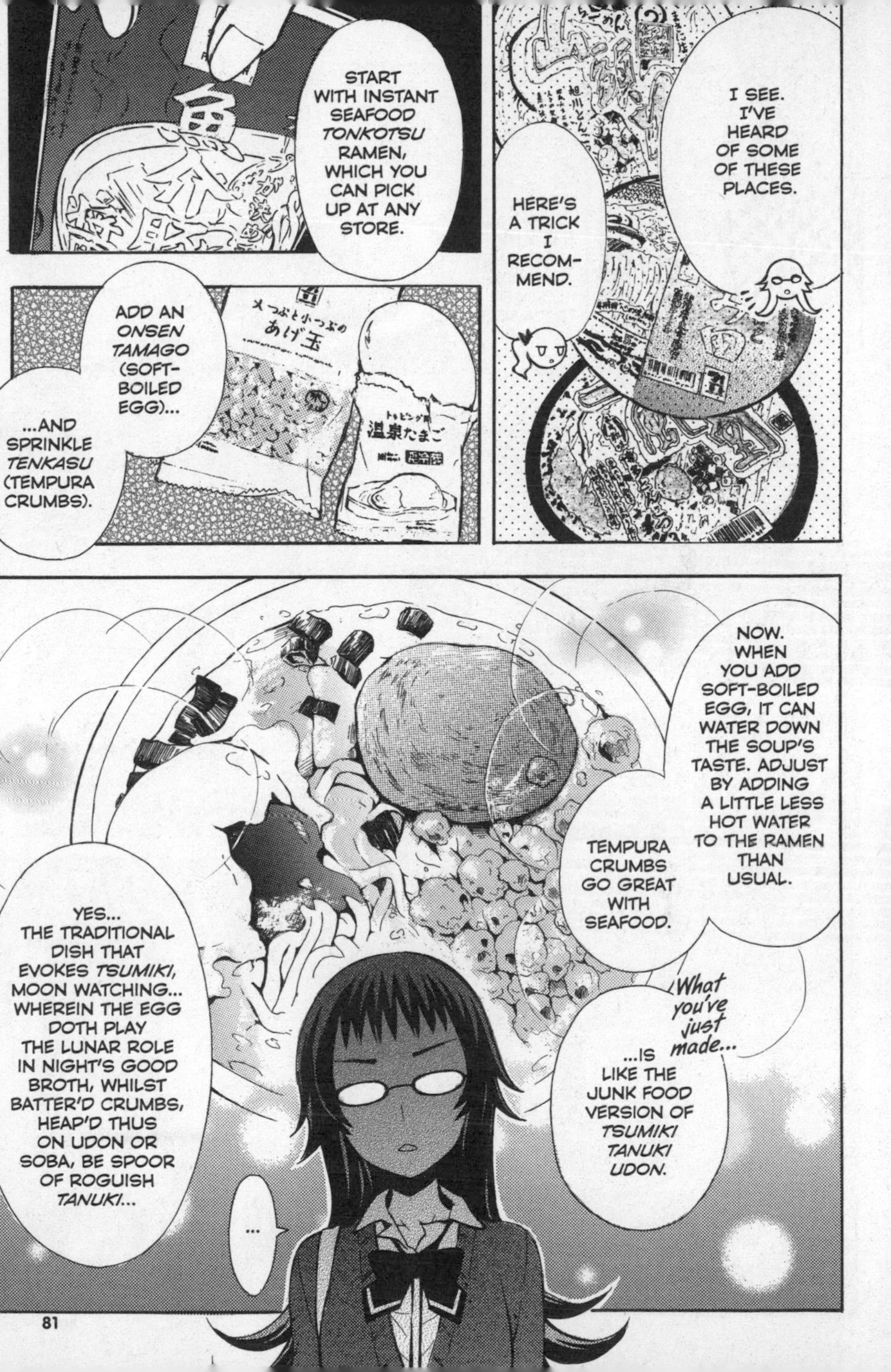
I SEE. I'VE HEARD OF SOME OF THESE PLACES.
HERE'S A TRICK I RECOMMEND.
START WITH INSTANT SEAFOOD *TONKOTSU* RAMEN, WHICH YOU CAN PICK UP AT ANY STORE.
ADD AN *ONSEN TAMAGO* (SOFT-BOILED EGG)...
...AND SPRINKLE *TENKASU* (TEMPURA CRUMBS).
あげ玉
温泉たまご
NOW. WHEN YOU ADD SOFT-BOILED EGG, IT CAN WATER DOWN THE SOUP'S TASTE. ADJUST BY ADDING A LITTLE LESS HOT WATER TO THE RAMEN THAN USUAL.
TEMPURA CRUMBS GO GREAT WITH SEAFOOD.
What you've just made...
...IS LIKE THE JUNK FOOD VERSION OF *TSUMIKI TANUKI UDON*.
YES... THE TRADITIONAL DISH THAT EVOKES *TSUMIKI*, MOON WATCHING... WHEREIN THE EGG DOTH PLAY THE LUNAR ROLE IN NIGHT'S GOOD BROTH, WHILST BATTER'D CRUMBS, HEAP'D THUS ON UDON OR SOBA, BE SPOOR OF ROGUISH *TANUKI*...
...

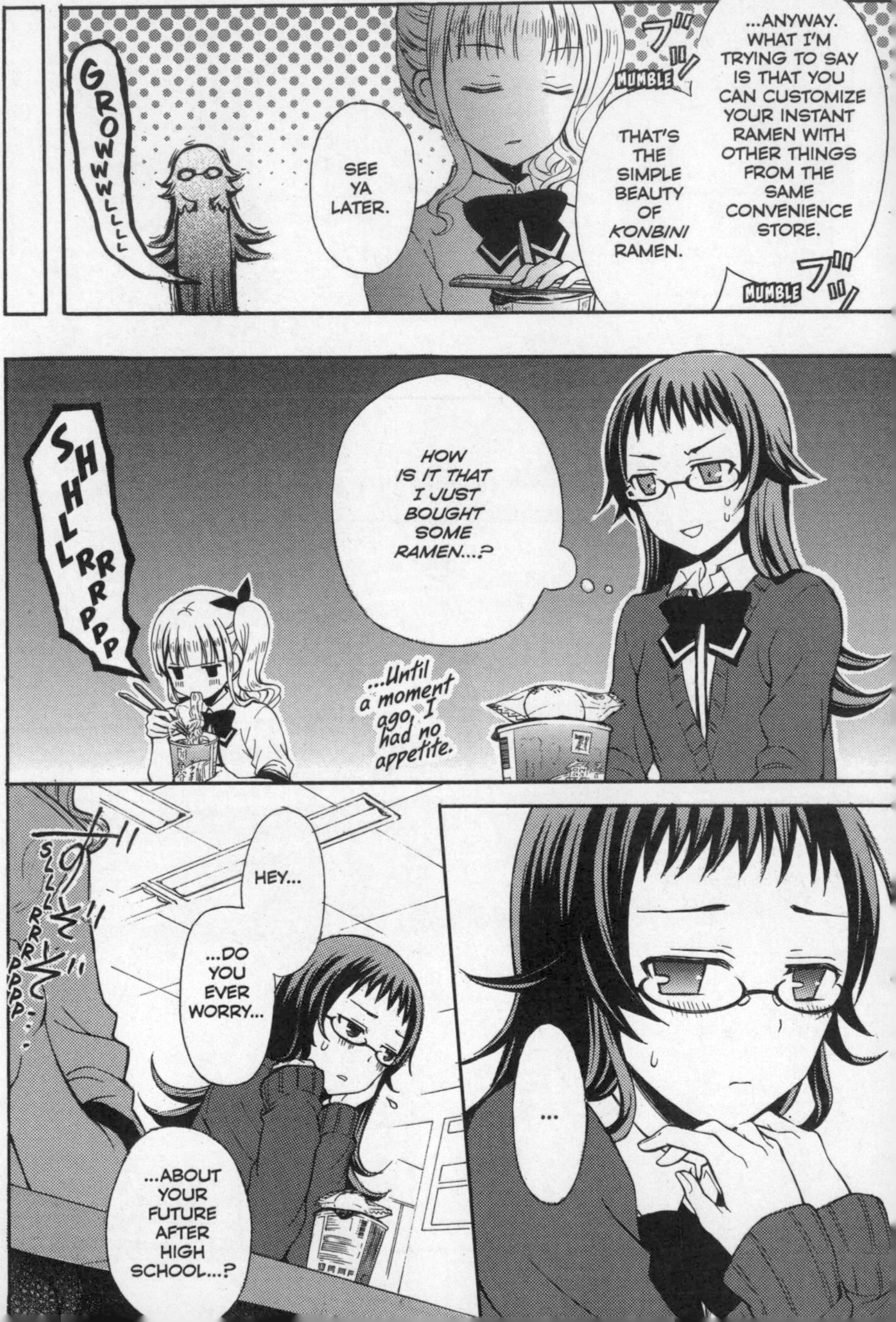
...ANYWAY. WHAT I'M TRYING TO SAY IS THAT YOU CAN CUSTOMIZE YOUR INSTANT RAMEN WITH OTHER THINGS FROM THE SAME CONVENIENCE STORE.
MUMBLE
THAT'S THE SIMPLE BEAUTY OF *KONBINI* RAMEN.
MUMBLE
SEE YA LATER.
GROWWWLLLLL
HOW IS IT THAT I JUST BOUGHT SOME RAMEN...?
...Until a moment ago, I had no appetite.
SHHLLRRRPPP
...
HEY...
...DO YOU EVER WORRY...
...ABOUT YOUR FUTURE AFTER HIGH SCHOOL...?
SLLLRRRRPPPP...

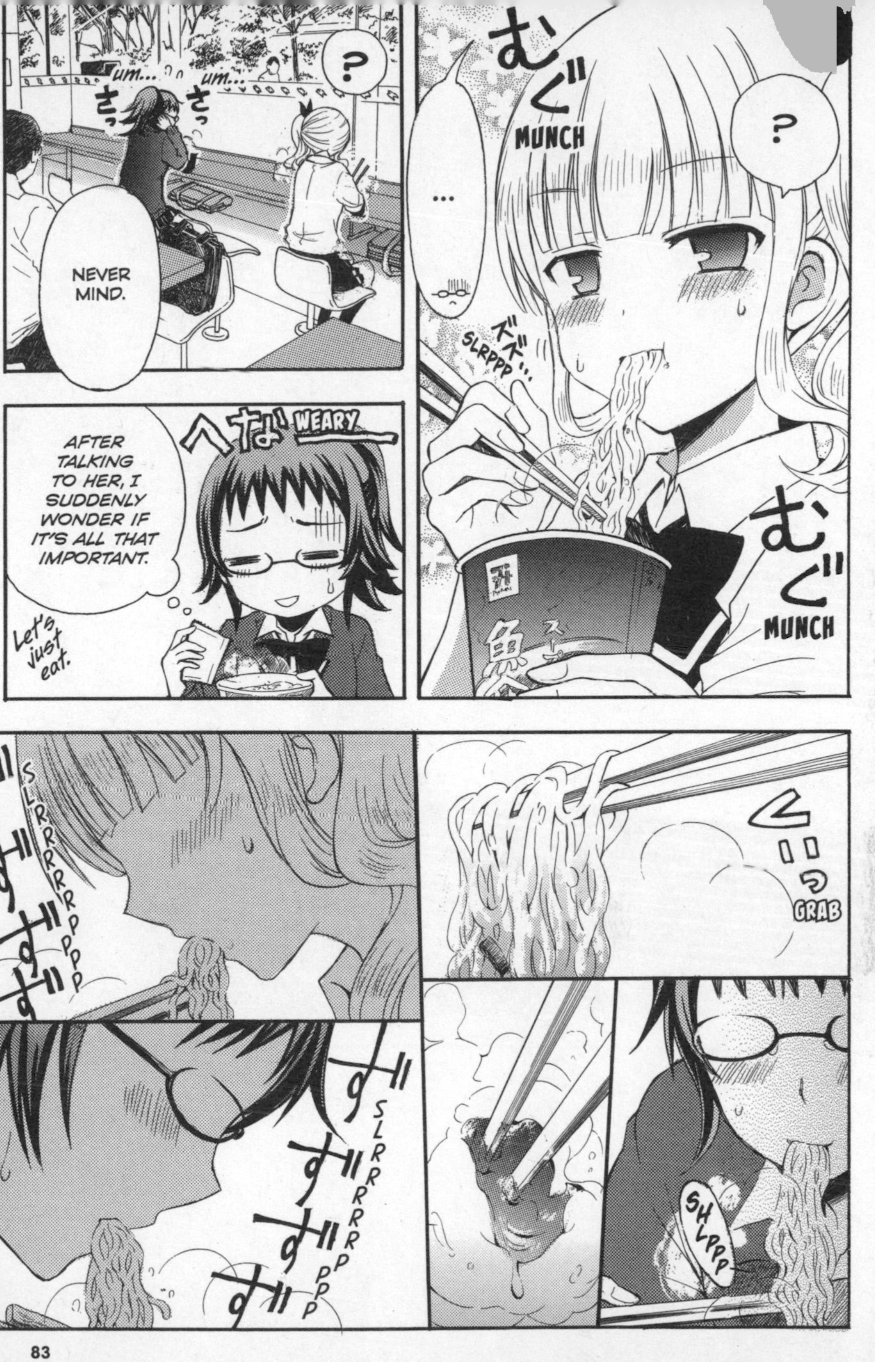

むぐ MUNCH
?
...
ズズ… SLRPPP…
むぐ MUNCH
?
um... さっ
um... さっ
NEVER MIND.
へな WEARY
AFTER TALKING TO HER, I SUDDENLY WONDER IF IT'S ALL THAT IMPORTANT.
Let's just eat.
ぐっ GRAB
すすすす SLRRRRRPPPP
SHLPPP
すすすす SLRRRRRPPPP

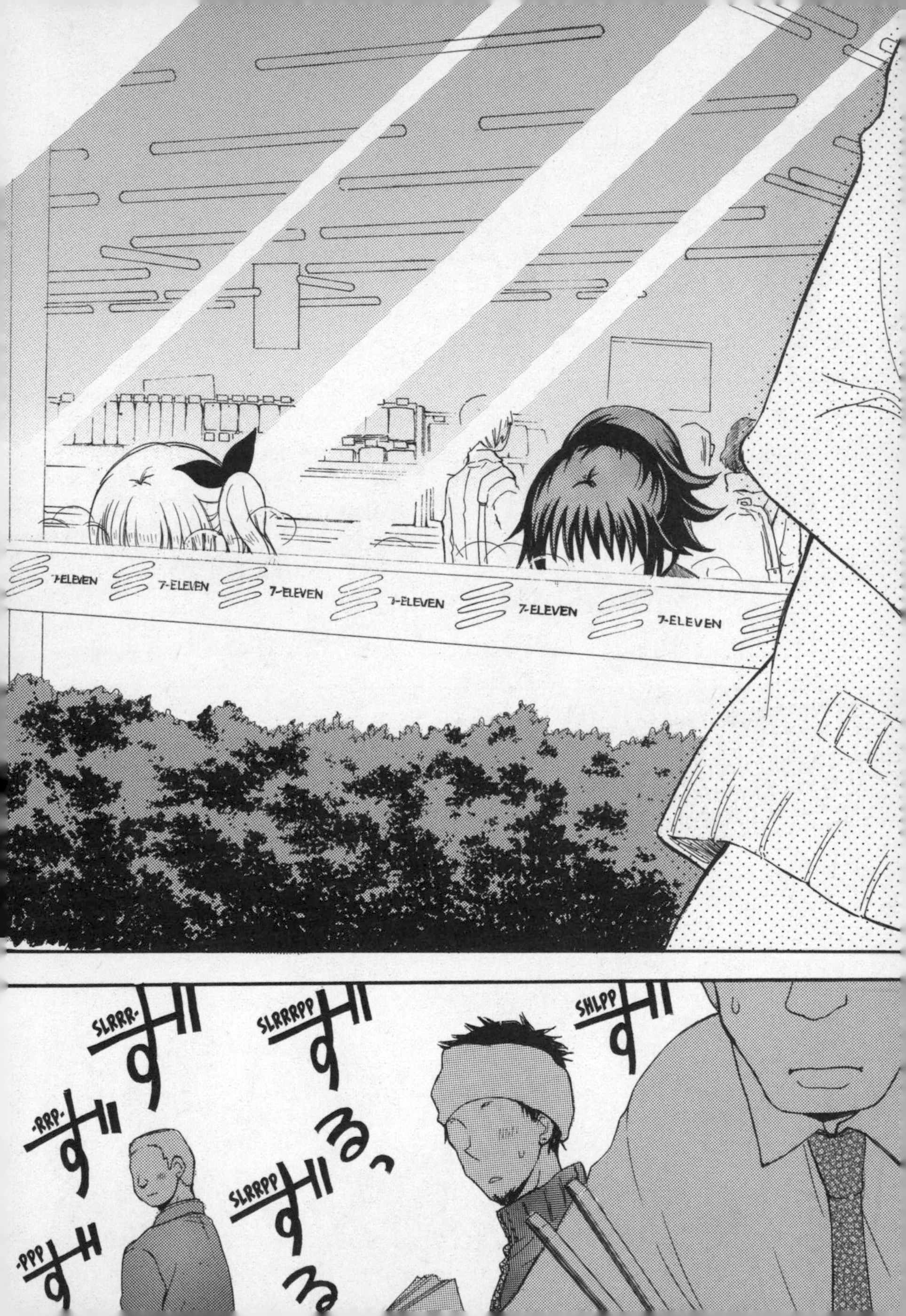
7-ELEVEN
7-ELEVEN
7-ELEVEN
7-ELEVEN
7-ELEVEN
7-ELEVEN
SHLPP
SLRRRPP
SLRRR-
-RRP-
SLRRPP
-PPP

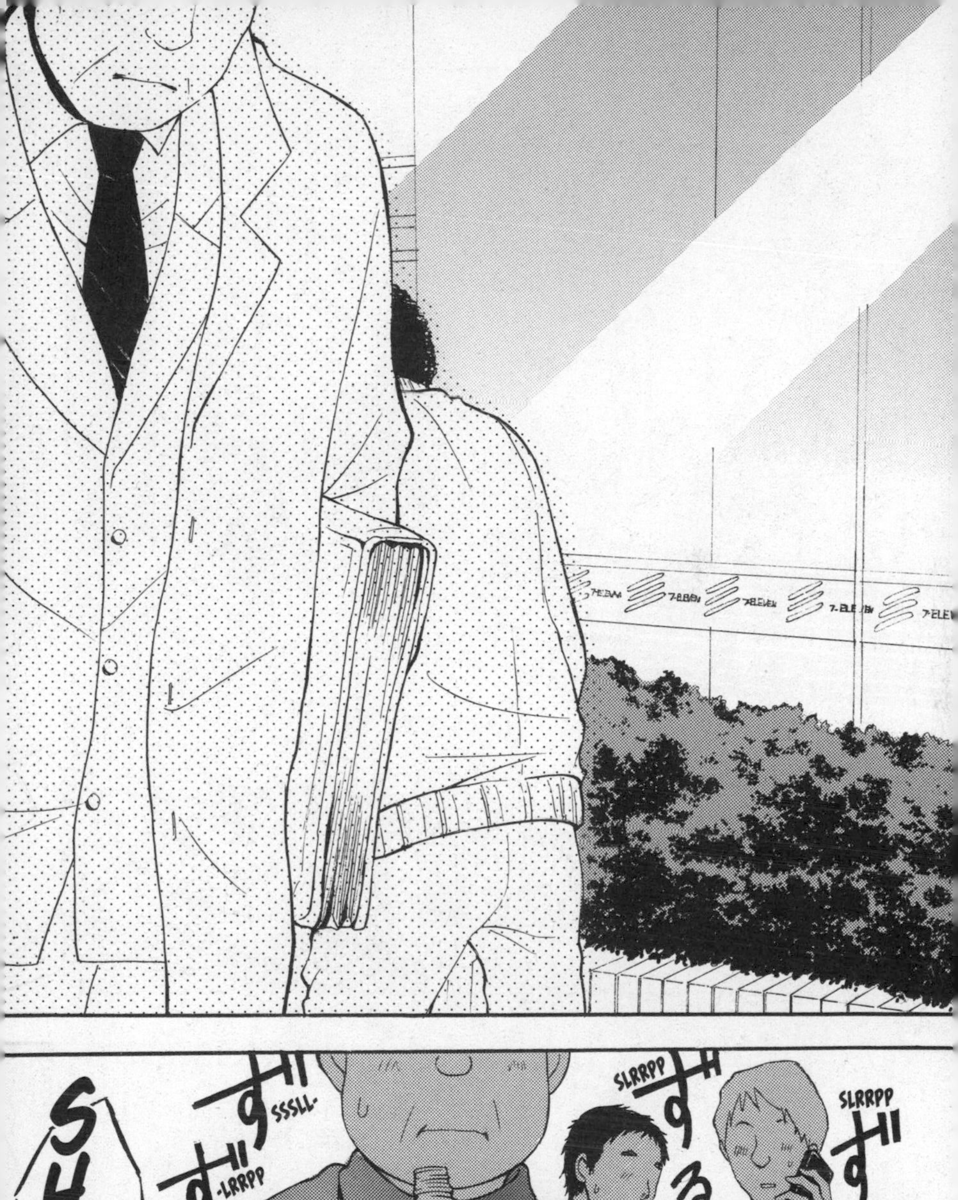

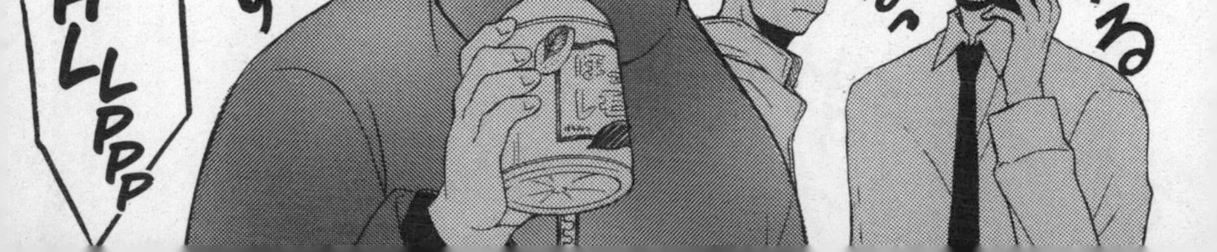
SLRRPP
ずる
SLRRPP
ずる
ず
SSSLL-
ず
-LRRPP
SHLLPPP

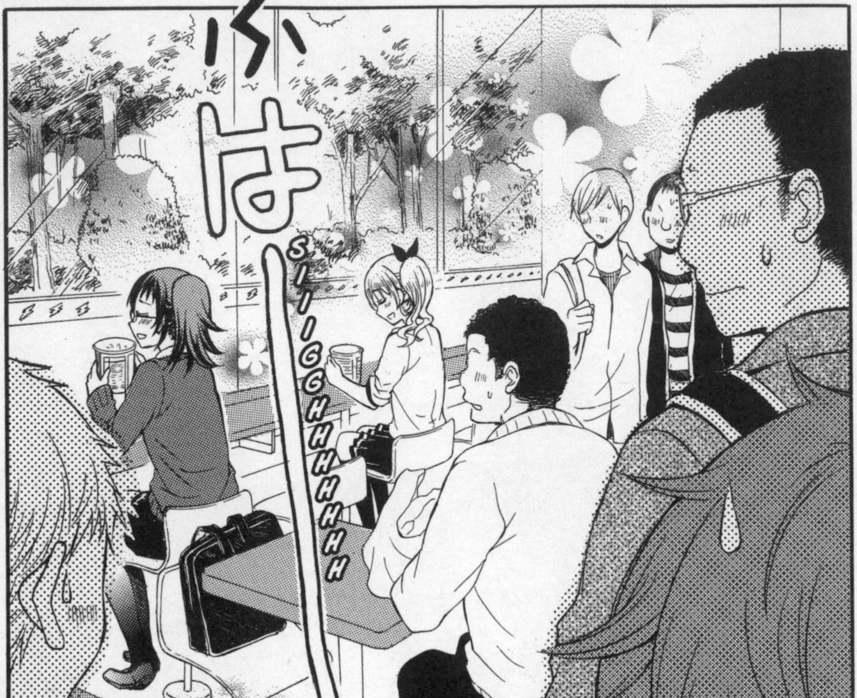
ふは
SI---IGGHHHHHHHHH
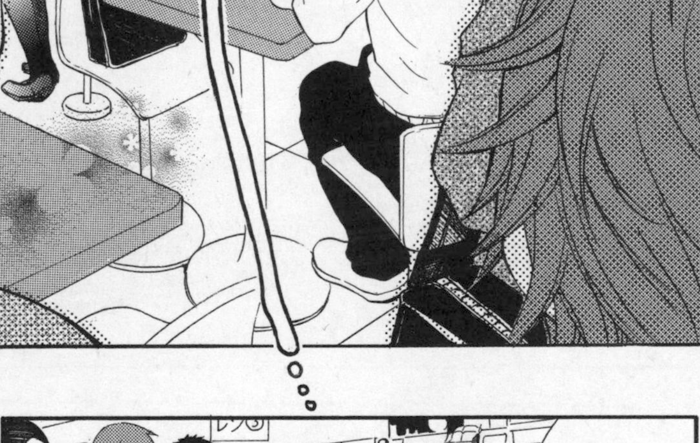
SEEMS LIKE EVERYONE'S BUYING INSTANT RAMEN TODAY...

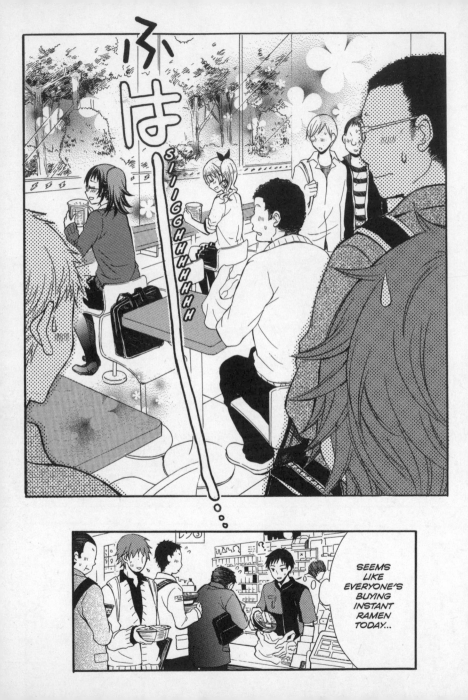

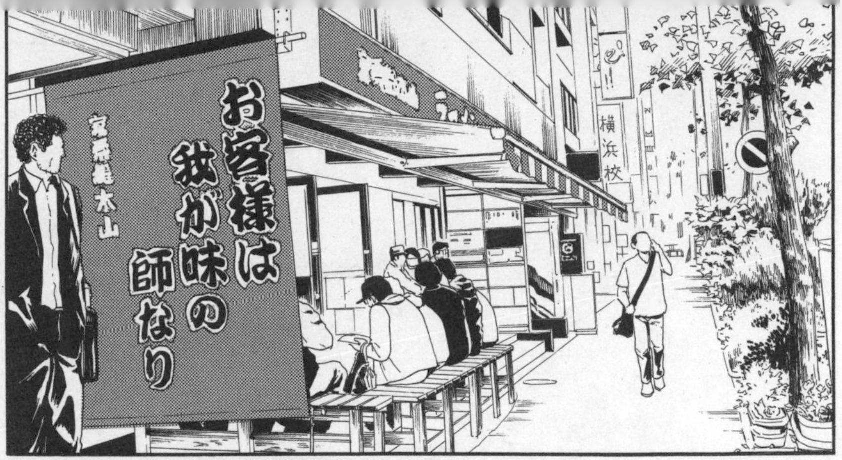
お客様は
我が味の
師なり
横浜校
BANNER: "CUSTOMERS ARE THE TEACHERS OF OUR TASTE."

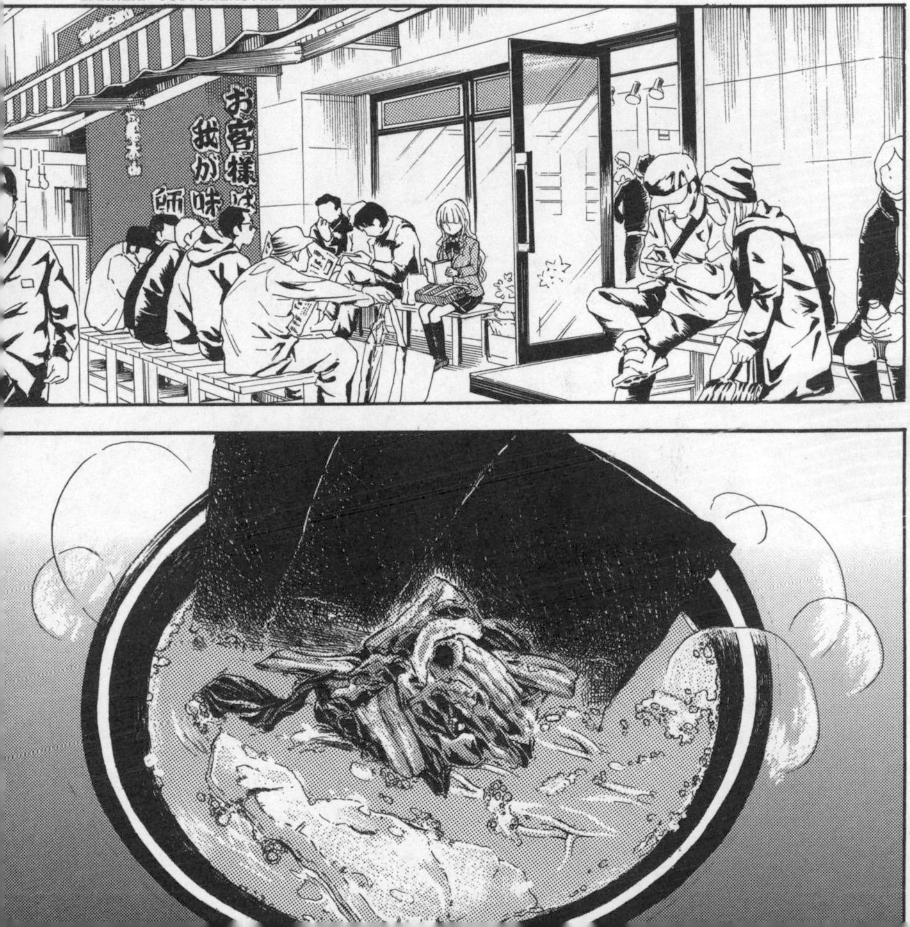

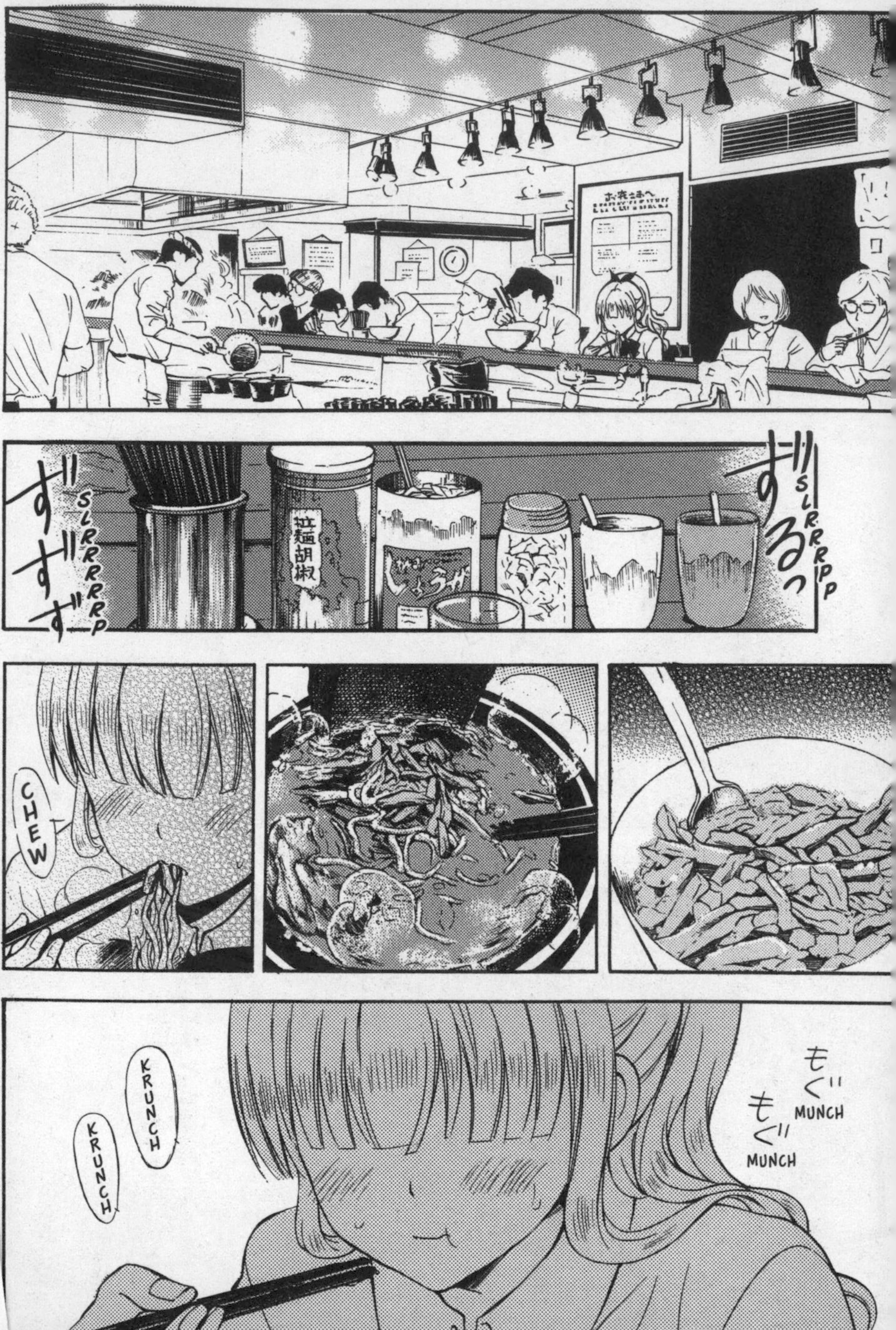
ずるっ
SLRRRPP
拉麺胡椒
ずずず
SLRRRRRP
CHEW
もぐもぐ
MUNCH
MUNCH
KRUNCH
KRUNCH

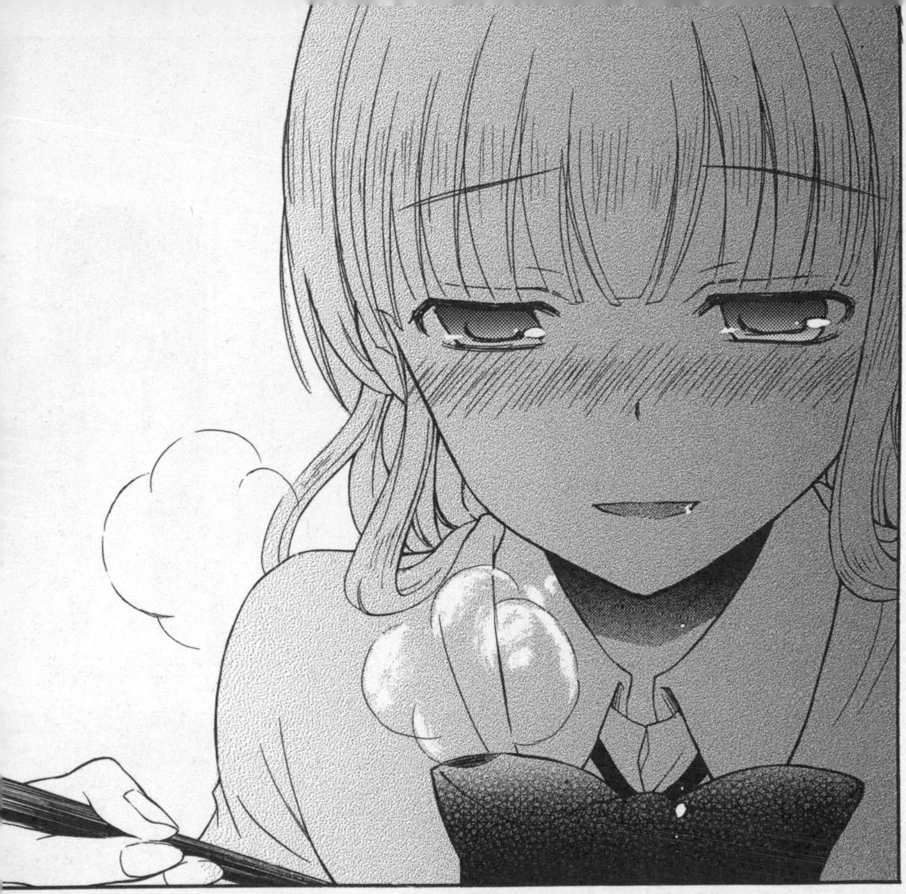

17th Bowl: Iekei

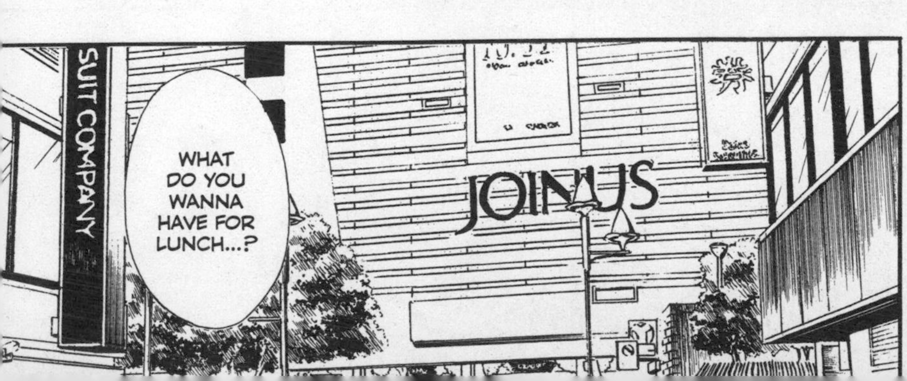
JOINUS
WHAT DO YOU WANNA HAVE FOR LUNCH...?
SUIT COMPANY

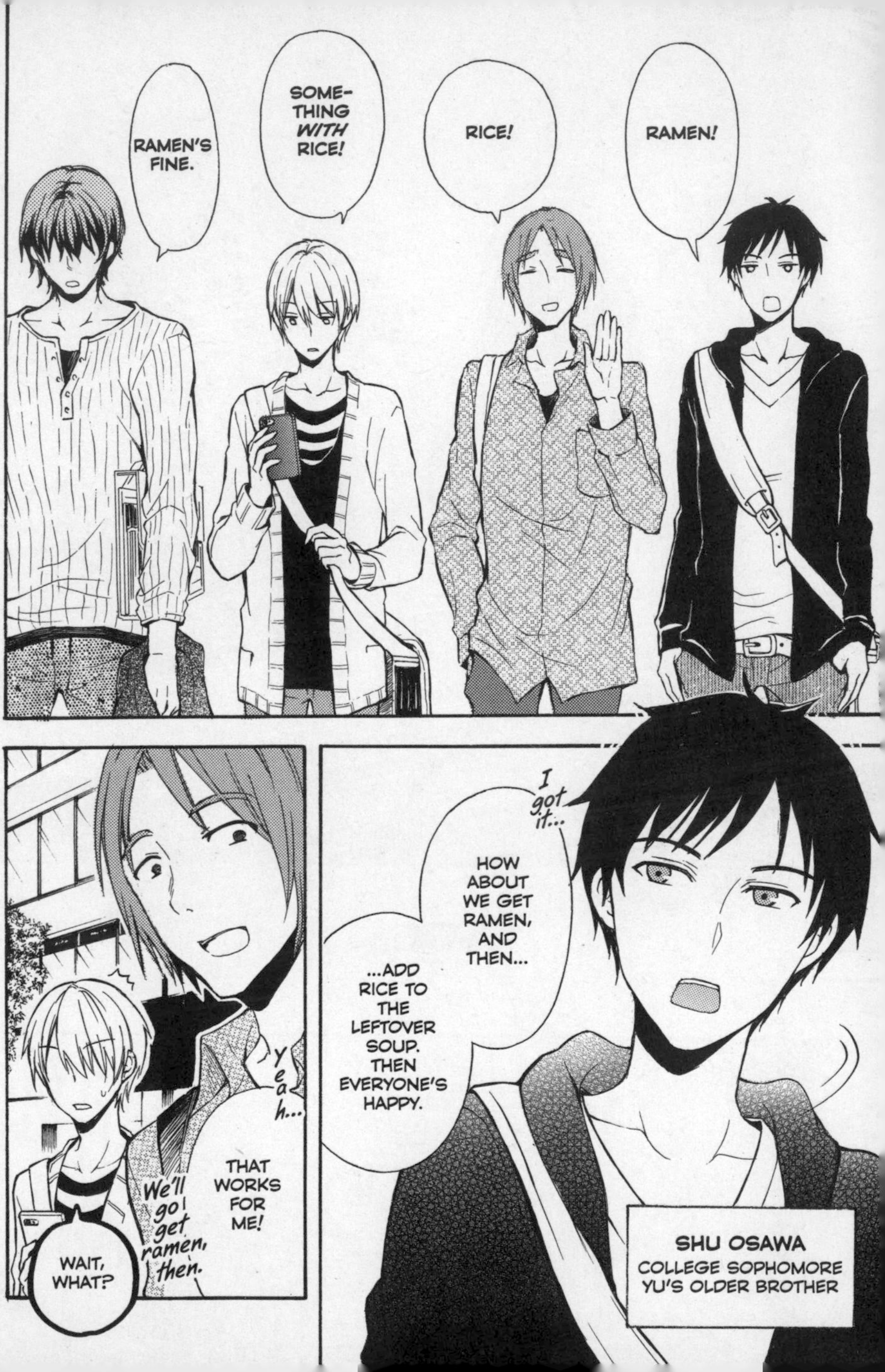
RAMEN!
RICE!
SOME-THING WITH RICE!
RAMEN'S FINE.
I got it...
HOW ABOUT WE GET RAMEN, AND THEN...
...ADD RICE TO THE LEFTOVER SOUP. THEN EVERYONE'S HAPPY.
SHU OSAWA
COLLEGE SOPHOMORE
YU'S OLDER BROTHER
Yeah...
THAT WORKS FOR ME!
We'll go! get ramen, then.
WAIT, WHAT?

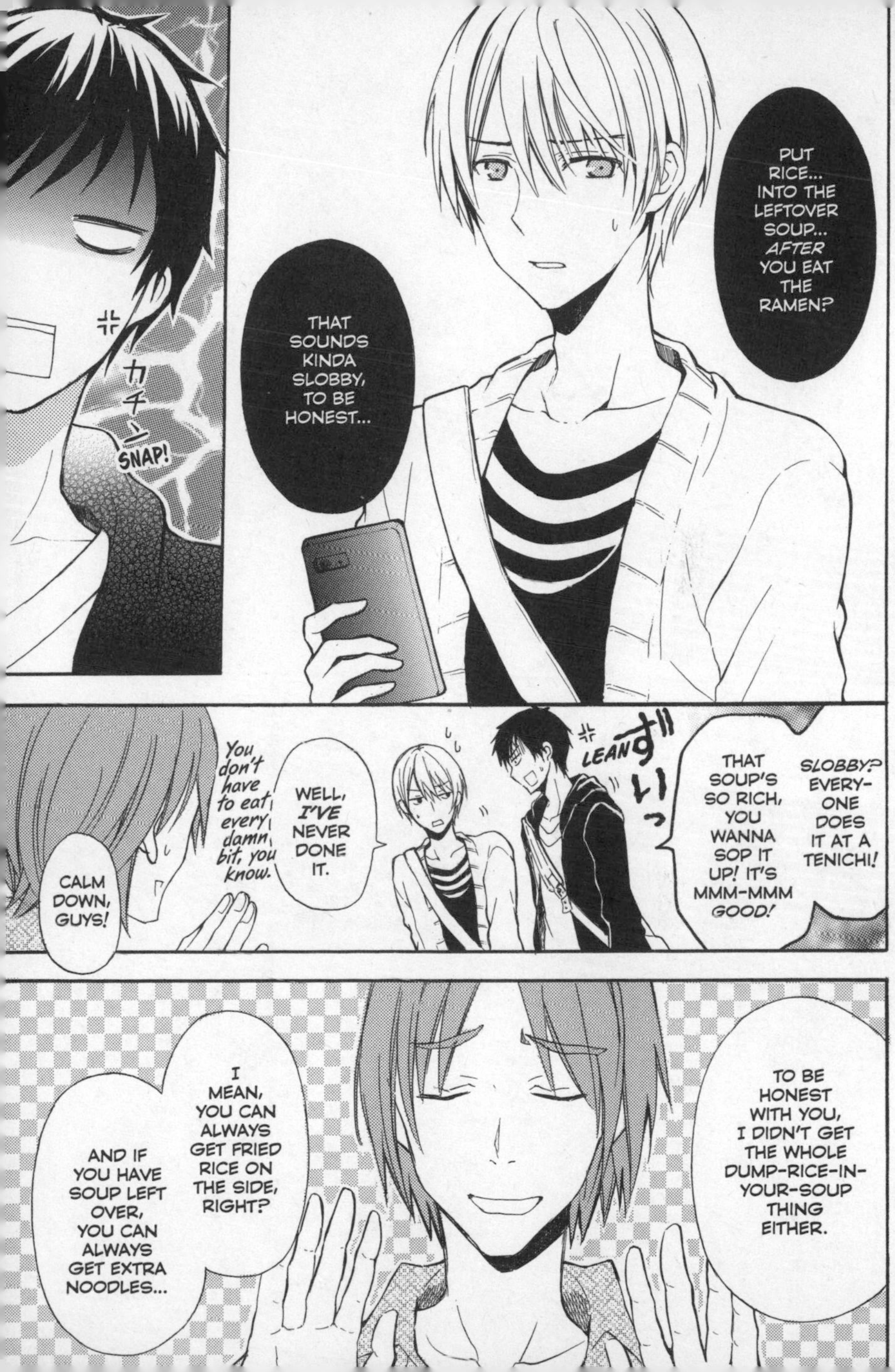
PUT RICE... INTO THE LEFTOVER SOUP... AFTER YOU EAT THE RAMEN?
THAT SOUNDS KINDA SLOBBY, TO BE HONEST...
カチン
SNAP!
SLOBBY? EVERY-ONE DOES IT AT A TENICHI!
THAT SOUP'S SO RICH, YOU WANNA SOP IT UP! IT'S MMM-MMM GOOD!
ずいっ
LEAN
WELL, I'VE NEVER DONE IT.
You don't have to eat every damn bit, you know.
CALM DOWN, GUYS!
TO BE HONEST WITH YOU, I DIDN'T GET THE WHOLE DUMP-RICE-IN-YOUR-SOUP THING EITHER.
I MEAN, YOU CAN ALWAYS GET FRIED RICE ON THE SIDE, RIGHT?
AND IF YOU HAVE SOUP LEFT OVER, YOU CAN ALWAYS GET EXTRA NOODLES...

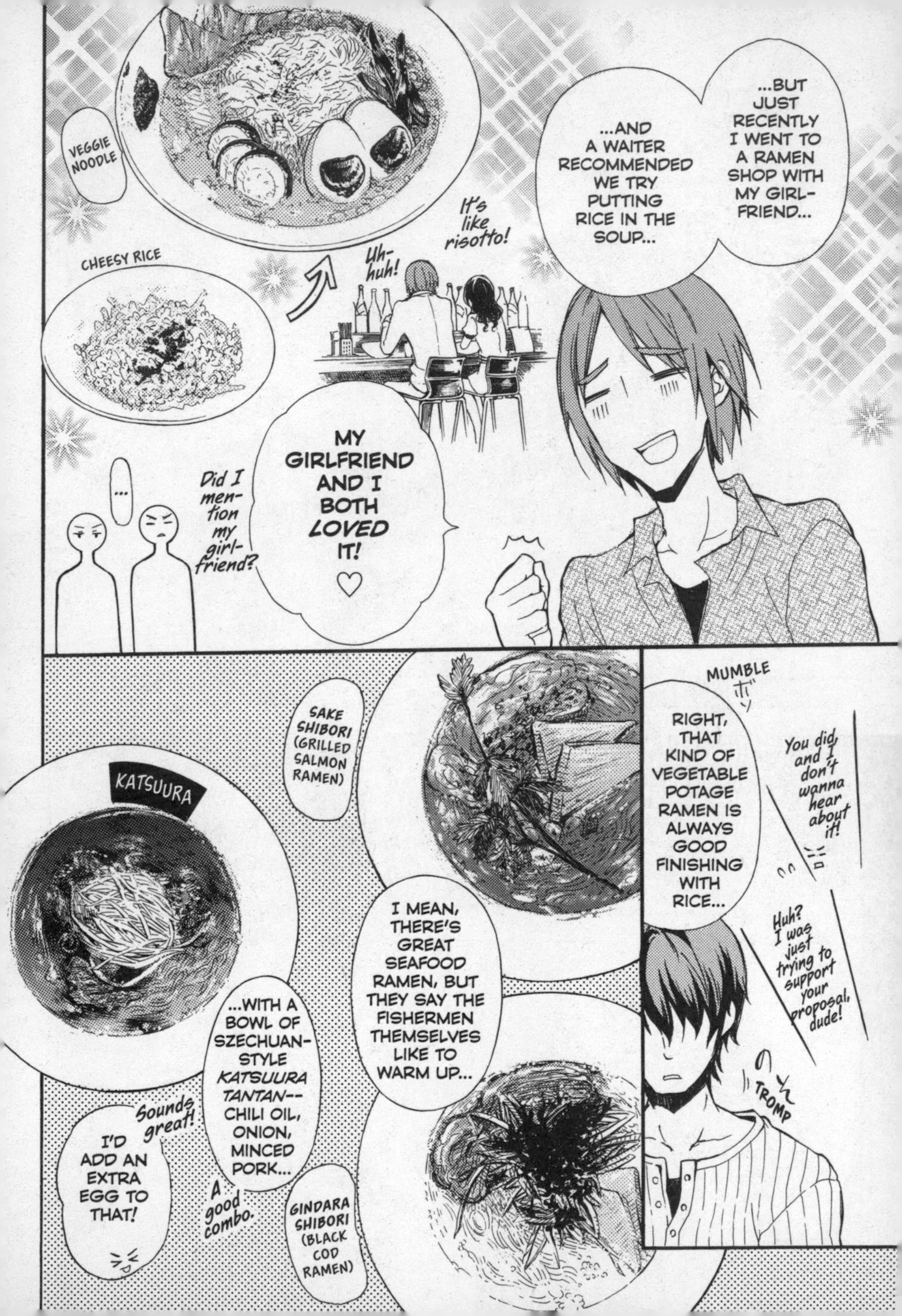
...BUT JUST RECENTLY I WENT TO A RAMEN SHOP WITH MY GIRLFRIEND...
...AND A WAITER RECOMMENDED WE TRY PUTTING RICE IN THE SOUP...
It's like risotto!
Uh-huh!
VEGGIE NOODLE
CHEESY RICE
MY GIRLFRIEND AND I BOTH *LOVED* IT! ♡
Did I mention my girlfriend?
...
MUMBLE
RIGHT, THAT KIND OF VEGETABLE POTAGE RAMEN IS ALWAYS GOOD FINISHING WITH RICE...
You did, and I don't wanna hear about it!
Huh? I was just trying to support your proposal, dude!
TROMP
SAKE SHIBORI (GRILLED SALMON RAMEN)
I MEAN, THERE'S GREAT SEAFOOD RAMEN, BUT THEY SAY THE FISHERMEN THEMSELVES LIKE TO WARM UP...
KATSUURA
...WITH A BOWL OF SZECHUAN-STYLE *KATSUURA TANTAN*--CHILI OIL, ONION, MINCED PORK...
Sounds great!
I'D ADD AN EXTRA EGG TO THAT!
A good combo.
GINDARA SHIBORI (BLACK COD RAMEN)

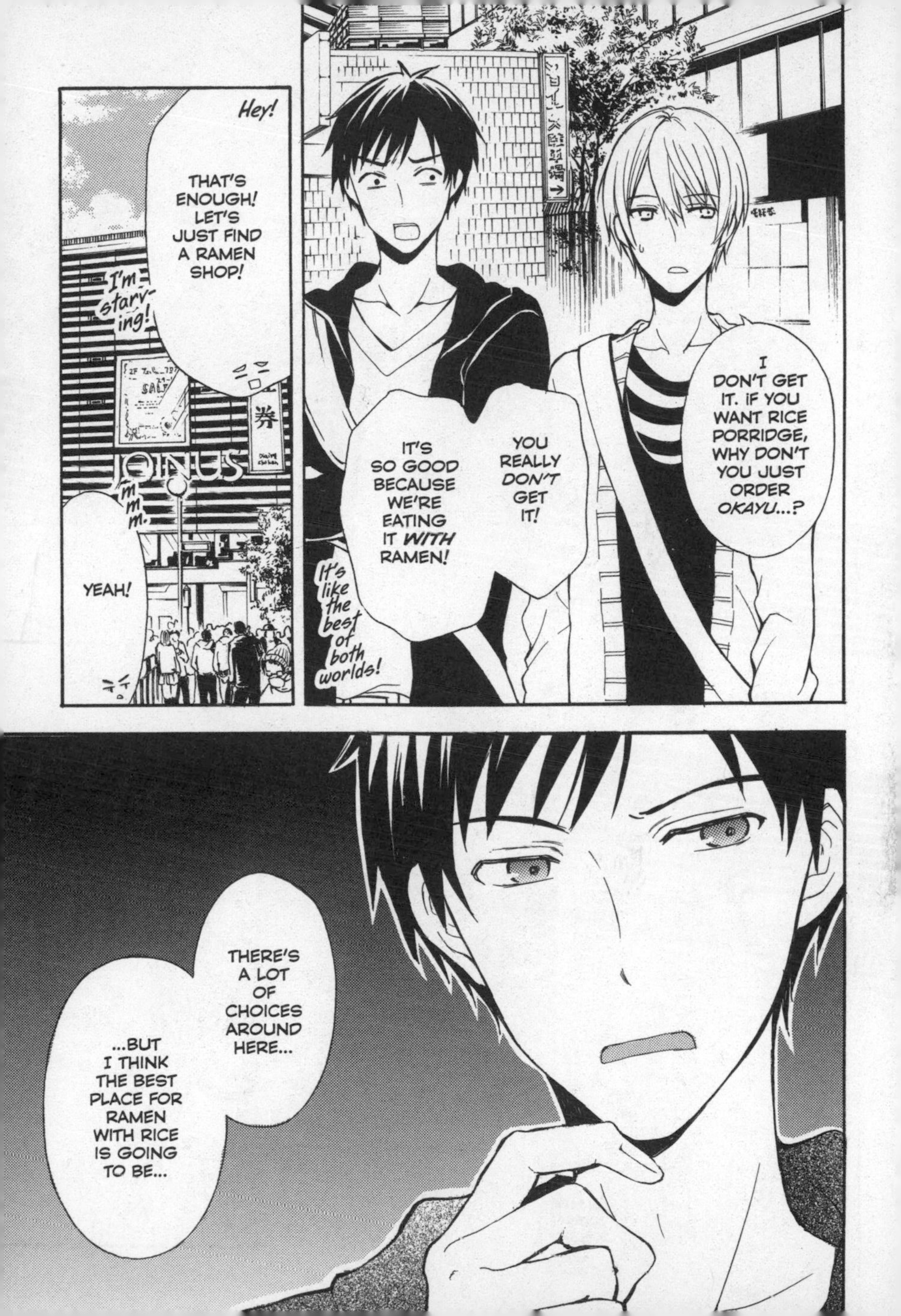
I DON'T GET IT. IF YOU WANT RICE PORRIDGE, WHY DON'T YOU JUST ORDER OKAYU...?
YOU REALLY DON'T GET IT!
IT'S SO GOOD BECAUSE WE'RE EATING IT WITH RAMEN!
It's like the best of both worlds!
Hey!
THAT'S ENOUGH! LET'S JUST FIND A RAMEN SHOP!
I'm starving!
JOINUS
mmm.
YEAH!
THERE'S A LOT OF CHOICES AROUND HERE...
...BUT I THINK THE BEST PLACE FOR RAMEN WITH RICE IS GOING TO BE...

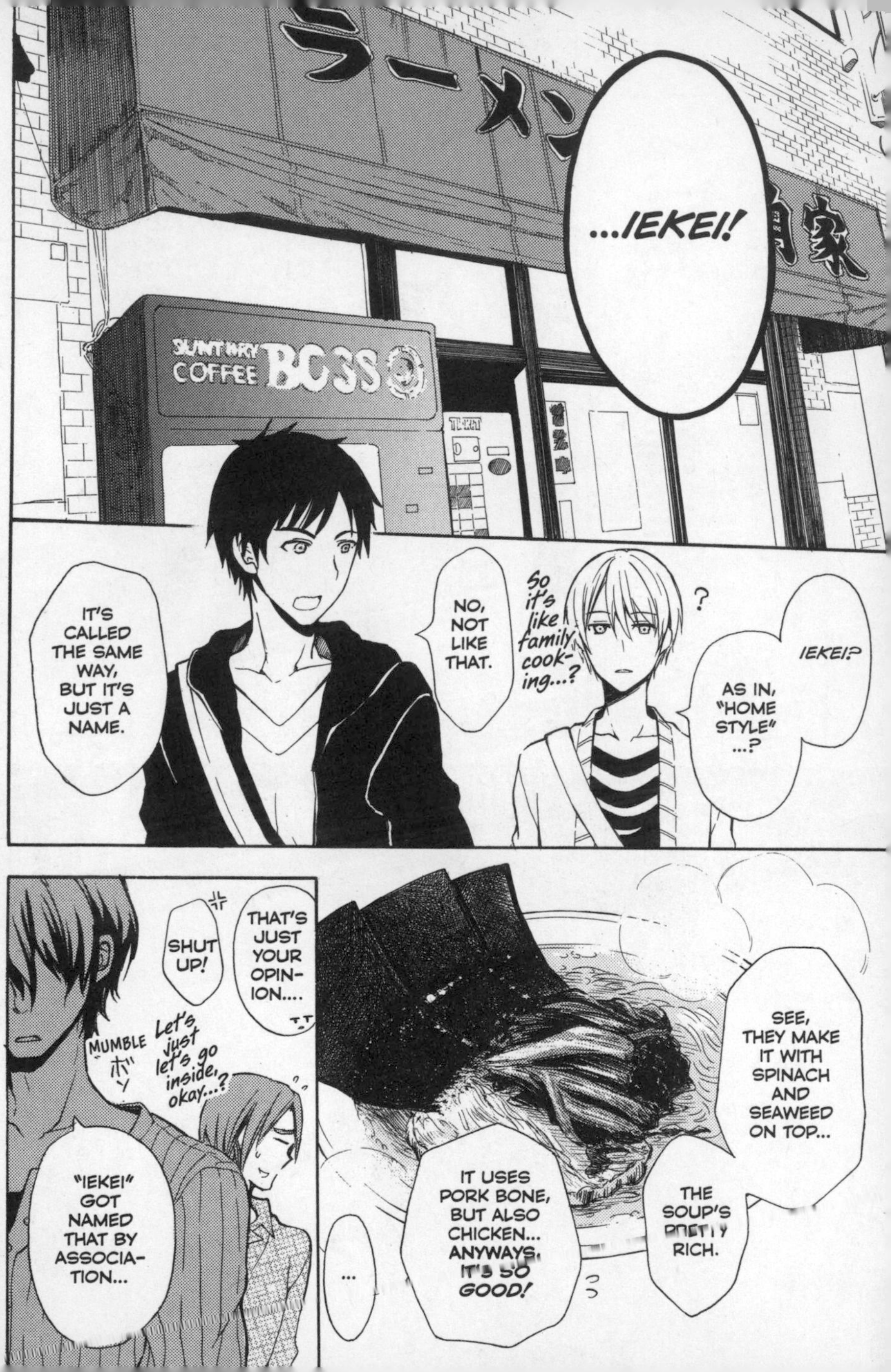
ラーメン
家
SUNTORY COFFEE BOSS
...IEKEI!
IEKEI? AS IN, "HOME STYLE" ...?
?
So it's like family cooking...?
NO, NOT LIKE THAT.
IT'S CALLED THE SAME WAY, BUT IT'S JUST A NAME.
SEE, THEY MAKE IT WITH SPINACH AND SEAWEED ON TOP...
THE SOUP'S PRETTY RICH.
IT USES PORK BONE, BUT ALSO CHICKEN... ANYWAYS, IT'S SO GOOD!
...
THAT'S JUST YOUR OPINION....
SHUT UP!
Let's just let's go inside, okay...?
MUMBLE ボソ
"IEKEI" GOT NAMED THAT BY ASSOCIATION...

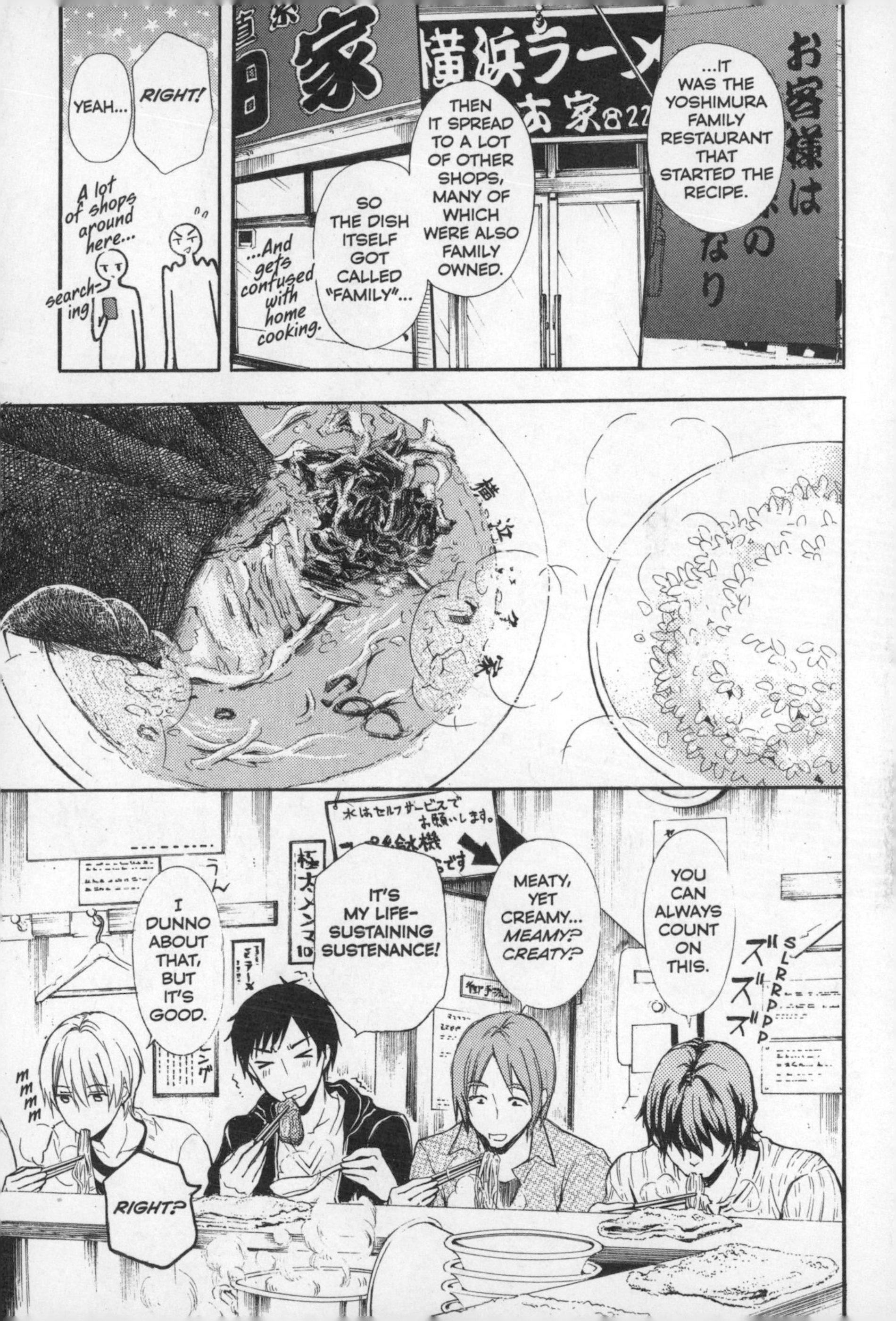
...IT WAS THE YOSHIMURA FAMILY RESTAURANT THAT STARTED THE RECIPE.
THEN IT SPREAD TO A LOT OF OTHER SHOPS, MANY OF WHICH WERE ALSO FAMILY OWNED.
SO THE DISH ITSELF GOT CALLED "FAMILY"...
...And gets confused with home cooking.
RIGHT!
YEAH...
A lot of shops around here...
searching
水はセルフサービスでお願いします。
YOU CAN ALWAYS COUNT ON THIS.
SLRRPP
ズズズ
MEATY, YET CREAMY... *MEAMY? CREATY?*
IT'S MY LIFE-SUSTAINING SUSTENANCE!
I DUNNO ABOUT THAT, BUT IT'S GOOD.
mmmm
RIGHT?

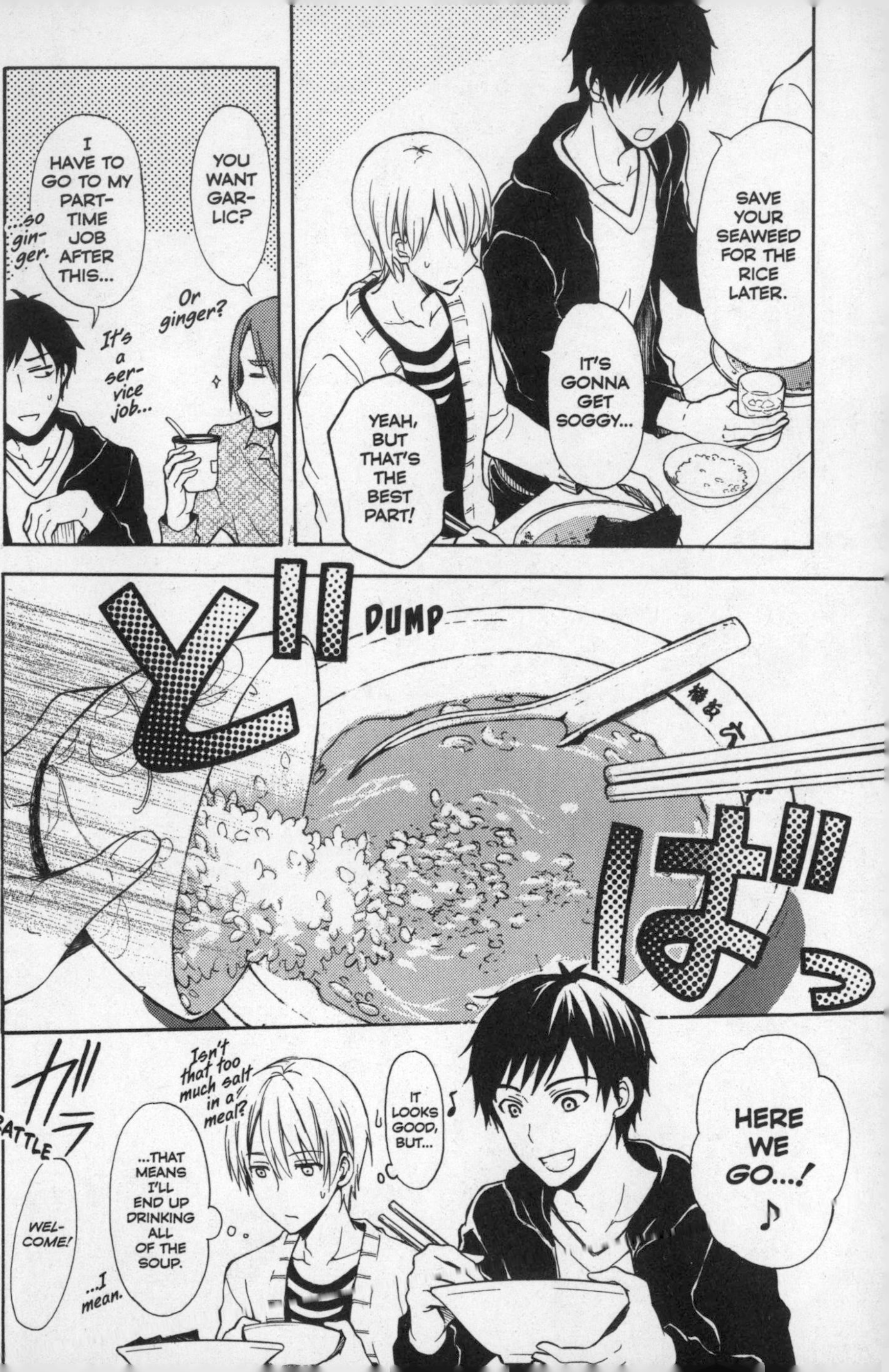
SAVE YOUR SEAWEED FOR THE RICE LATER.
IT'S GONNA GET SOGGY...
YEAH, BUT THAT'S THE BEST PART!
YOU WANT GARLIC?
Or ginger?
I HAVE TO GO TO MY PART-TIME JOB AFTER THIS...
It's a service job...
...so ginger.
ど
DUMP
ばっ
HERE WE GO...! ♪
IT LOOKS GOOD, BUT...
Isn't that too much salt in a meal?
...THAT MEANS I'LL END UP DRINKING ALL OF THE SOUP.
ガラ
RATTLE
WELCOME!
...I mean.

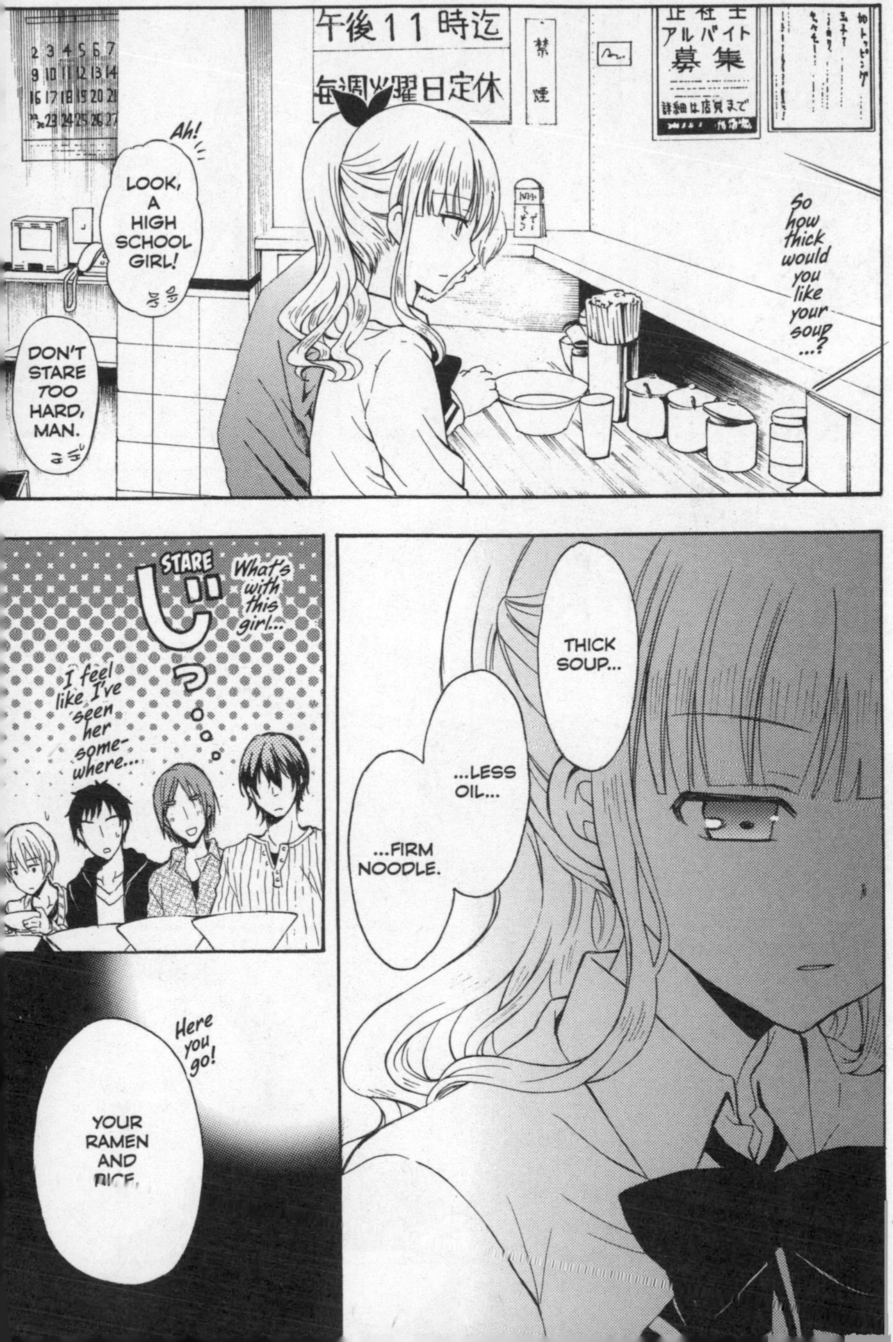

正社員
アルバイト
募集
詳細は店員まで
禁煙
午後11時迄
毎週火曜日定休
So how thick would you like your soup...?
Ah!
LOOK, A HIGH SCHOOL GIRL!
DON'T STARE TOO HARD, MAN.
THICK SOUP...
...LESS OIL...
...FIRM NOODLE.
What's with this girl...
STARE
I feel like I've seen her some-where...
Here you go!
YOUR RAMEN AND RICE.

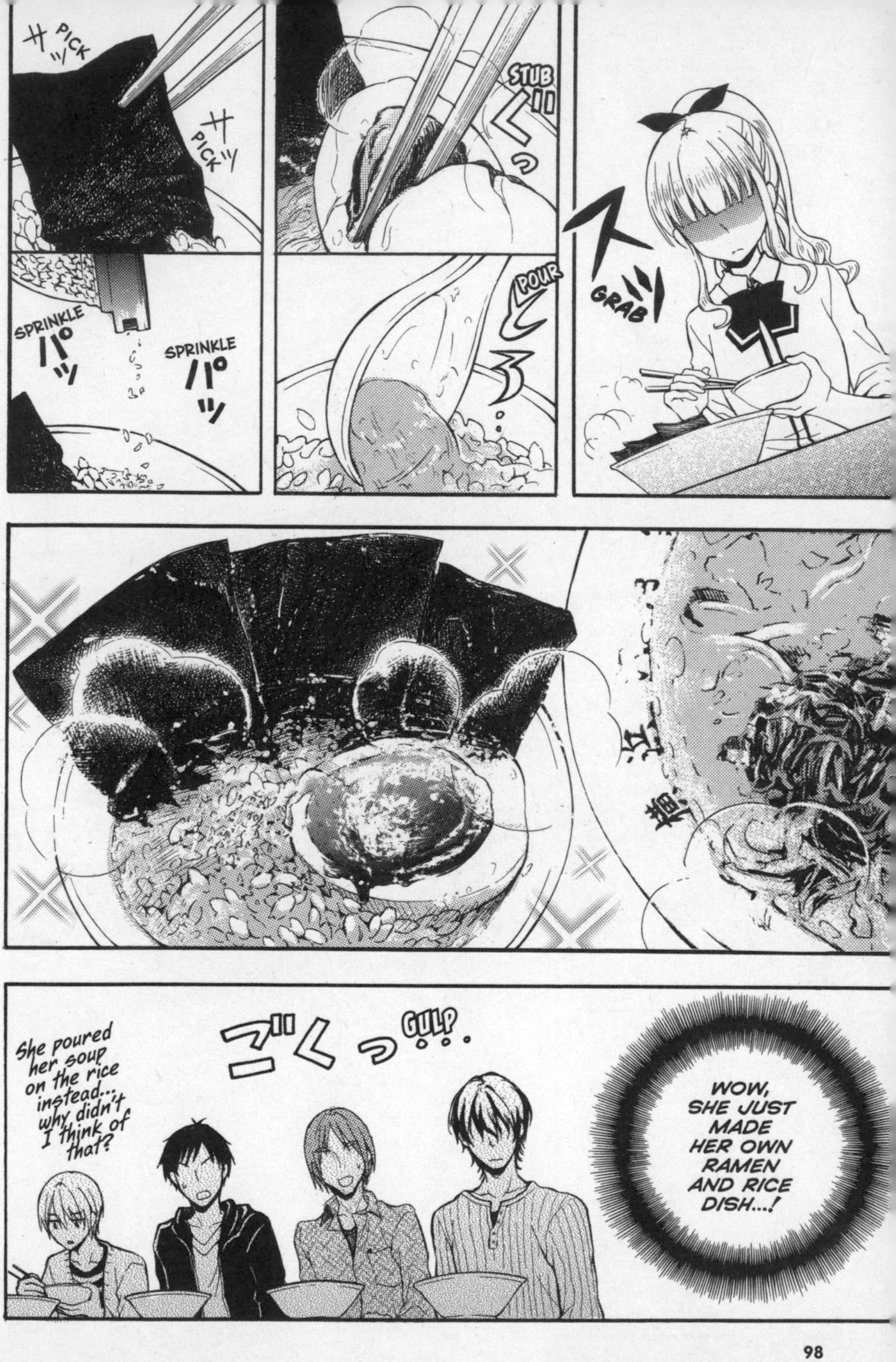
GRAB
STUB
ぐっ
POUR
どろ
PICK
サッ
PICK
サッ
SPRINKLE
パッ
SPRINKLE
パッ
WOW, SHE JUST MADE HER OWN RAMEN AND RICE DISH...!
ごくっ GULP...
She poured her soup on the rice instead... why didn't I think of that?

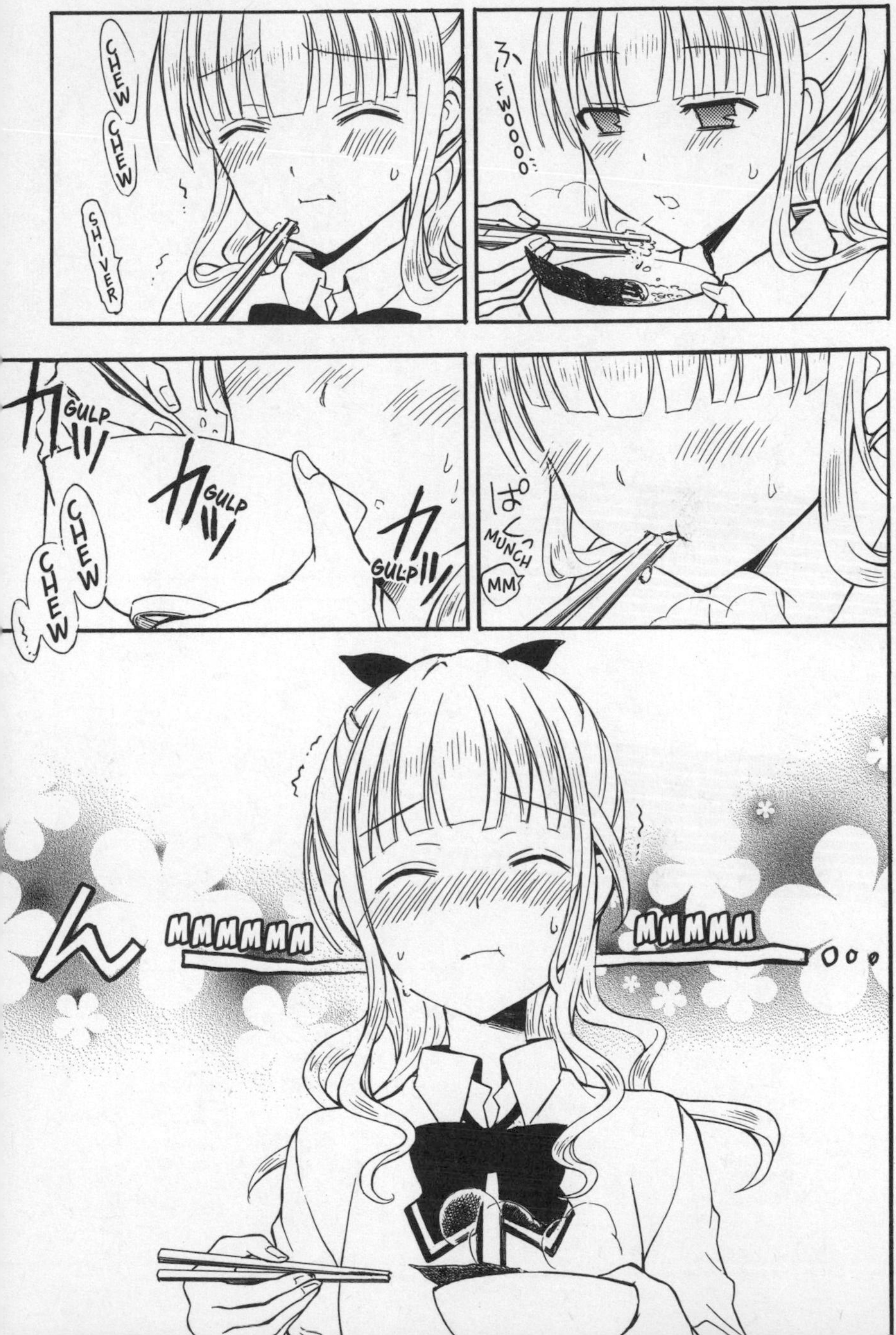
ふ
FWOOOOO
CHEW
CHEW
CHEW
SHIVER
ぱく
MUNCH
MM
カ
GULP
カ
GULP
カ
GULP
CHEW
CHEW
CHEW
ん
MMMMMM
MMMMM
ooo

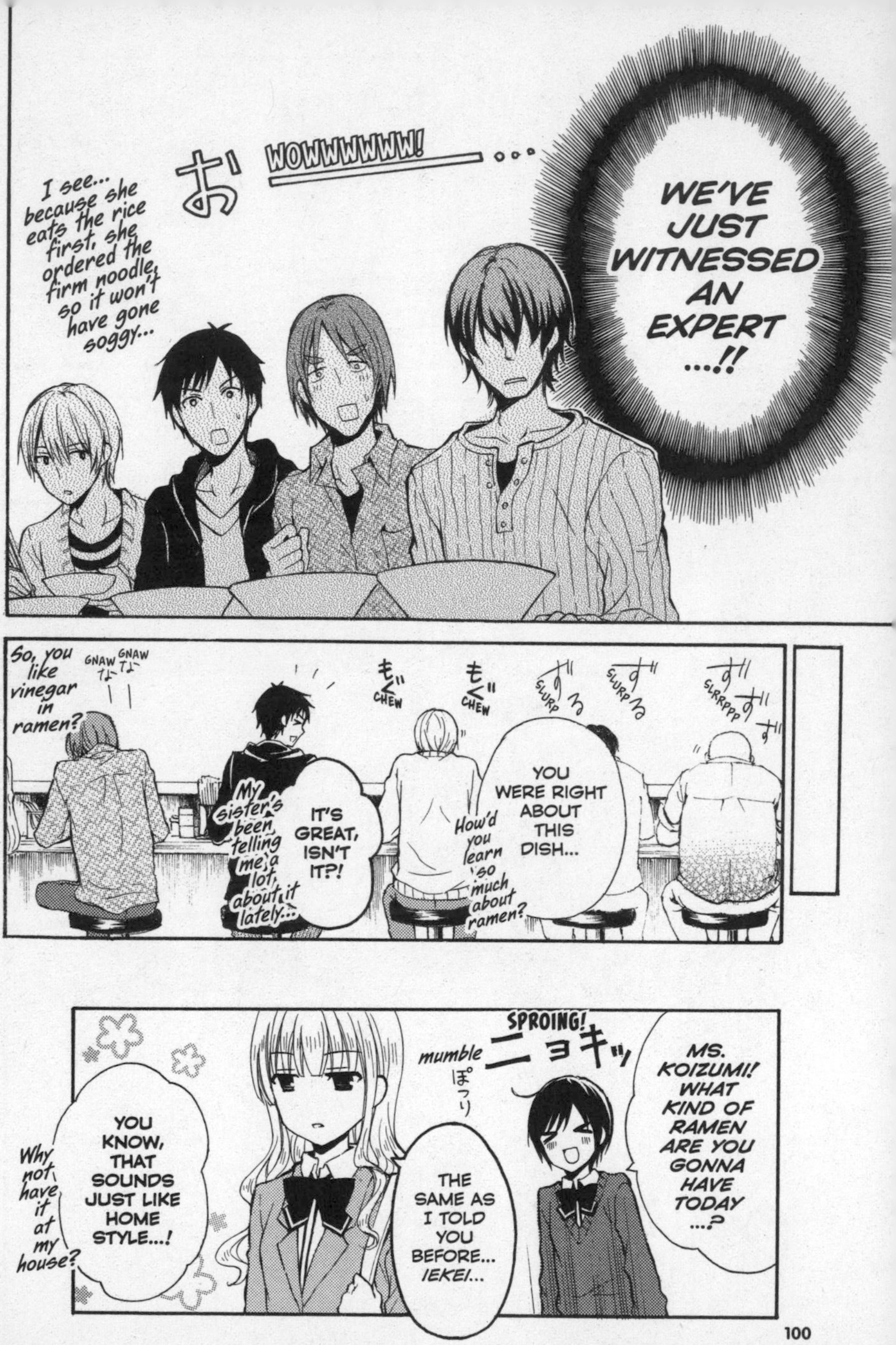
WE'VE JUST WITNESSED AN EXPERT ...!!
お WOWWWWWWW! ...
I see... because she eats the rice first, she ordered the firm noodle, so it won't have gone soggy...
ずず SLRRPPP
ずる SLURP
ずる SLURP
もぐ CHEW
もぐ CHEW
YOU WERE RIGHT ABOUT THIS DISH...
How'd you learn so much about ramen?
IT'S GREAT, ISN'T IT?!
My sister's been telling me a lot about it lately...
GNAW GNAW
So, you like vinegar in ramen?
MS. KOIZUMI! WHAT KIND OF RAMEN ARE YOU GONNA HAVE TODAY ...?
SPROING! ニョキッ
mumble ぽつり
THE SAME AS I TOLD YOU BEFORE... IEKEI...
YOU KNOW, THAT SOUNDS JUST LIKE HOME STYLE...!
Why not have it at my house?

Like it lighter...?
Use the free toppings on the table to give Iekei a lighter taste!
One month later
Here's a tip. Most of the shops have free ginger, both julienne and grated. They help a lot with making it lighter.
The other day I found a shop that has sliced onions. It made the ramen so light and delicious. It was really unexpected!
He's become an Iekei boy!
Extra oil, rich flavor, and sliced onions are a golden combination!
The tsubamesanjo style ramen from Niigata uses the same principle.
Yep.
Yep.

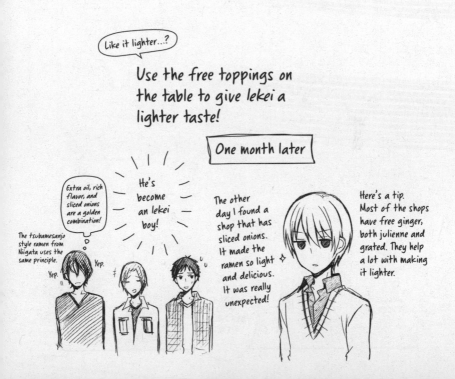

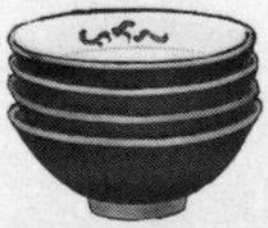

Ms. Koizumi loves ramen noodles

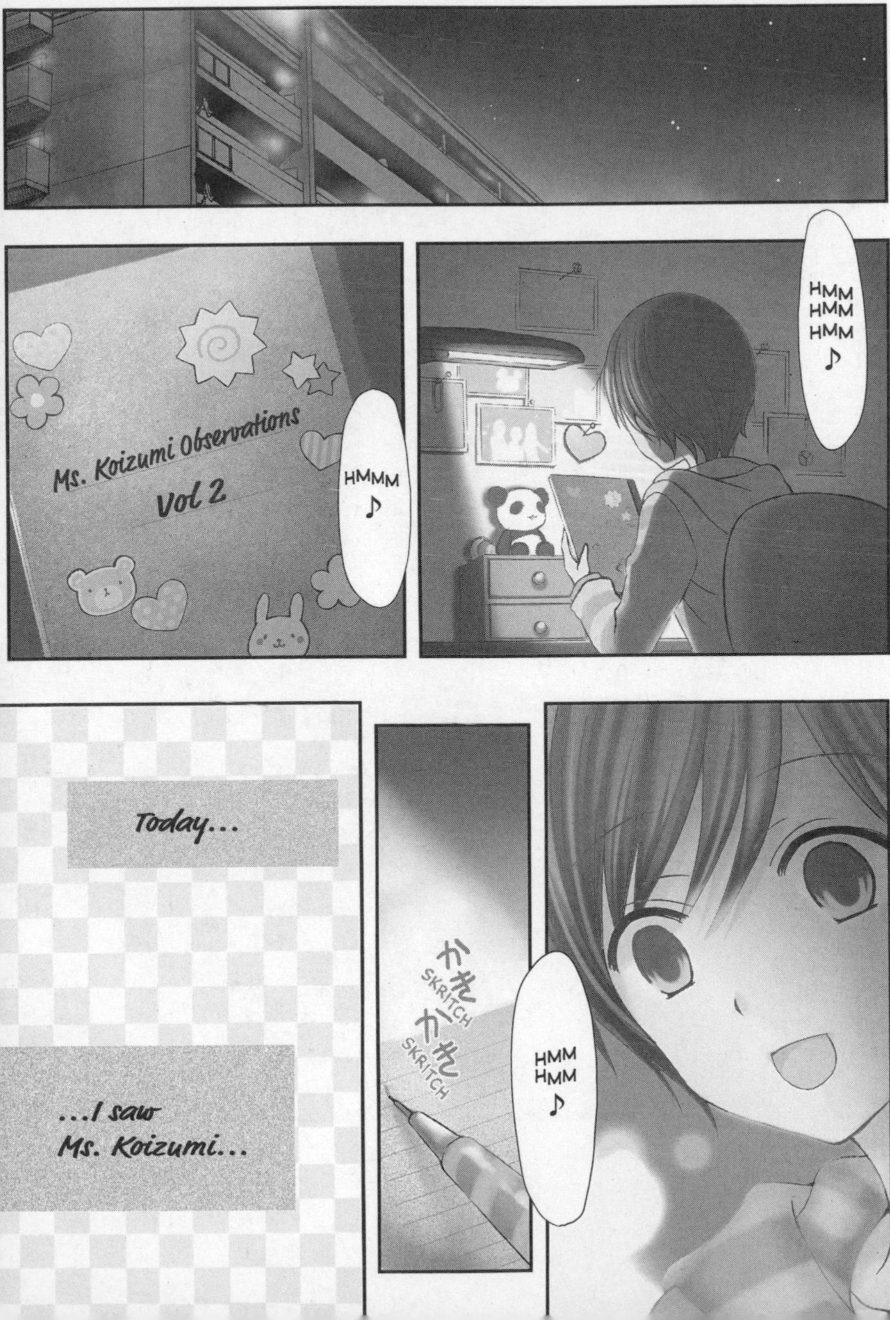
HMM HMM HMM ♪
Ms. Koizumi Observations Vol 2
HMMM ♪
HMM HMM ♪
かき SKRITCH
かき SKRITCH
Today...
...I saw Ms. Koizumi...

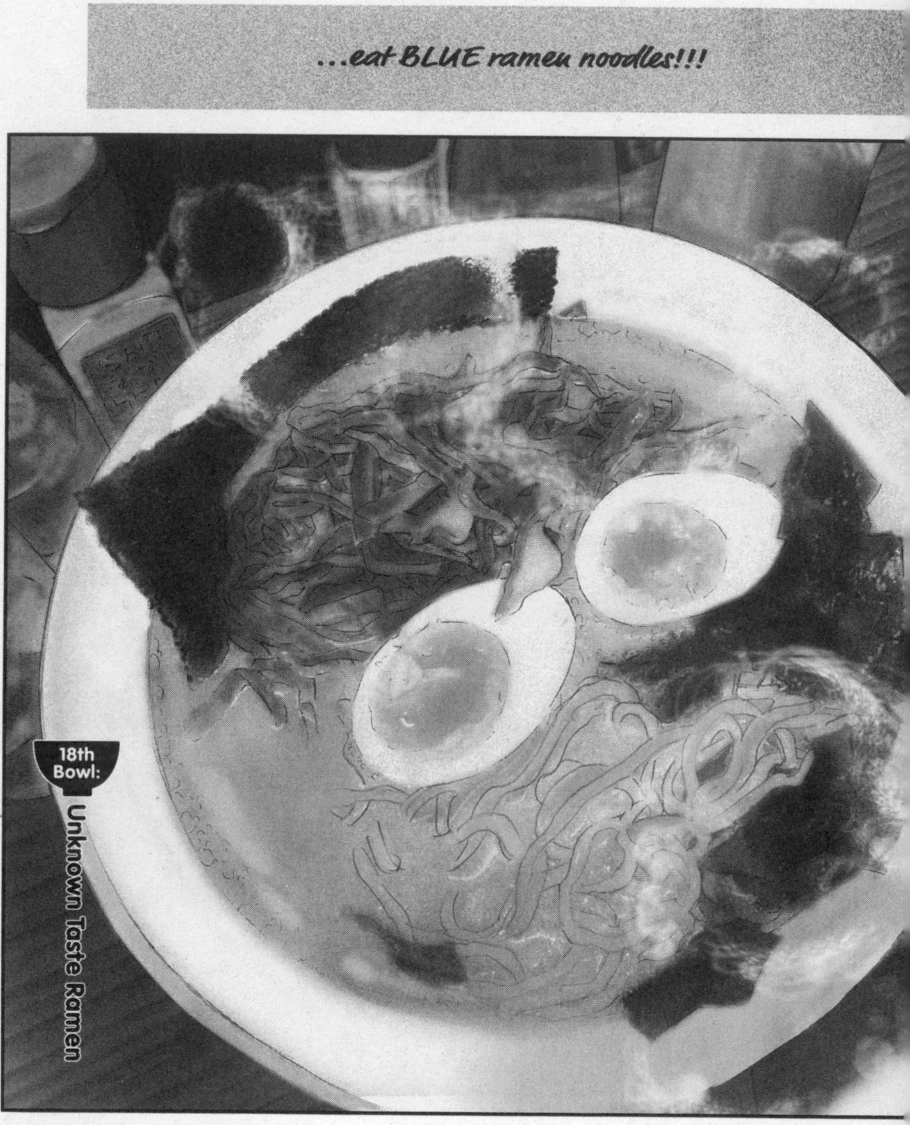
...eat BLUE ramen noodles!!!

18th Bowl: Unknown Taste Ramen

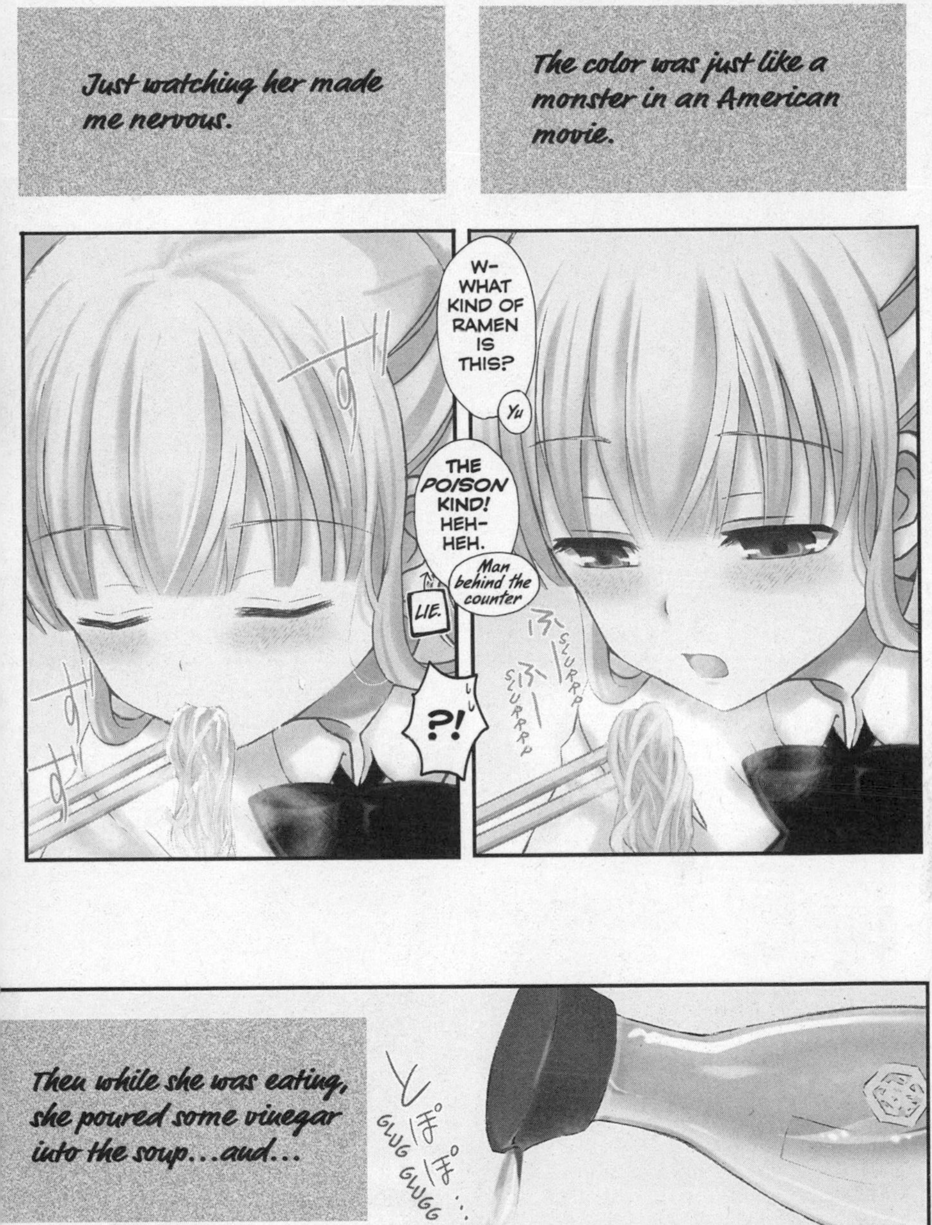
The color was just like a monster in an American movie.
Just watching her made me nervous.
W-WHAT KIND OF RAMEN IS THIS?
Yu
THE POISON KIND! HEH-HEH.
Man behind the counter
LIE.
SLURRP
SLURRRP
?!
GLUG GLUGG
Then while she was eating, she poured some vinegar into the soup...and...

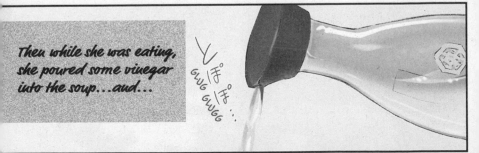

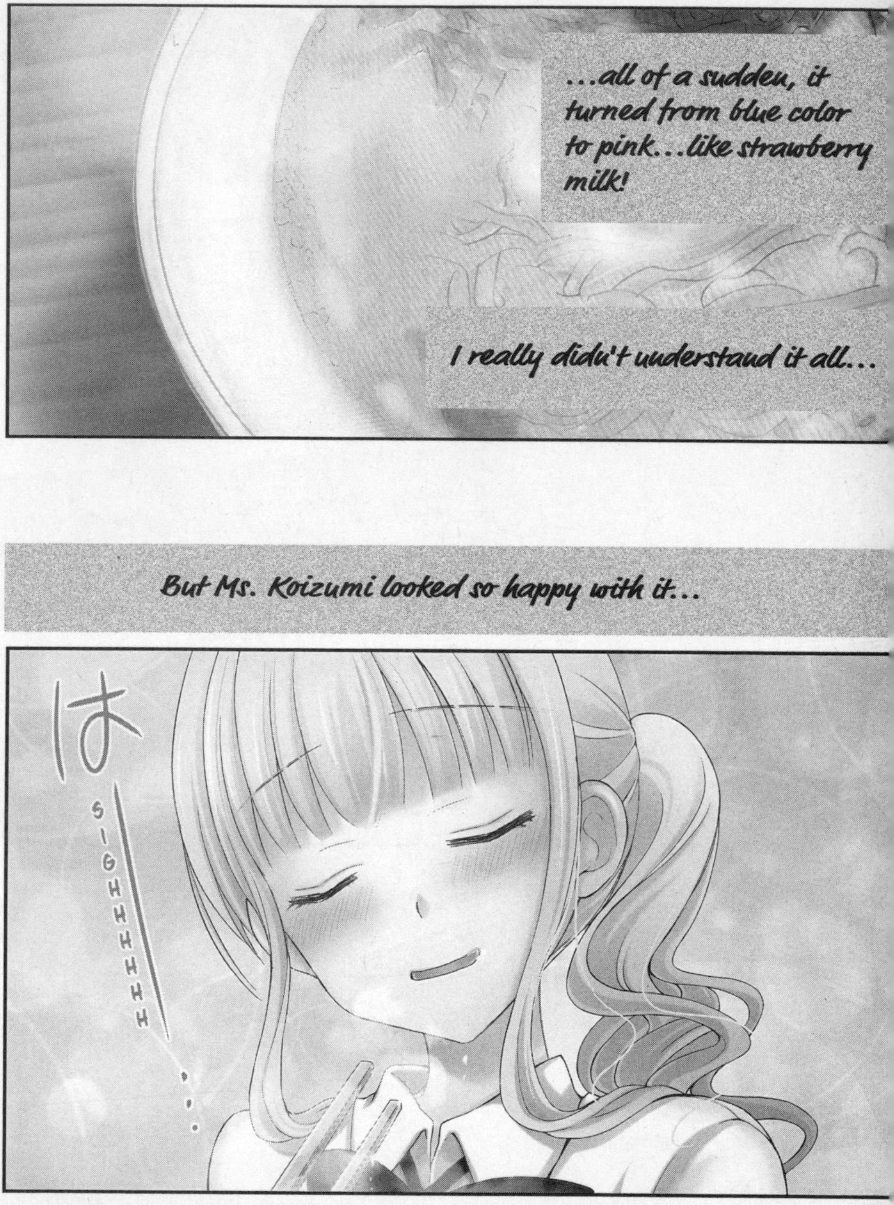
...all of a sudden, it turned from blue color to pink...like strawberry milk!
I really didn't understand it all...
But Ms. Koizumi looked so happy with it...
は
SIGHHHHHHH...
...and that's all I need to know.

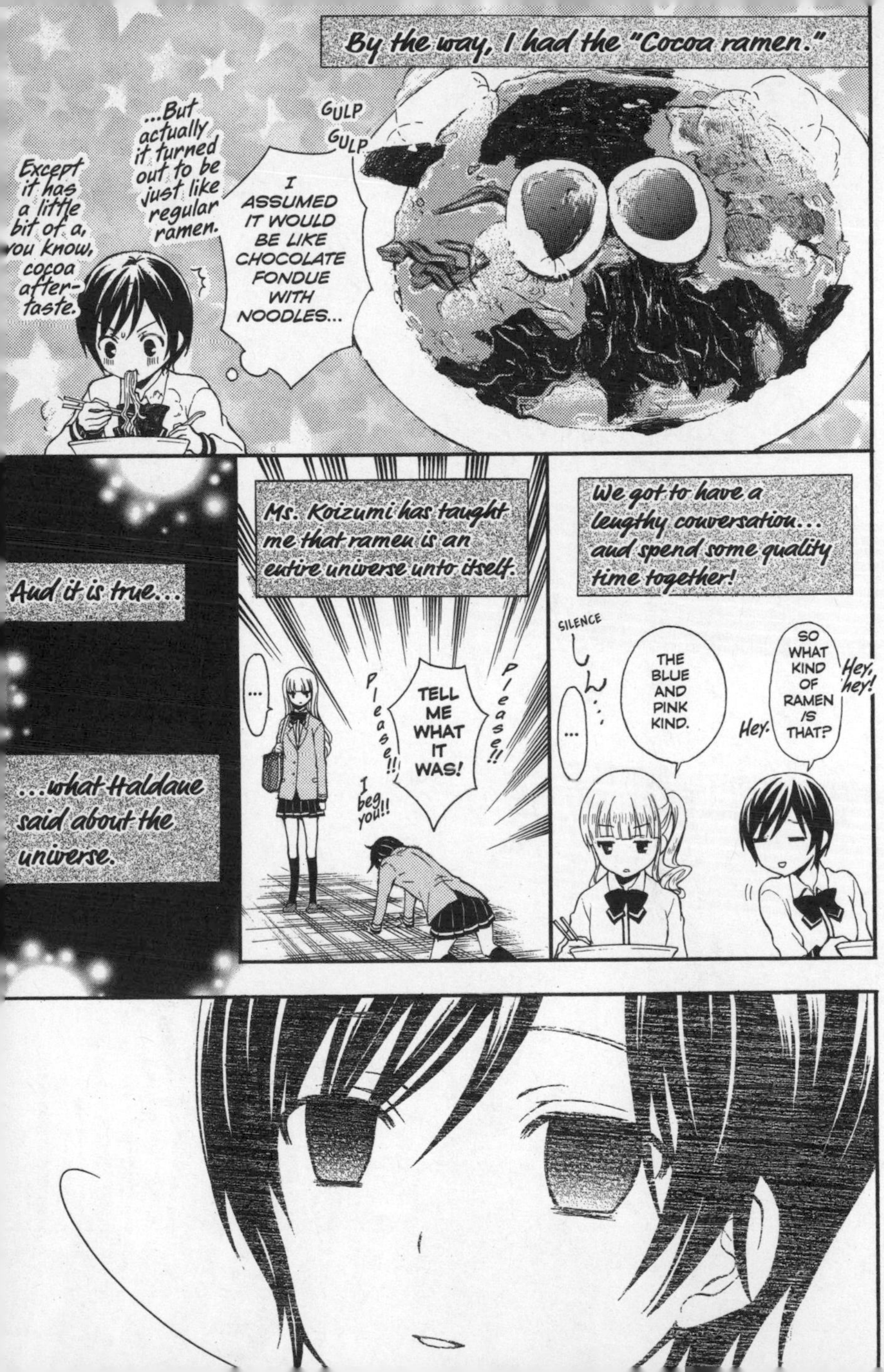
By the way, I had the "Cocoa ramen."
GULP GULP
I ASSUMED IT WOULD BE LIKE CHOCOLATE FONDUE WITH NOODLES...
...But actually it turned out to be just like regular ramen.
Except it has a little bit of a, you know, cocoa after-taste.
We got to have a lengthy conversation... and spend some quality time together!
Hey, hey!
SO WHAT KIND OF RAMEN IS THAT?
Hey.
THE BLUE AND PINK KIND.
SILENCE
...
Ms. Koizumi has taught me that ramen is an entire universe unto itself.
Please!!
TELL ME WHAT IT WAS!
Please!!
I beg you!!
...
And it is true...
...what Haldane said about the universe.

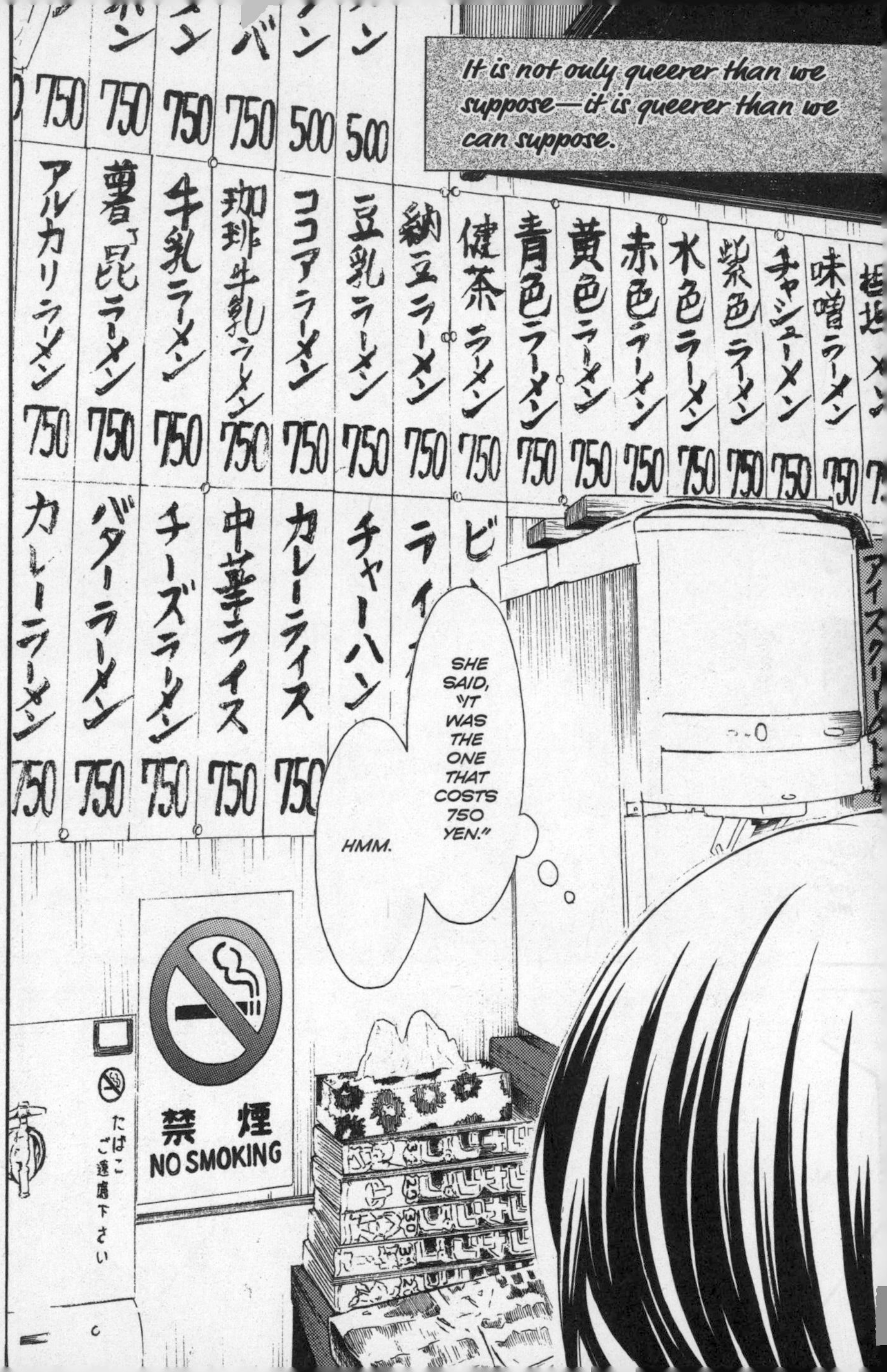
It is not only queerer than we suppose—it is queerer than we can suppose.
味噌ラーメン 750
チャシューメン 750
紫色ラーメン 750
水色ラーメン 750
赤色ラーメン 750
黄色ラーメン 750
青色ラーメン 750
健茶ラーメン 750
納豆ラーメン 750
豆乳ラーメン 750
ココアラーメン 750
珈琲牛乳ラーメン 750
牛乳ラーメン 750
アルカリラーメン 750
チャーハン
カレーライス 750
中華ライス 750
チーズラーメン 750
バターラーメン 750
カレーラーメン 750
SHE SAID, "IT WAS THE ONE THAT COSTS 750 YEN."
HMM.
禁煙
NO SMOKING
たばこ ご遠慮下さい

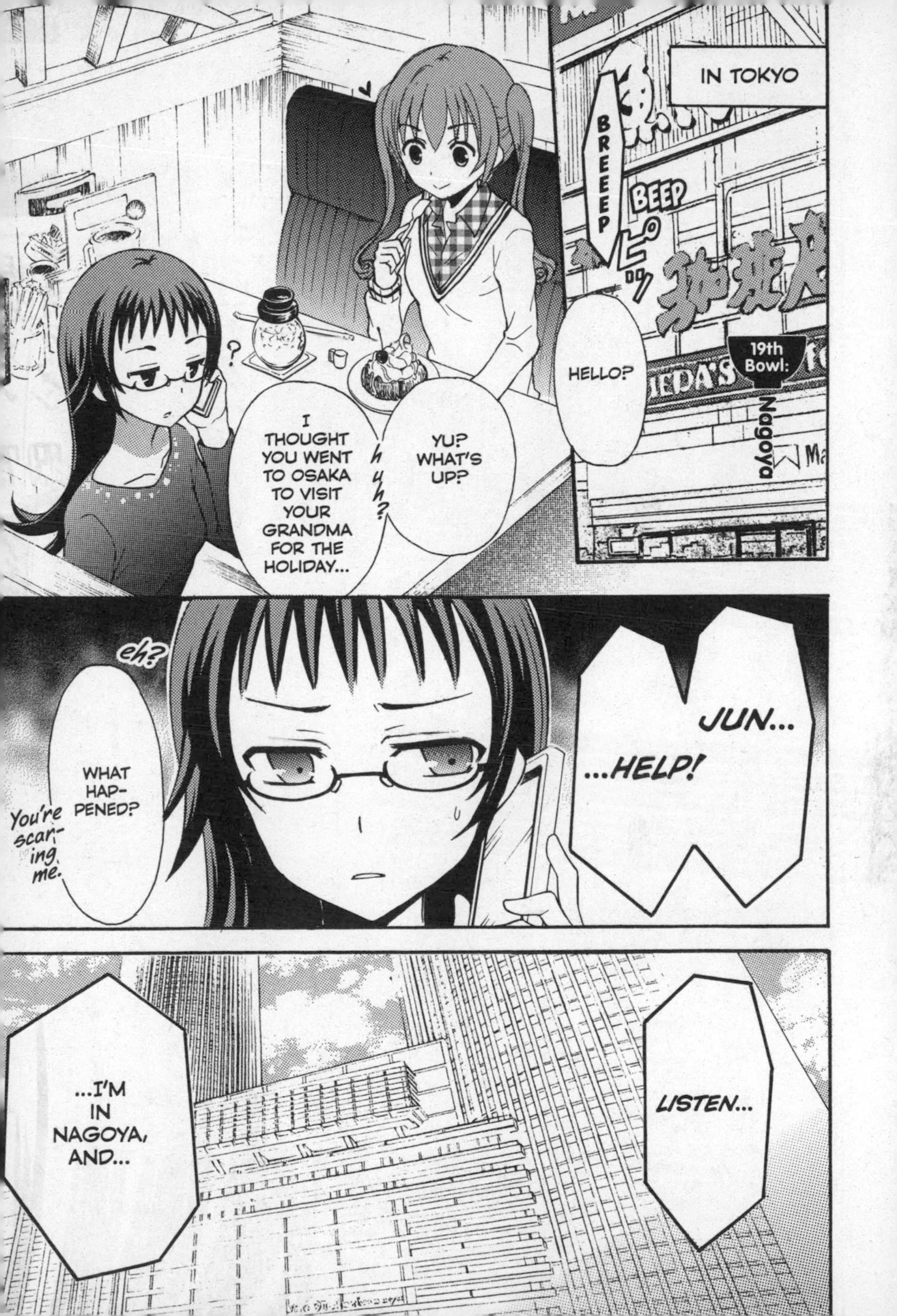
IN TOKYO
BREEEP
BEEP
19th Bowl: Nagoya
HELLO?
YU? WHAT'S UP?
huh?
I THOUGHT YOU WENT TO OSAKA TO VISIT YOUR GRANDMA FOR THE HOLIDAY...
?
JUN... ...HELP!
eh?
WHAT HAP-PENED?
You're scar-ing me.
LISTEN...
...I'M IN NAGOYA, AND...

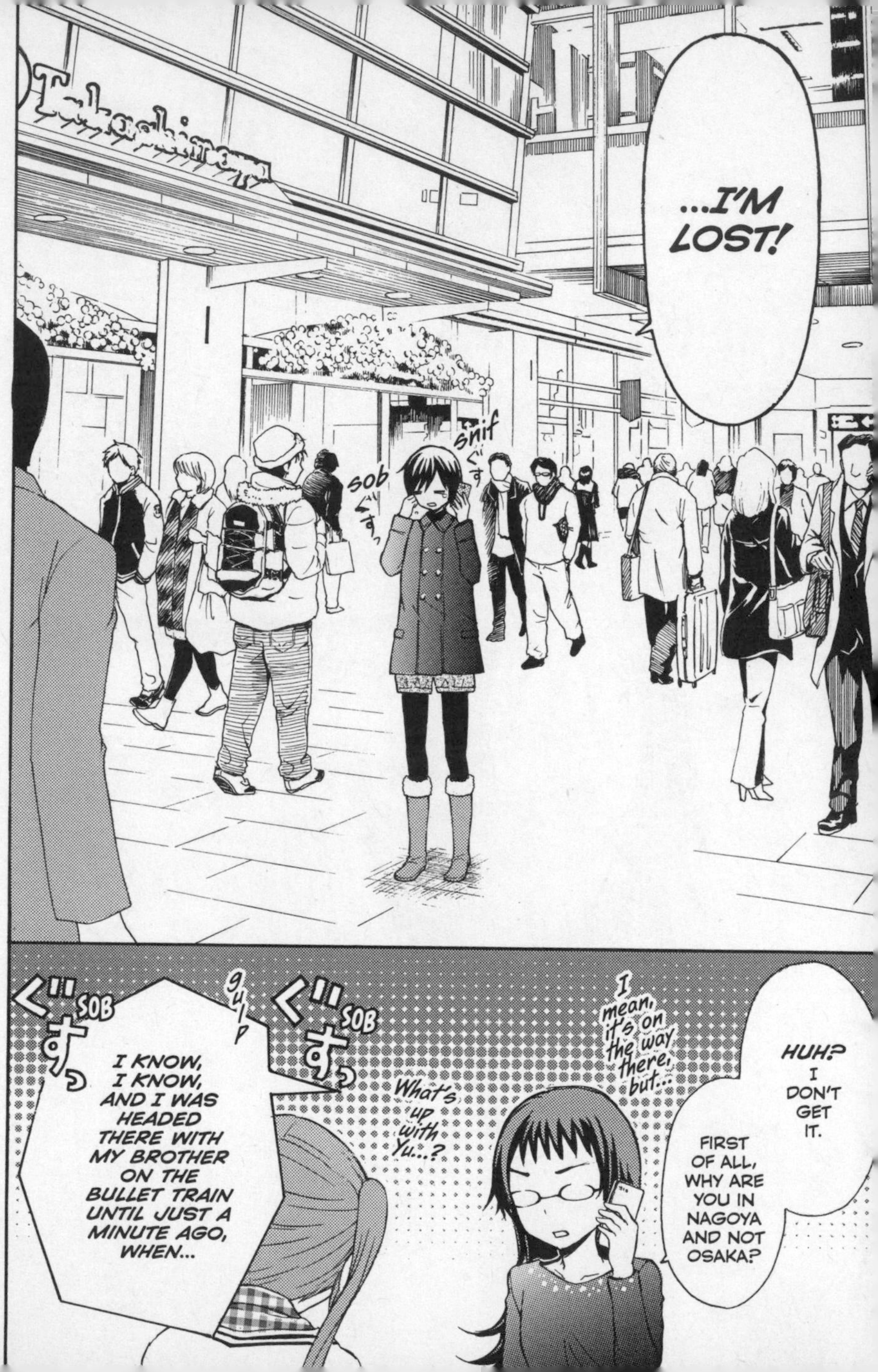
...I'M LOST!
snif ぐす
sob ぐすっ
HUH? I DON'T GET IT.
FIRST OF ALL, WHY ARE YOU IN NAGOYA AND NOT OSAKA?
I mean, it's on the way there, but...
What's up with Yu...?
ぐすっ SOB
gulp
I KNOW, I KNOW, AND I WAS HEADED THERE WITH MY BROTHER ON THE BULLET TRAIN UNTIL JUST A MINUTE AGO, WHEN...
ぐすっ SOB

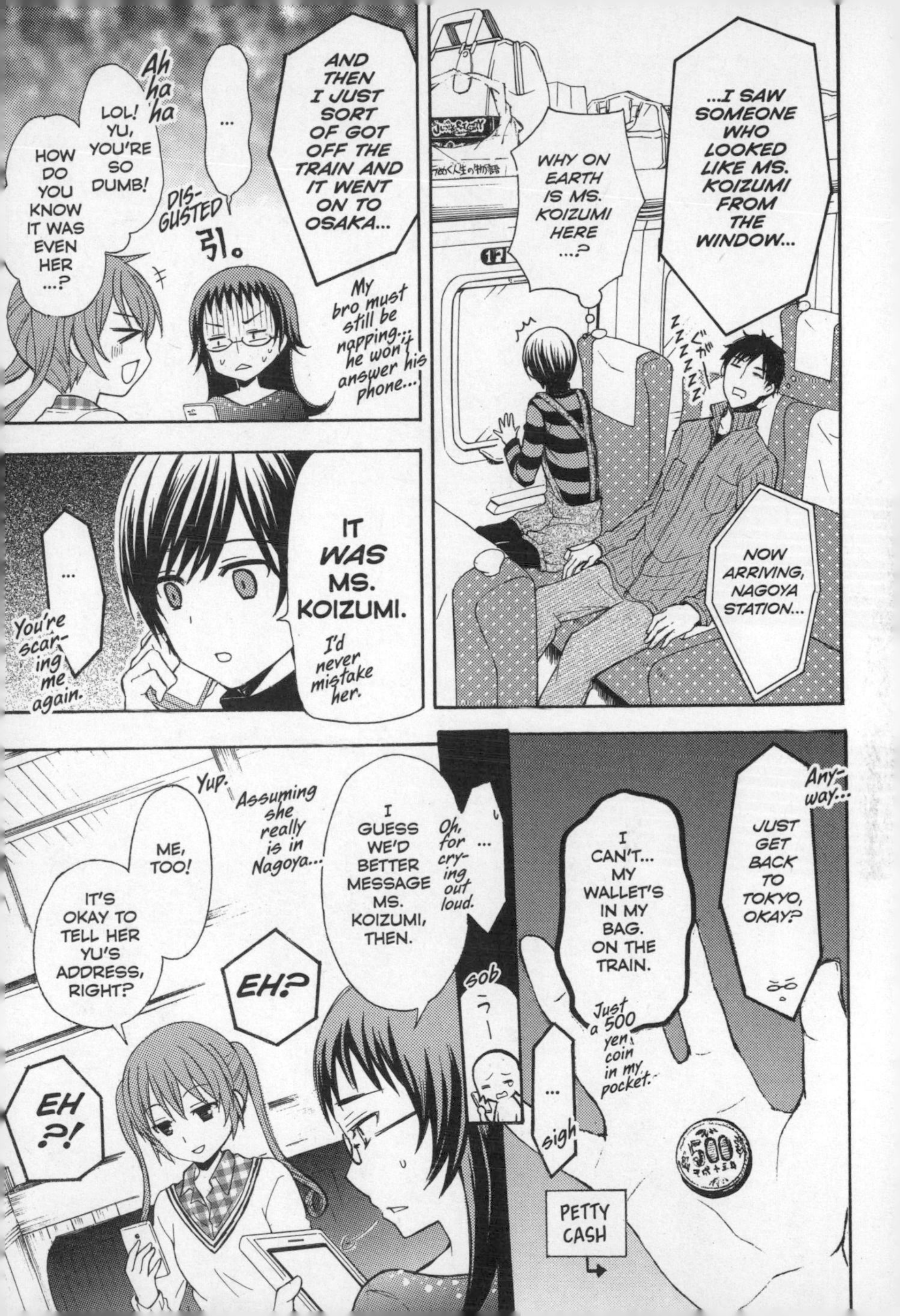
...I SAW SOMEONE WHO LOOKED LIKE MS. KOIZUMI FROM THE WINDOW...
WHY ON EARTH IS MS. KOIZUMI HERE ...?
NOW ARRIVING, NAGOYA STATION...
AND THEN I JUST SORT OF GOT OFF THE TRAIN AND IT WENT ON TO OSAKA...
...
Ah ha ha
LOL! YU, YOU'RE SO DUMB!
HOW DO YOU KNOW IT WAS EVEN HER ...?
DIS-GUSTED
引。
My bro must still be napping... he won't answer his phone...
IT WAS MS. KOIZUMI.
I'd never mistake her.
...
You're scar-ing me again.
Any-way...
JUST GET BACK TO TOKYO, OKAY?
I CAN'T... MY WALLET'S IN MY BAG. ON THE TRAIN.
Just a 500 yen coin in my pocket.
...
sigh
sob
PETTY CASH
...
Oh, for cry-ing out loud.
I GUESS WE'D BETTER MESSAGE MS. KOIZUMI, THEN.
Assuming she really is in Nagoya...
Yup.
ME, TOO!
IT'S OKAY TO TELL HER YU'S ADDRESS, RIGHT?
EH?
EH ?!

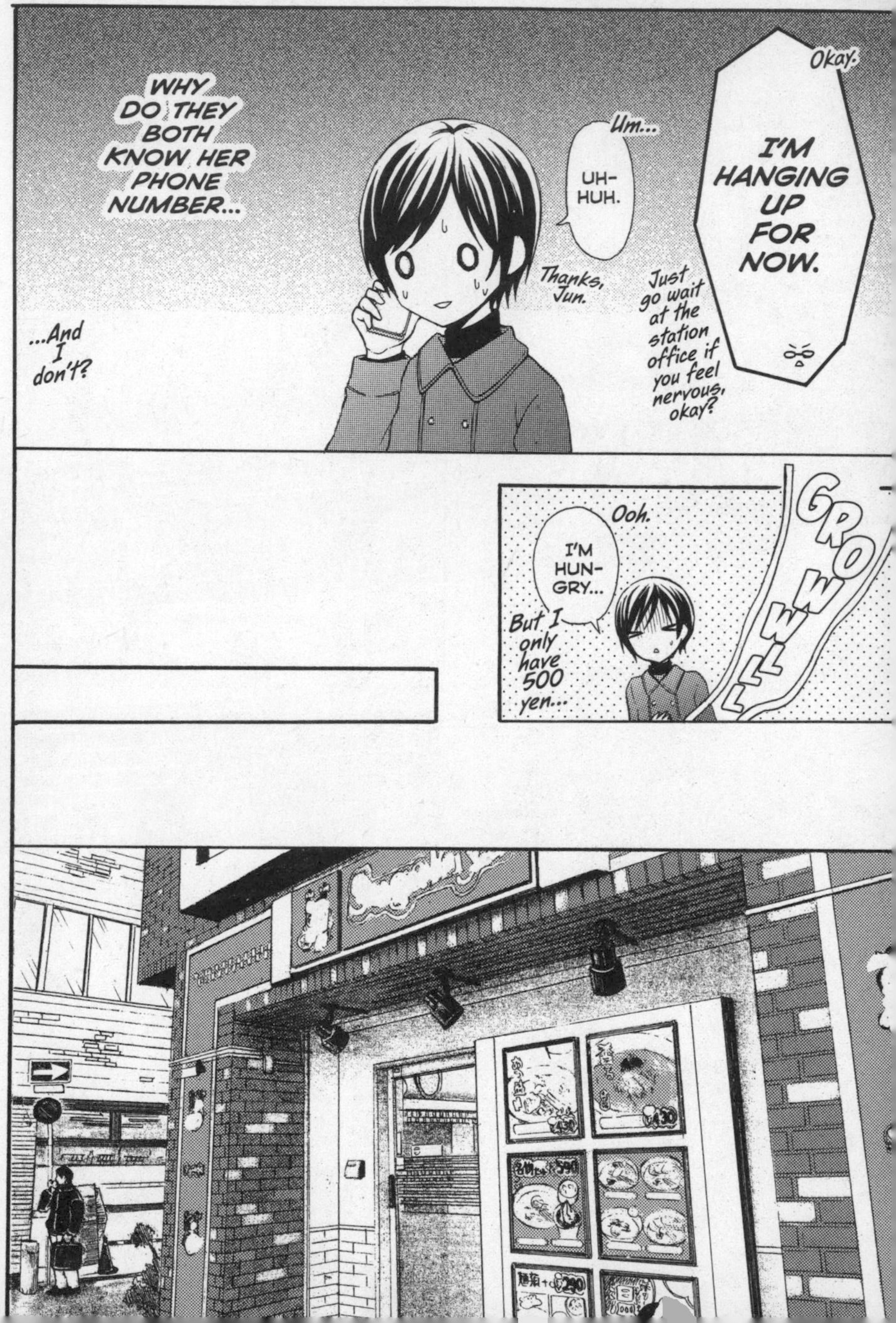
Okay.
I'M HANGING UP FOR NOW.
Just go wait at the station office if you feel nervous, okay?
Um...
UH-HUH.
Thanks, Jun.
WHY DO THEY BOTH KNOW HER PHONE NUMBER...
...And I don't?
GROWWLL
Ooh.
I'M HUNGRY...
But I only have 500 yen...

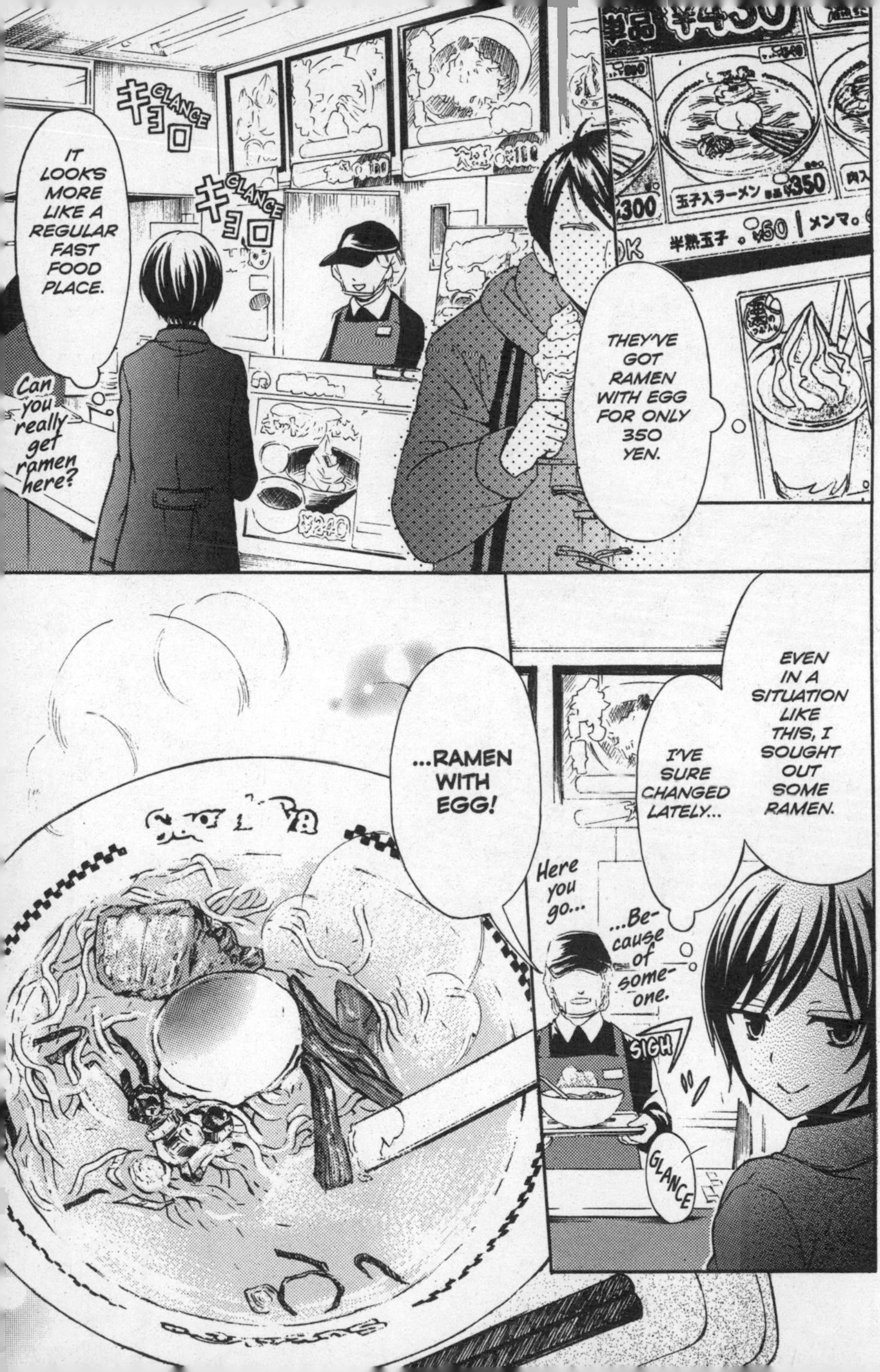

玉子入ラーメン ¥350
半熟玉子 ¥50
メンマ
THEY'VE GOT RAMEN WITH EGG FOR ONLY 350 YEN.
キョロ GLANCE
キョロ GLANCE
IT LOOKS MORE LIKE A REGULAR FAST FOOD PLACE.
Can you really get ramen here?
EVEN IN A SITUATION LIKE THIS, I SOUGHT OUT SOME RAMEN.
I'VE SURE CHANGED LATELY...
...Be-cause of some-one.
SIGH
GLANCE
Here you go...
...RAMEN WITH EGG!

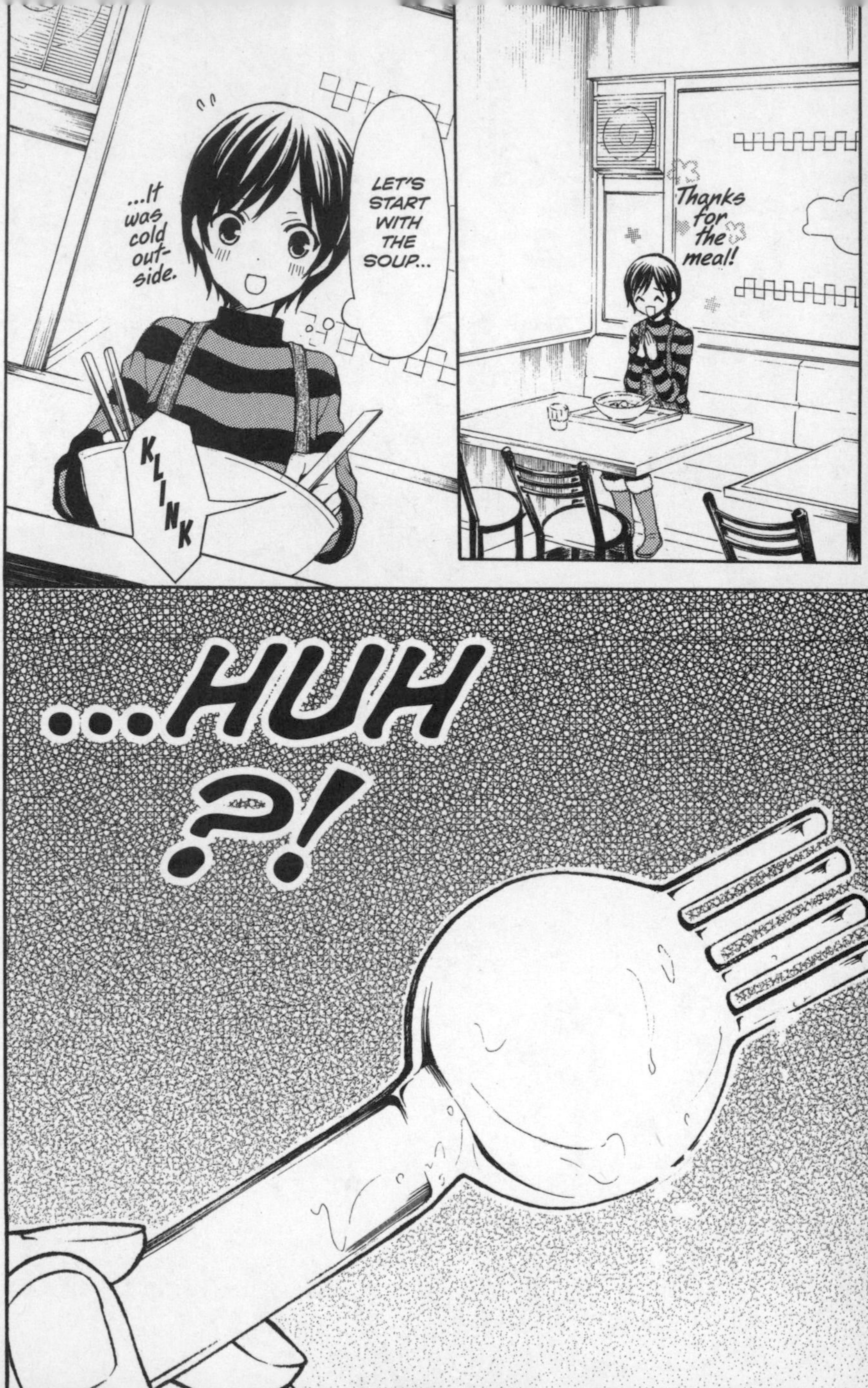
Thanks for the meal!
LET'S START WITH THE SOUP...
...It was cold out-side.
KLINK
...HUH ?!

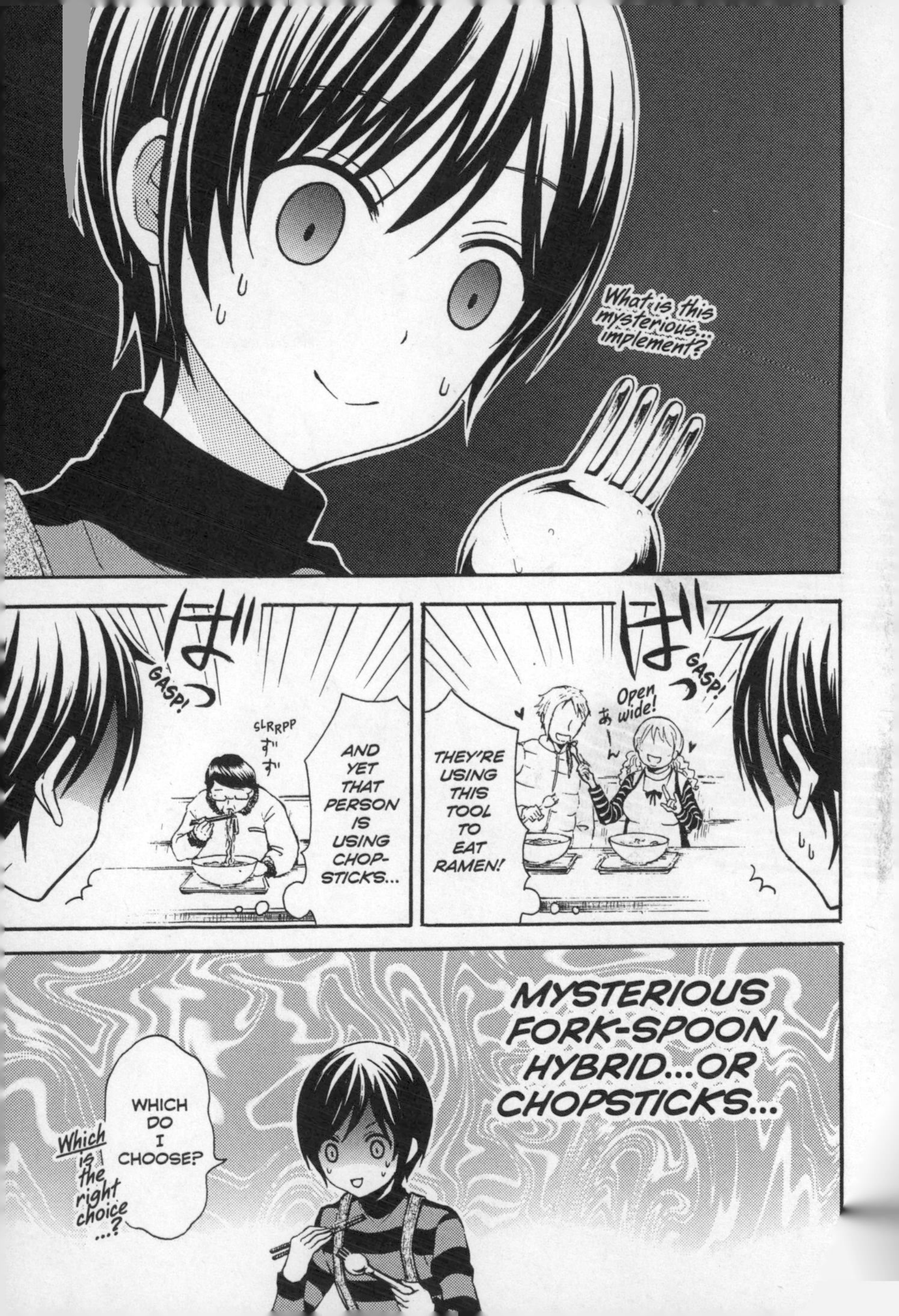
What is this mysterious... implement?
GASP!
Open wide!
あ～ん
THEY'RE USING THIS TOOL TO EAT RAMEN!
GASP!
SLRRPP
ずず
AND YET THAT PERSON IS USING CHOP-STICKS...
MYSTERIOUS FORK-SPOON HYBRID...OR CHOPSTICKS...
WHICH DO I CHOOSE?
Which is the right choice...?

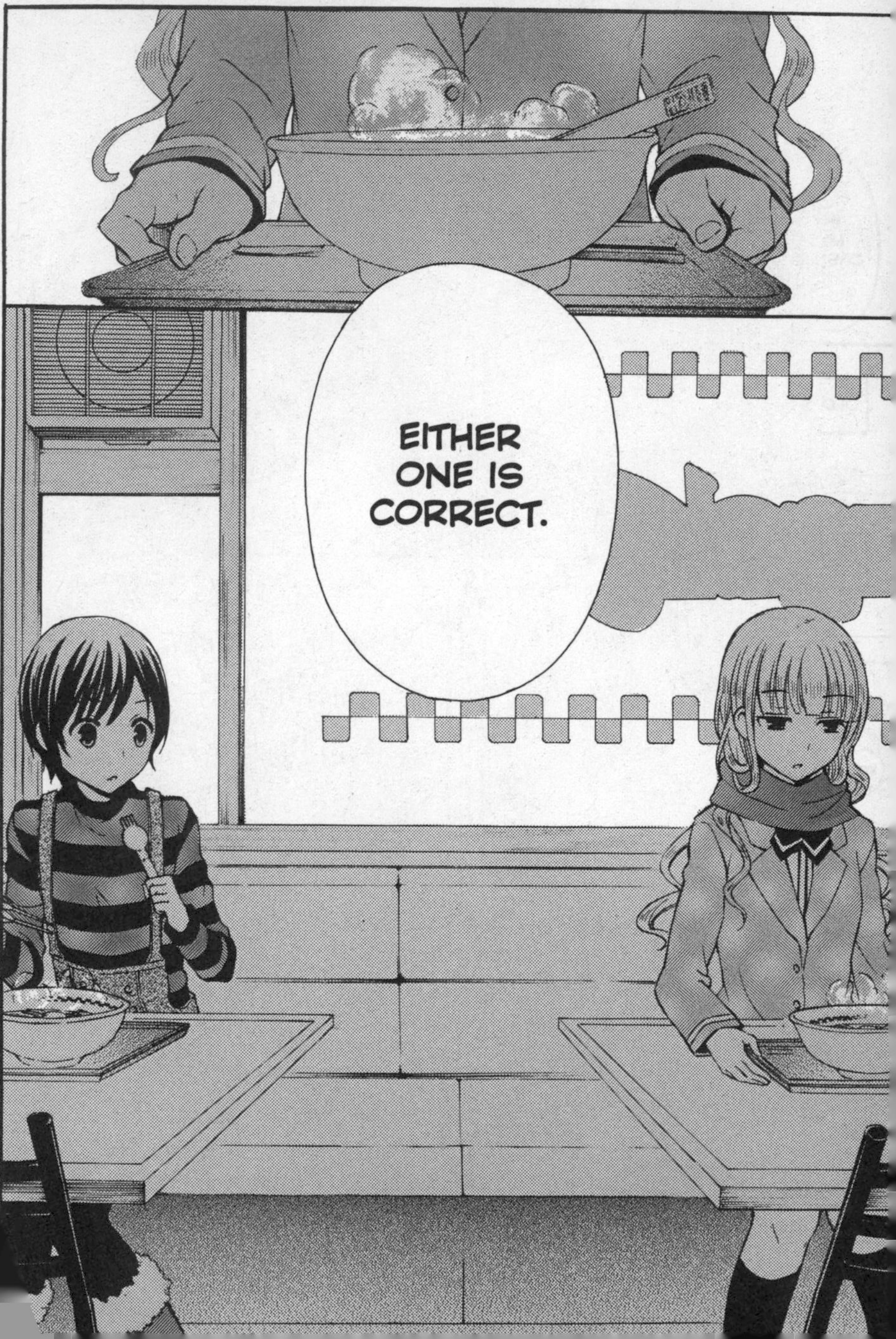
EITHER ONE IS CORRECT.

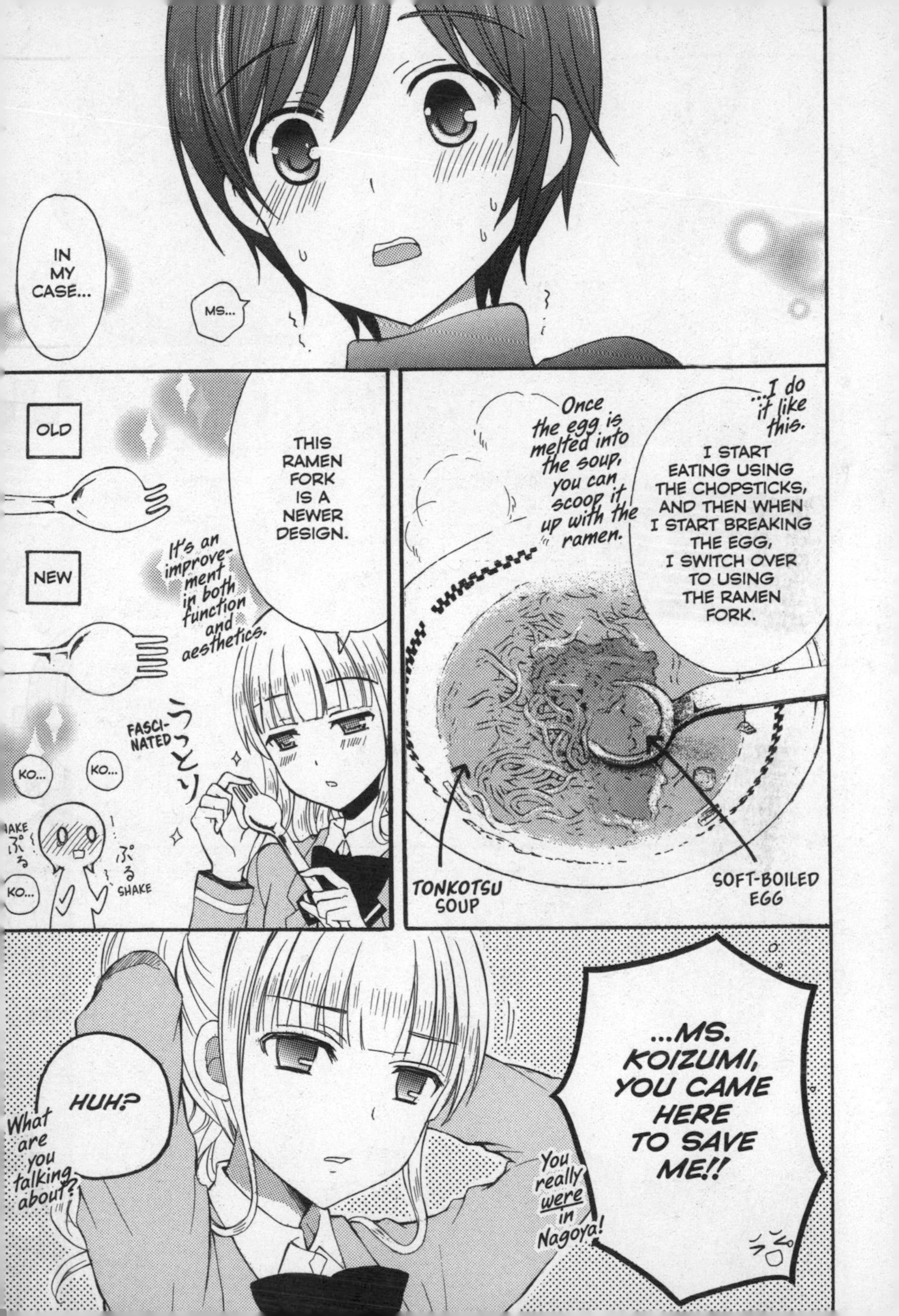
MS...
IN MY CASE...
...I do it like this.
I START EATING USING THE CHOPSTICKS, AND THEN WHEN I START BREAKING THE EGG, I SWITCH OVER TO USING THE RAMEN FORK.
Once the egg is melted into the soup, you can scoop it up with the ramen.
SOFT-BOILED EGG
TONKOTSU SOUP
THIS RAMEN FORK IS A NEWER DESIGN.
It's an improvement in both function and aesthetics.
OLD
NEW
FASCINATED うっとり
KO...
KO...
ぷる SHAKE
SHAKE ぷる
KO...
...MS. KOIZUMI, YOU CAME HERE TO SAVE ME!!
You really were in Nagoya!
HUH?
What are you talking about?

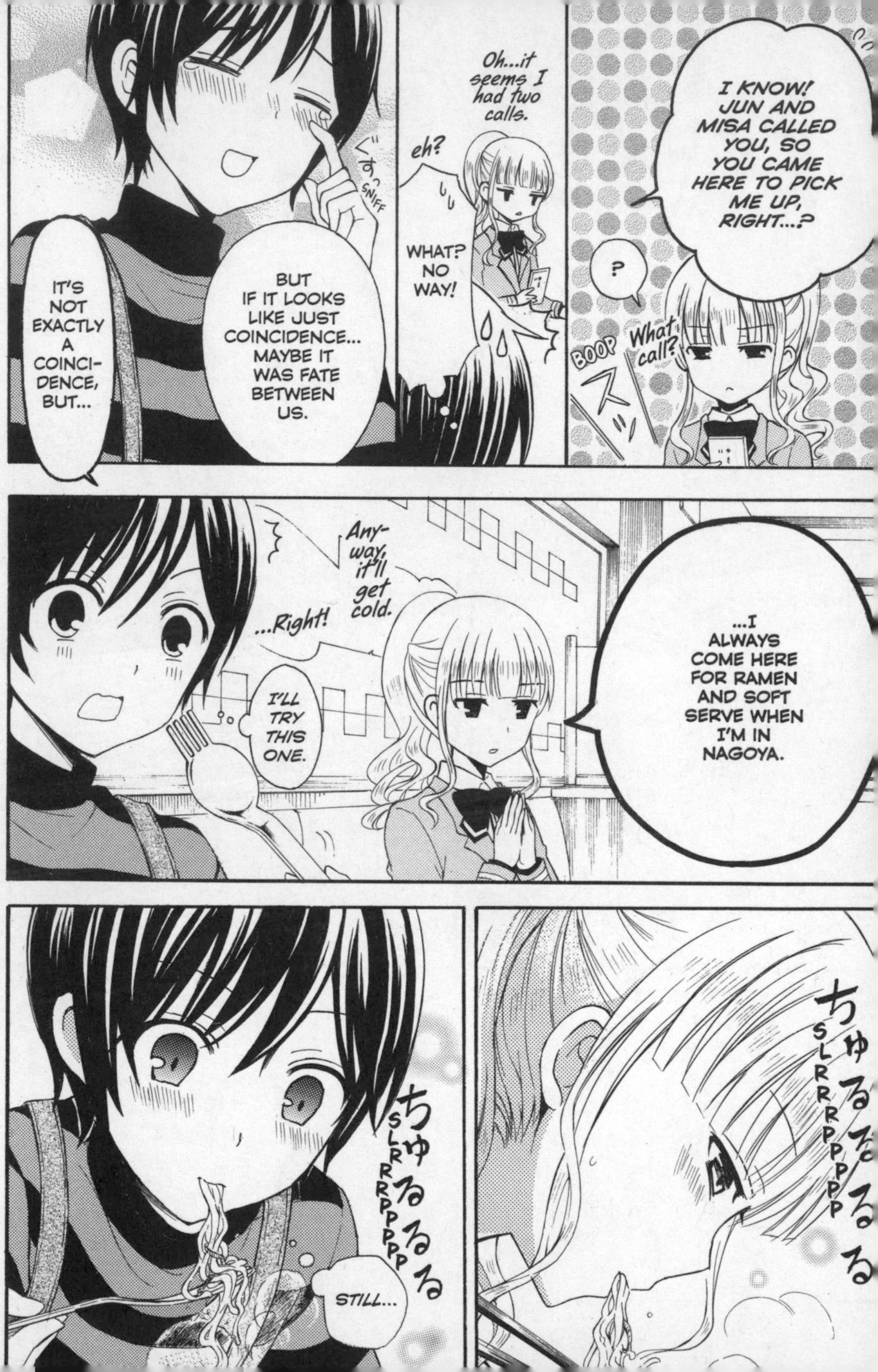

I KNOW! JUN AND MISA CALLED YOU, SO YOU CAME HERE TO PICK ME UP, RIGHT...?
?
What call?
スッ
BOOP
Oh...it seems I had two calls.
eh?
WHAT? NO WAY!
ぐすっ
SNIFF
BUT IF IT LOOKS LIKE JUST COINCIDENCE... MAYBE IT WAS FATE BETWEEN US.
IT'S NOT EXACTLY A COINCIDENCE, BUT...
...I ALWAYS COME HERE FOR RAMEN AND SOFT SERVE WHEN I'M IN NAGOYA.
Any-way, it'll get cold.
...Right!
I'LL TRY THIS ONE.
ちゅるるるる
SLRRRPPPPP
ちゅるるる
SLRRRPPPP
STILL...

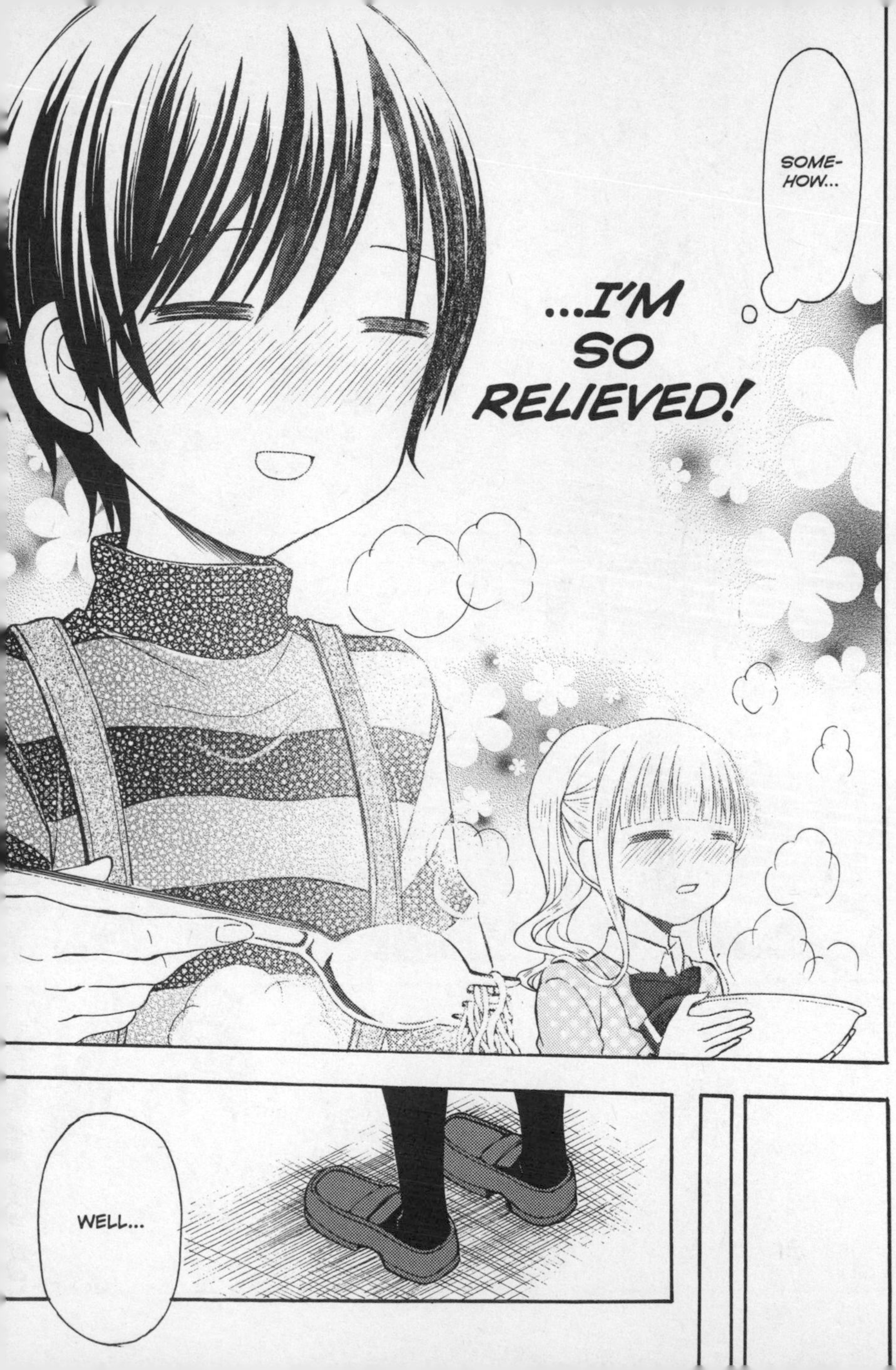
SOME-HOW...
...I'M SO RELIEVED!
WELL...

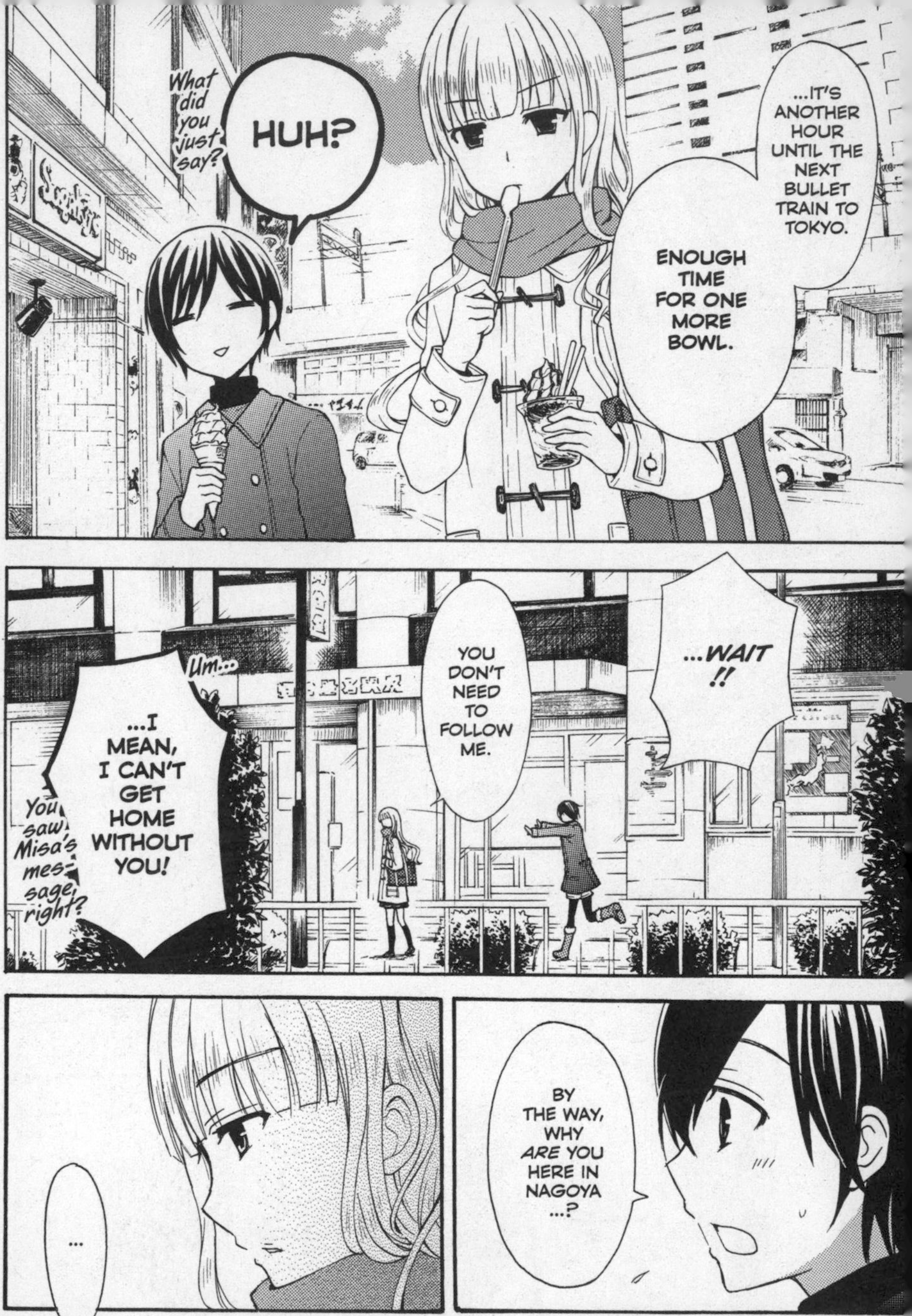
...IT'S ANOTHER HOUR UNTIL THE NEXT BULLET TRAIN TO TOKYO.
ENOUGH TIME FOR ONE MORE BOWL.
HUH?
What did you just say?
...WAIT!!
YOU DON'T NEED TO FOLLOW ME.
Um...
...I MEAN, I CAN'T GET HOME WITHOUT YOU!
You saw Misa's mes-sage, right?
BY THE WAY, WHY *ARE* YOU HERE IN NAGOYA ...?
...

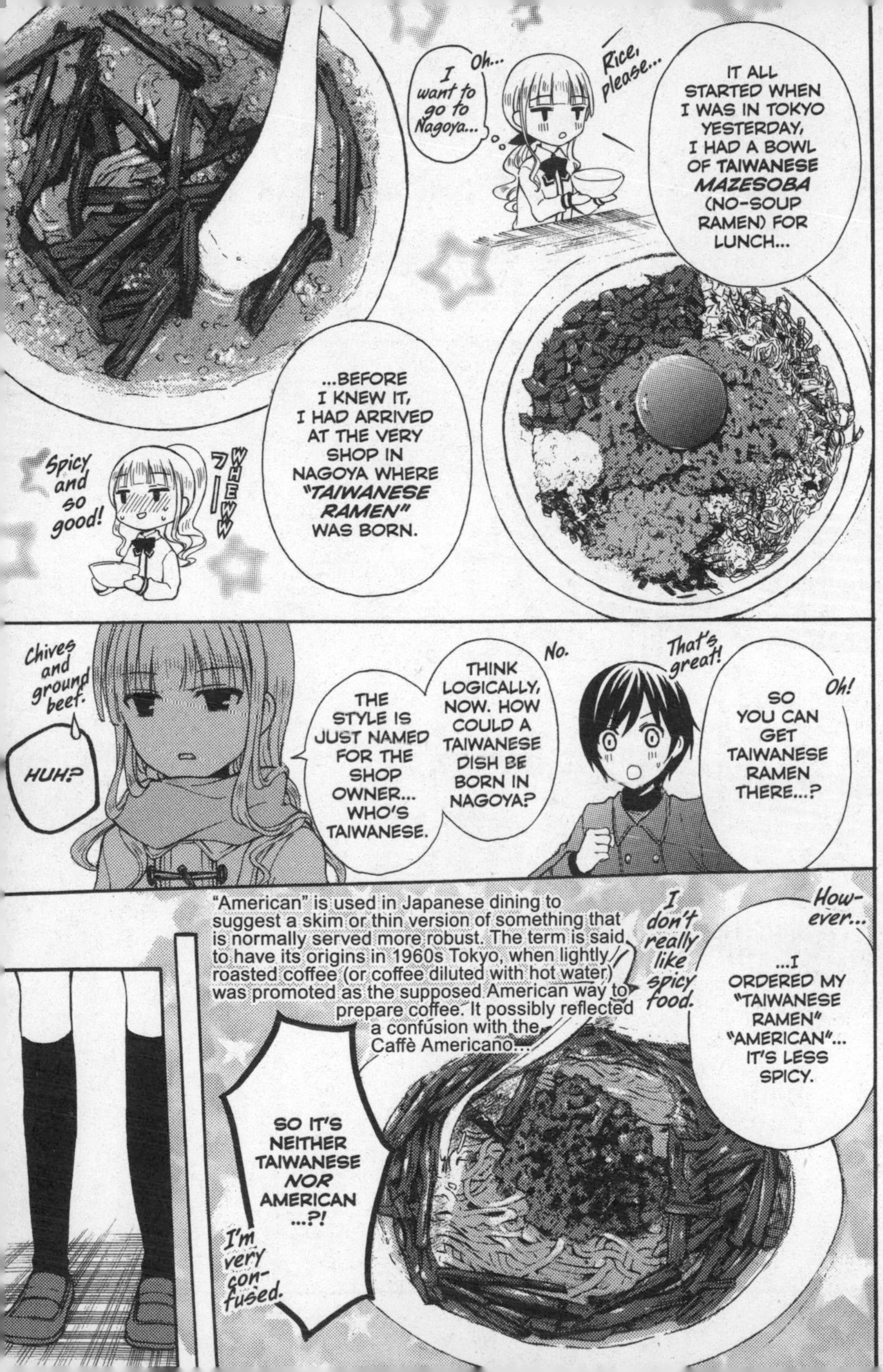

IT ALL STARTED WHEN I WAS IN TOKYO YESTERDAY, I HAD A BOWL OF TAIWANESE *MAZESOBA* (NO-SOUP RAMEN) FOR LUNCH...
Rice, please...
Oh... I want to go to Nagoya...
...BEFORE I KNEW IT, I HAD ARRIVED AT THE VERY SHOP IN NAGOYA WHERE *"TAIWANESE RAMEN"* WAS BORN.
WHEEW
Spicy and so good!
Oh!
SO YOU CAN GET TAIWANESE RAMEN THERE...?
That's great!
No.
THINK LOGICALLY, NOW. HOW COULD A TAIWANESE DISH BE BORN IN NAGOYA?
THE STYLE IS JUST NAMED FOR THE SHOP OWNER... WHO'S TAIWANESE.
Chives and ground beef.
HUH?
How-ever...
...I ORDERED MY "TAIWANESE RAMEN" "AMERICAN"... IT'S LESS SPICY.
I don't really like spicy food.
"American" is used in Japanese dining to suggest a skim or thin version of something that is normally served more robust. The term is said to have its origins in 1960s Tokyo, when lightly roasted coffee (or coffee diluted with hot water) was promoted as the supposed American way to prepare coffee. It possibly reflected a confusion with the Caffè Americano...
SO IT'S NEITHER TAIWANESE *NOR* AMERICAN ...?!
I'm very con-fused.

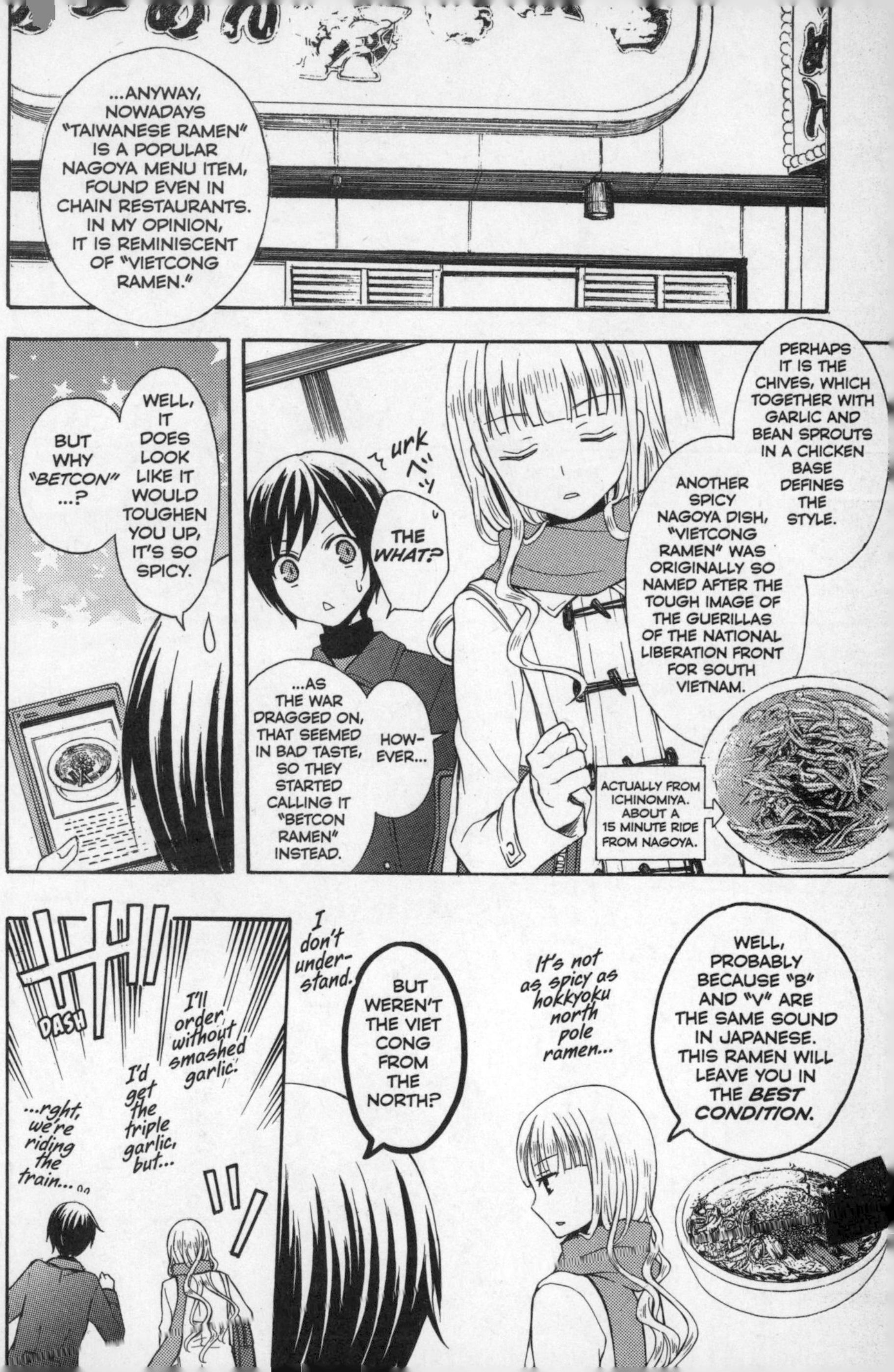
...ANYWAY, NOWADAYS "TAIWANESE RAMEN" IS A POPULAR NAGOYA MENU ITEM, FOUND EVEN IN CHAIN RESTAURANTS. IN MY OPINION, IT IS REMINISCENT OF "VIETCONG RAMEN."
PERHAPS IT IS THE CHIVES, WHICH TOGETHER WITH GARLIC AND BEAN SPROUTS IN A CHICKEN BASE DEFINES THE STYLE.
ANOTHER SPICY NAGOYA DISH, "VIETCONG RAMEN" WAS ORIGINALLY SO NAMED AFTER THE TOUGH IMAGE OF THE GUERILLAS OF THE NATIONAL LIBERATION FRONT FOR SOUTH VIETNAM.
urk
THE *WHAT?*
ACTUALLY FROM ICHINOMIYA. ABOUT A 15 MINUTE RIDE FROM NAGOYA.
HOW-EVER...
...AS THE WAR DRAGGED ON, THAT SEEMED IN BAD TASTE, SO THEY STARTED CALLING IT "BETCON RAMEN" INSTEAD.
WELL, IT DOES LOOK LIKE IT WOULD TOUGHEN YOU UP, IT'S SO SPICY.
BUT WHY "*BETCON*" ...?
WELL, PROBABLY BECAUSE "B" AND "V" ARE THE SAME SOUND IN JAPANESE. THIS RAMEN WILL LEAVE YOU IN THE *BEST CONDITION.*
It's not as spicy as hokkyoku north pole ramen...
BUT WEREN'T THE VIET CONG FROM THE NORTH?
I don't under-stand.
DASH
I'll order without smashed garlic.
I'd get the triple garlic, but...
...rght, we're riding the train...

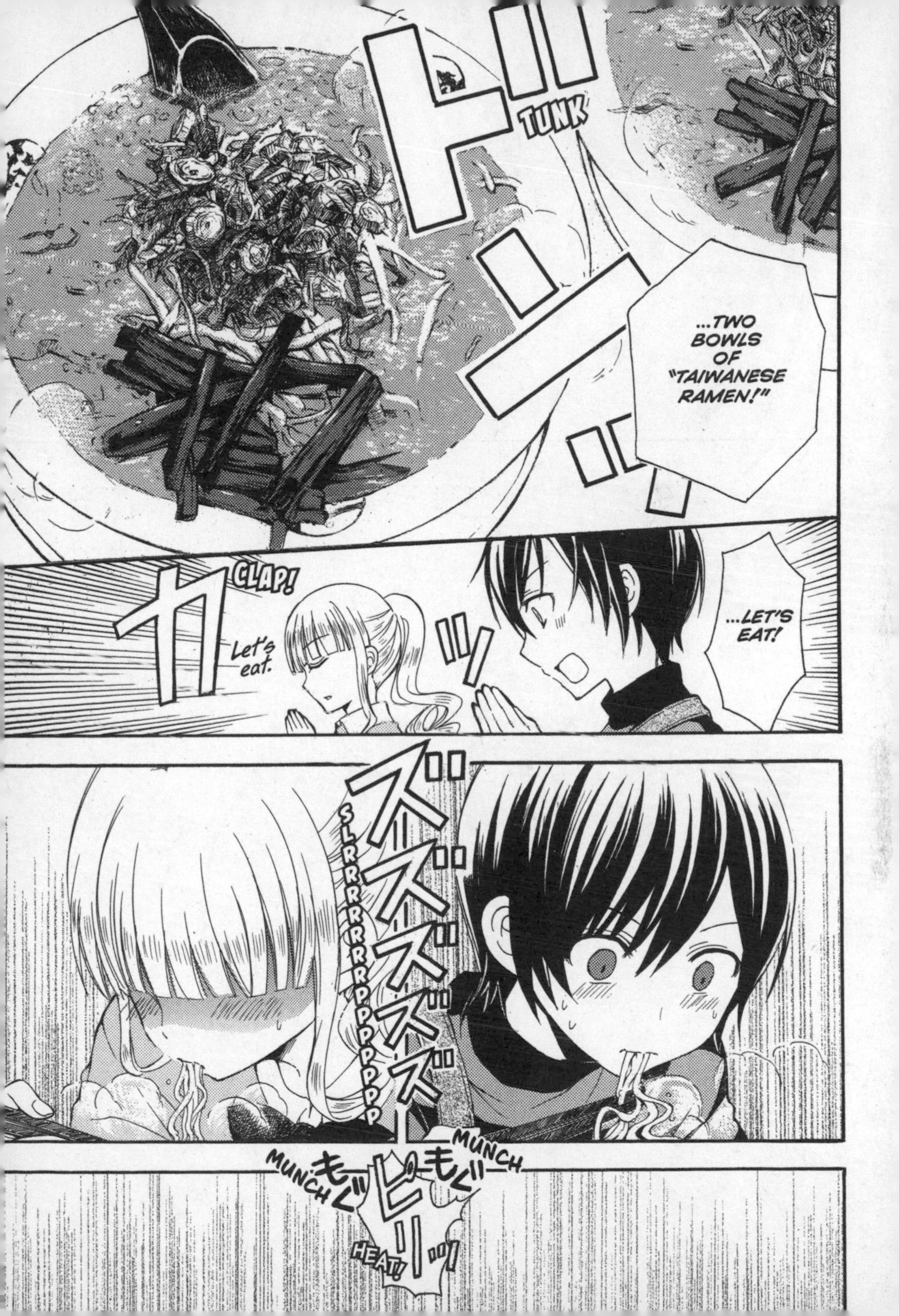
TUNK
...TWO BOWLS OF "TAIWANESE RAMEN!"
...LET'S EAT!
CLAP!
Let's eat.
SLRRRRRRRPPPPPPPP
MUNCH
MUNCH
HEAT!

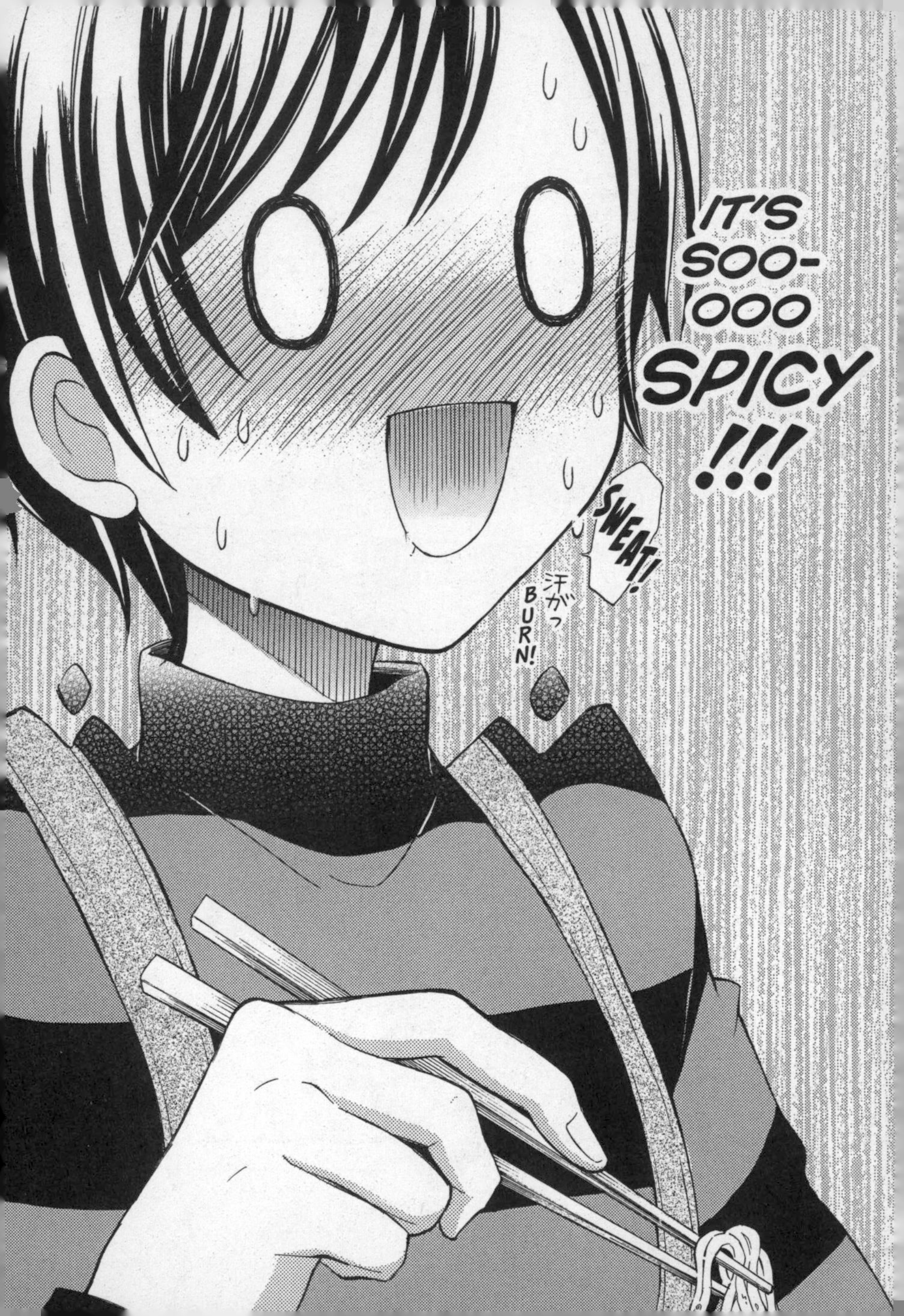
IT'S SOO-OOO SPICY!!!
SWEAT!
汗がっ
BURN!

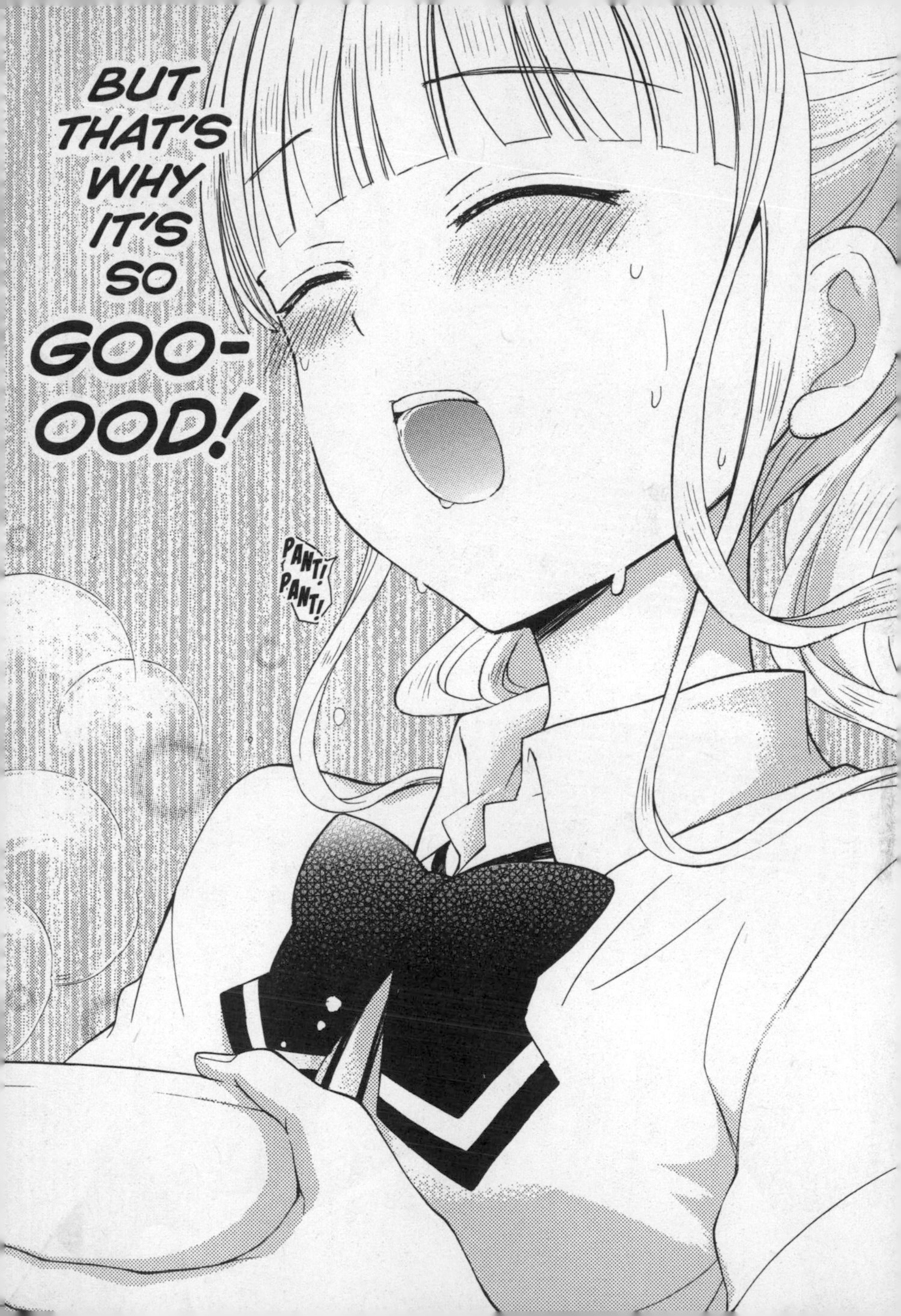
BUT THAT'S WHY IT'S SO GOO-OOD!
PANT! PANT!

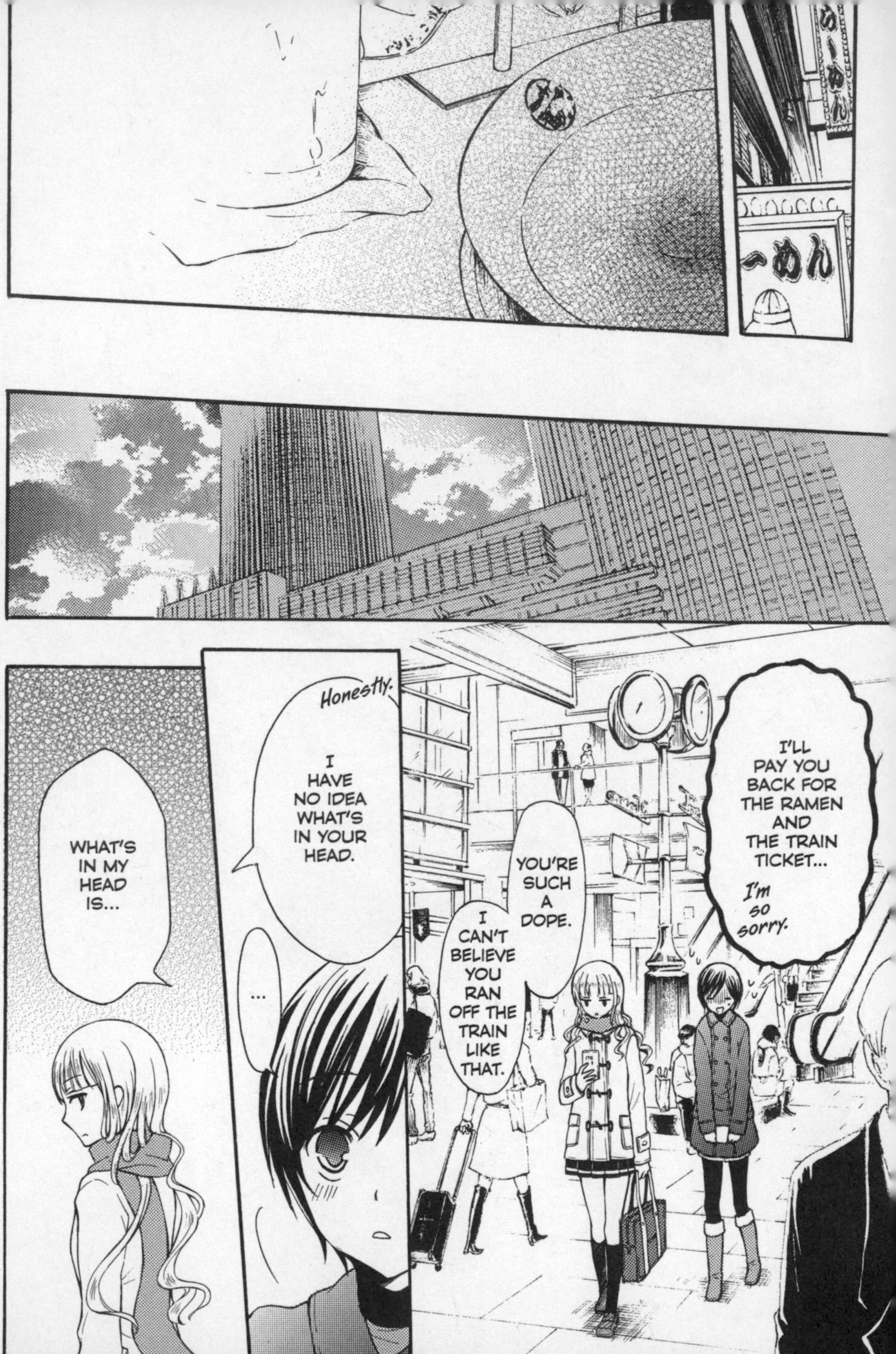
I'LL PAY YOU BACK FOR THE RAMEN AND THE TRAIN TICKET...
I'm so sorry.
YOU'RE SUCH A DOPE.
I CAN'T BELIEVE YOU RAN OFF THE TRAIN LIKE THAT.
Honestly.
I HAVE NO IDEA WHAT'S IN YOUR HEAD.
...
WHAT'S IN MY HEAD IS...

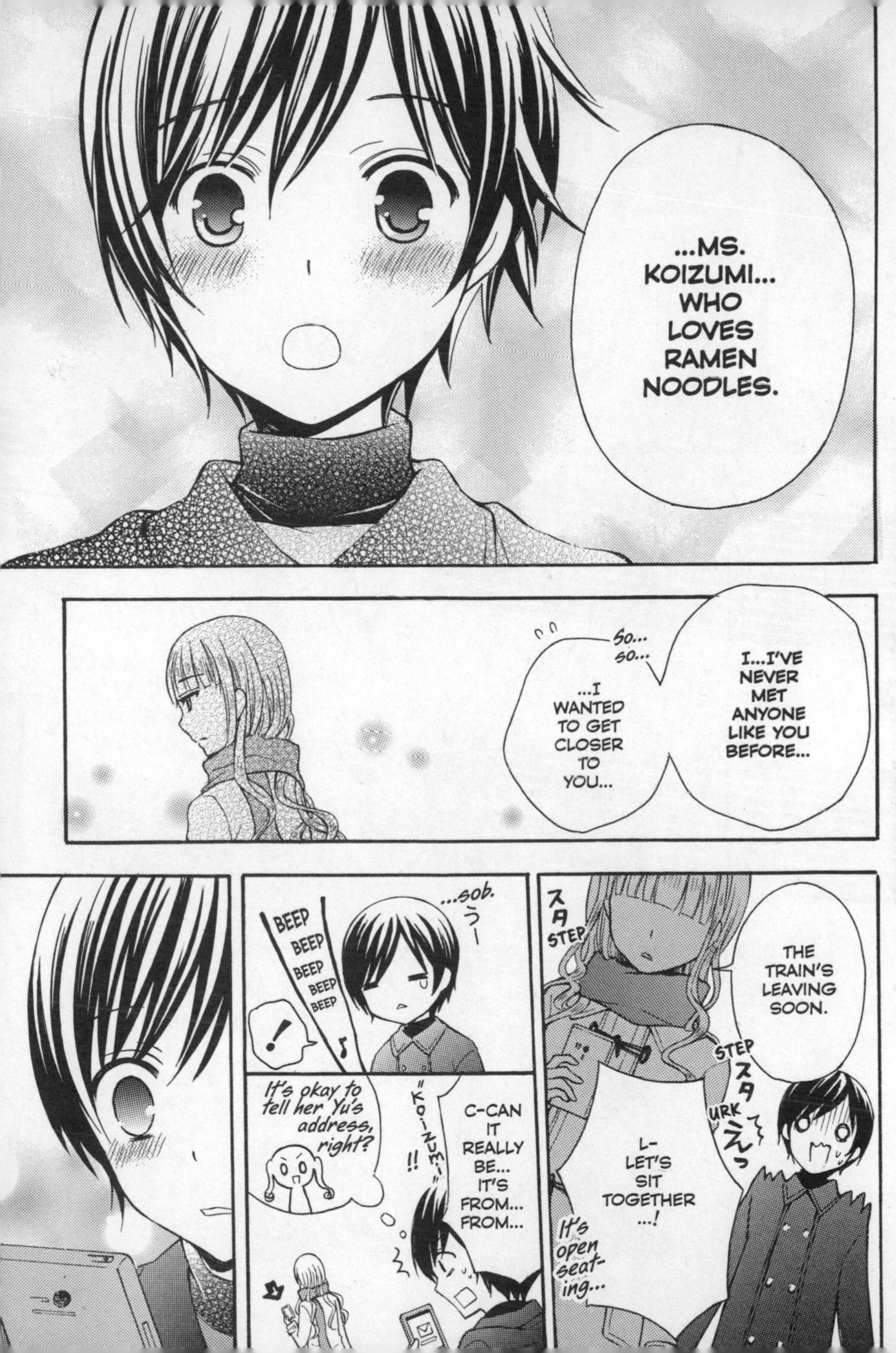
...MS. KOIZUMI... WHO LOVES RAMEN NOODLES.
I...I'VE NEVER MET ANYONE LIKE YOU BEFORE...
So... so...
...I WANTED TO GET CLOSER TO YOU...
スタ STEP
THE TRAIN'S LEAVING SOON.
STEP スタ
URK えっ
L-LET'S SIT TOGETHER ...!
It's open seating...
...sob. うー
BEEP BEEP BEEP BEEP BEEP
!
C-CAN IT REALLY BE... IT'S FROM... FROM...
"KOIZUMI"!!
It's okay to tell her Yu's address, right?

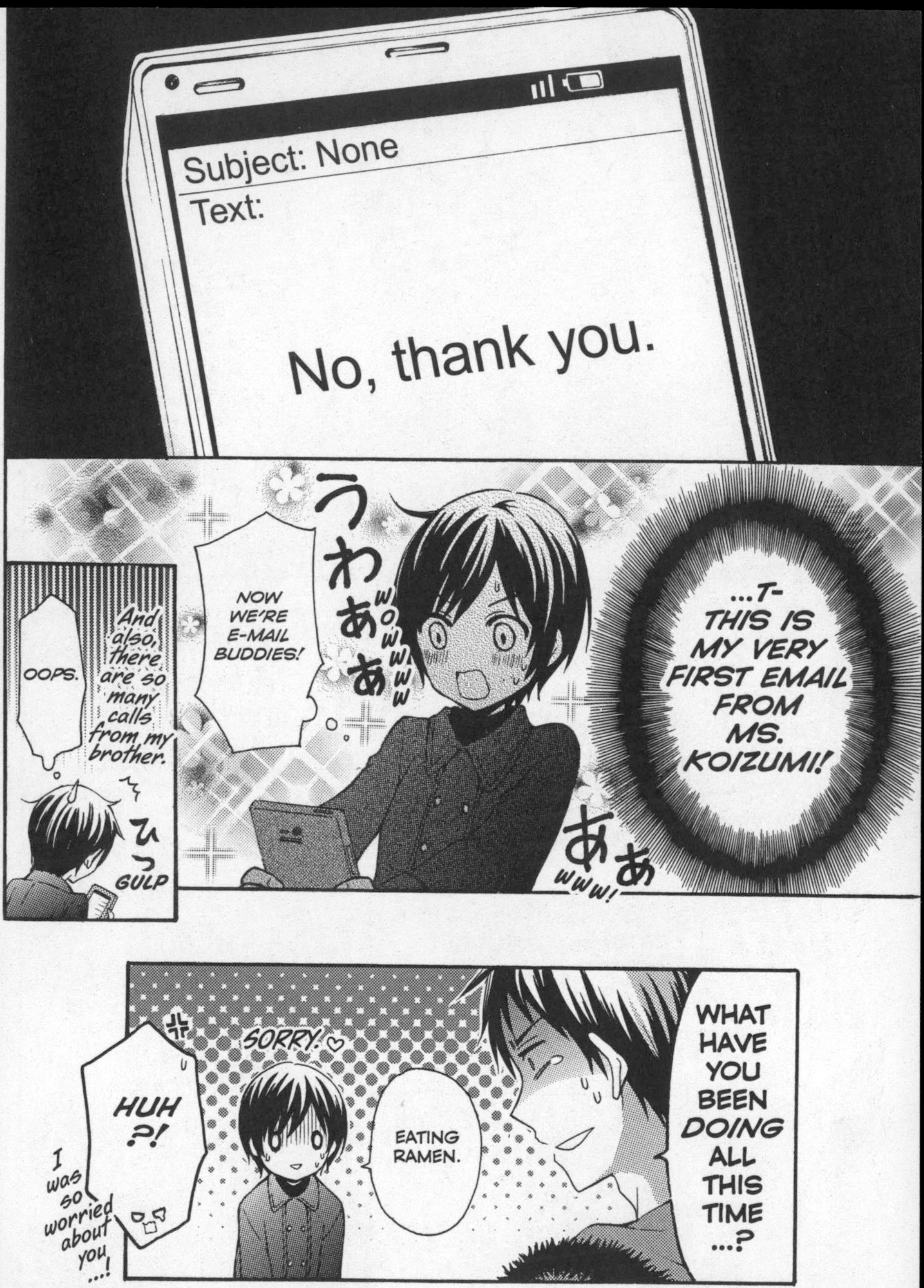
Subject: None
Text:
No, thank you.
...T- THIS IS MY VERY FIRST EMAIL FROM MS. KOIZUMI!
うわあぁ
WOWWWWW
NOW WE'RE E-MAIL BUDDIES!
あぁ
WWW!
And also, there are so many calls from my brother.
OOPS.
ひっ
GULP
WHAT HAVE YOU BEEN DOING ALL THIS TIME ...?
EATING RAMEN.
SORRY ♡
HUH ?!
I was so worried about you ...!

After that, Ms. Koizumi never emailed me again.

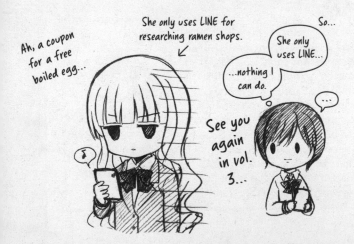

So...
She only uses LINE...
...nothing I can do.
...
See you again in vol. 3...
She only uses LINE for researching ramen shops.
Ah, a coupon for a free boiled egg...

p o s t s c r i p t

Finally Volume 2 has been published! Fortunately the magazine has also been continued. Thank you to all the fans who have supported *Ms. Koizumi*. While I was preparing for Vol. 2 of the manga, I was so excited, and my heart started beating fast.

After the first book came out, many people reached out to me through Twitter and email. And many people mentioned that after reading *Ms. Koizumi*, they went to ramen shops near them or made their own ramen, and it made me very happy! (Of course I was also happy to hear their reviews of the manga as well :))

Just having them add ramen to their daily meals makes me think it was worth it to create *Ms. Koizumi*. Please do help yourself to some ramen after reading the manga—nothing can beat ramen in the real world!

And the best thing someone told me so far was, "While I was on a diet I read *Ms. Koizumi*, and I could imagine that I had eaten ramen without actually eating it!" That's a new way of using this manga!

It might be too soon to say this but I'll work hard on Volume 3 as well!

—naru narumi

P.S. *Manga Life Storia* (*Storia* for short), the print manga magazine that serialized *Ms. Koizumi Loves Ramen Noodles*, in fact did cease publication in 2019, after six years. However, the various manga being serialized in the print magazine, including *Ms. Koizumi*, have continued to be serialized on the Storia Dash website. The print graphic novels (*tankobon*) continue to come out in Japan, too—in fact, the latest is vol. 8! We hope we can go all the way with the English version!

twitter:
@naruminaru3

I'll tweet about
Ms. Koizumi there!

The most important thing when planning a ramen tour is making sure to check your travel time relative to the shop hours of the places you want to visit. Consider for your itinerary the correct balance between light and rich ramen styles—and scheduling a break between ramen shops is also important! You need to organize your schedule well so you can have as much good ramen as possible within the limits of your available time. In this volume, I'm going to recommend some bowls to try in the Nagoya area. All of them are near train stations, to aid in your logistics.

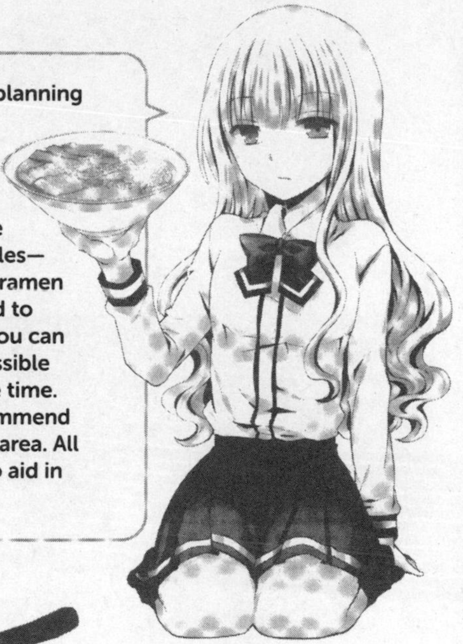

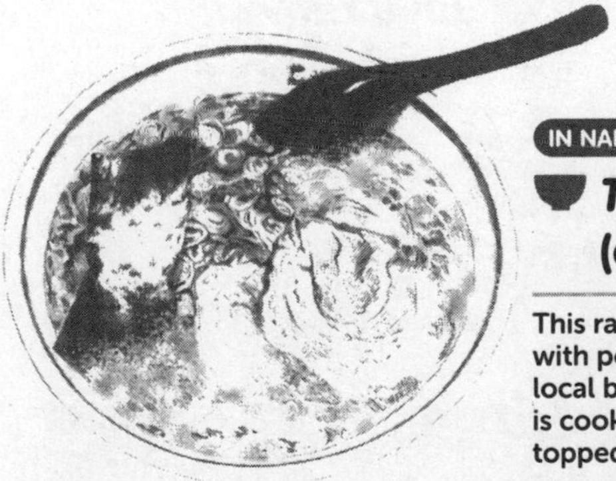

IN NAKAMURA WARD

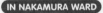

Tamagotoji (egg drop) ramen

This ramen has a soup made not only with pork, but with chicken from the local breed, Nagoya Cochin. The soup is cooked for a very long time, and then topped with a fluffy egg drop.

Manchinken, over 40 years in business, is a shop known for this dish. The ramen is very rich despite being covered with fluffy eggs. The noodle itself is very thin, and has a mild taste. Once you try this, you'll be more curious to check out other egg drop ramen. If you like it spicy, I recommend Manchinken's *tamagotoji* tantanmen style.

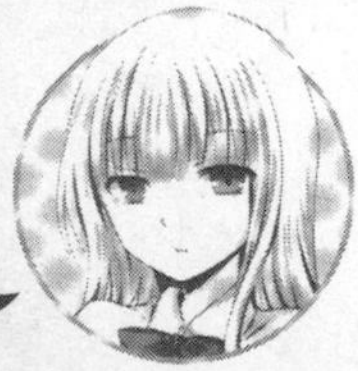

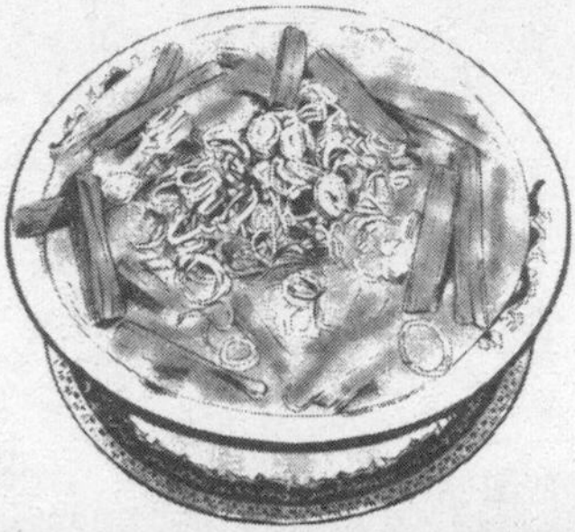

IN THE FUKIAGE NEIGHBORHOOD

Korai style ramen

This ramen style takes its name from the shop that originated it, Korai. The options are *matsu* (pine), *take* (bamboo), and *kotobuki* (longevity). The basic option is *matsu*, which is *chashu* ramen.

This time, I ordered *take* which, as the name suggests, comes with very thick *menma* (bamboo shoots). The soup is made from many different root vegetables, and made me think of *nikomi* udon (udon cooked in the pot) because of its light, mild nature. It's good to have when your stomach needs a break. When you add some ginseng vinegar to the soup, it gets even lighter and more refreshing.

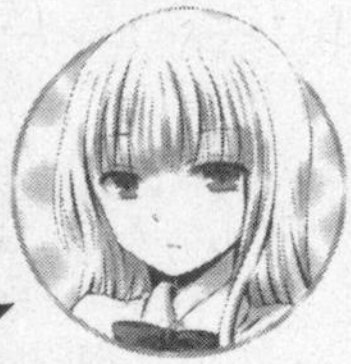

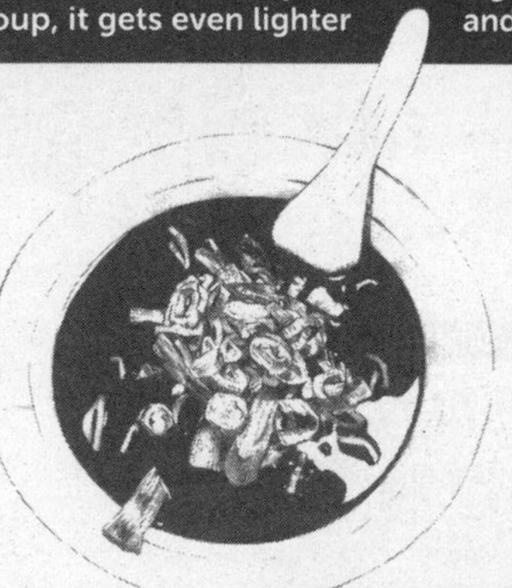

IN THE IMAIKE NEIGHBORHOOD

Juyu ramen

This ramen, served at Nomisuke, is a legend for the soup base that's been around for over 60 years, with ingredients gradually added to it.

Their menu consists of:

a.) traditional oily rich ramen (aka *juyu* ramen)

b.) light *shoyu* ramen.

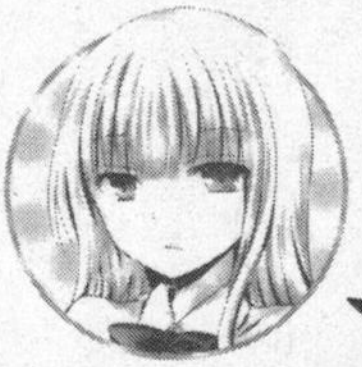

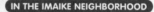

Juyu looks like black curry. Once you put chopsticks into the soup, you'll see the clear pork oil floating atop. Even before getting your first bite, you'll know you're in for a very rich and heavy satisfying ramen. It has a very strong aftertaste, like drinking hard water. It's quite unique among ramen. Please be careful not to get addicted. Even as I write about it, I get a craving for it.

In Nagoya, there are many cafés, so it's easy to take a break between bowls. Enjoy your ramen life!

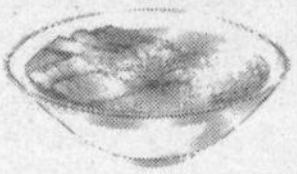

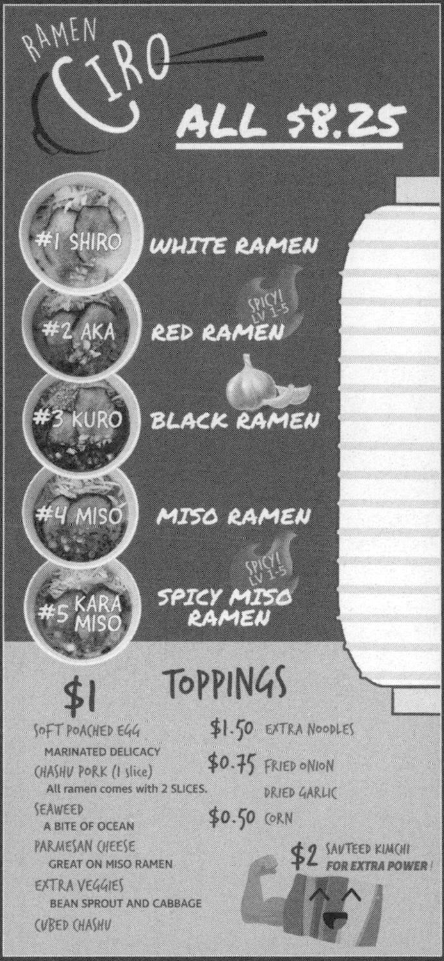
RAMEN
CIRO
ALL $8.25
#1 SHIRO
WHITE RAMEN
#2 AKA
RED RAMEN
SPICY! LV 1-5
#3 KURO
BLACK RAMEN
#4 MISO
MISO RAMEN
SPICY! LV 1-5
#5 KARA MISO
SPICY MISO RAMEN
TOPPINGS
$1
SOFT POACHED EGG
MARINATED DELICACY
CHASHU PORK (1 slice)
All ramen comes with 2 SLICES.
SEAWEED
A BITE OF OCEAN
PARMESAN CHEESE
GREAT ON MISO RAMEN
EXTRA VEGGIES
BEAN SPROUT AND CABBAGE
CUBED CHASHU
$1.50 EXTRA NOODLES
$0.75 FRIED ONION
DRIED GARLIC
$0.50 CORN
$2 SAUTEED KIMCHI
FOR EXTRA POWER!

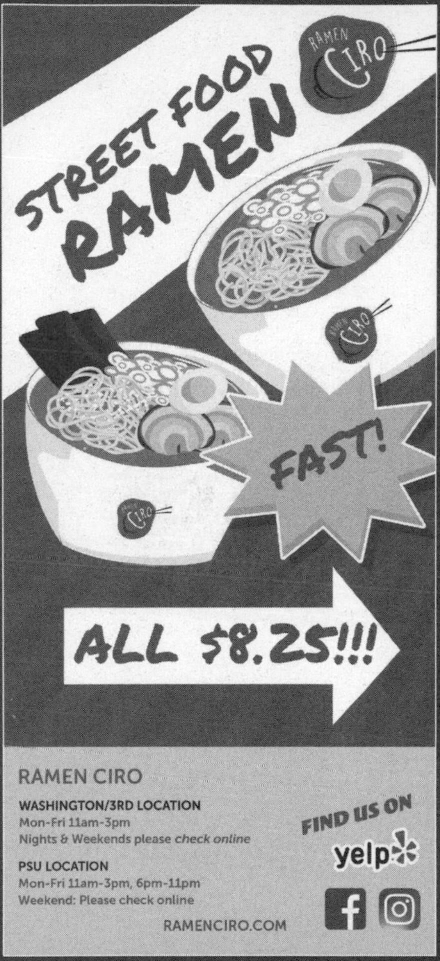
STREET FOOD
RAMEN
RAMEN CIRO
FAST!
ALL $8.25!!!
RAMEN CIRO
WASHINGTON/3RD LOCATION
Mon-Fri 11am-3pm
Nights & Weekends please check online
PSU LOCATION
Mon-Fri 11am-3pm, 6pm-11pm
Weekend: Please check online
RAMENCIRO.COM
FIND US ON
yelp

Visit Ramen Ciro in downtown Portland!

Have you spotted the cover of *Ms. Koizumi Loves Ramen Noodles* vol. 1 in downtown Portland? Then that's thanks to someone else who loves ramen noodles—Shoji Suzuki, proprietor of Ramen Ciro, a food cart with two locations downtown—one on SW 3rd near the Morrison Bridge, and one on SW 4th across from the Engineering Building at PSU. Shoji was kind enough to post images and info about *Ms. Koizumi* on his carts! "I grew up in Tokyo reading manga every day," says Shoji, whose first restaurant was a sushi bar in Minneapolis. Now he's helping to make Portland a town known both for its ramen and its ramen manga, so check out Ramen Ciro—and thank you, Shoji!

president and publisher **Mike Richardson**

editor **Carl Gustav Horn**

lettering and retouch **Susie Lee**

designers **Anita Magaña** and **Cindy Cacerez-Sprague**

digital art technician **Ann Gray**

english-language version produced by dark horse comics

Ms. Koizumi Loves Ramen Noodles Vol. 2

Published by
Dark Horse Manga
A division of Dark Horse Comics LLC
10956 SE Main Street
Milwaukie, OR 97222

DarkHorse.com
To find a comics shop in your area visit comicshoplocator.com

First edition: September 2020
Ebook ISBN 978-1-50672-158-3
Trade paperback ISBN 978-1-50671-328-1
1 2 3 4 5 6 7 8 9 10